GOD'S FOOL

by the same author

*

TIBETAN JOURNEY

Author in Tibetan dress, taken on arrival in India after crossing
Tibet from China.

GOD'S FOOL

by

George N. Patterson

FABER AND FABER
24 Russell Square
London

First published in mcmlvi
by Faber and Faber Limited
24 Russell Square London W.C.1
Printed in Great Britain by
Latimer Trend & Co Ltd Plymouth

GOD'S FOOLS

Let me stand with the conquered who assayed
A greater thing than sane men can imagine
Or pious hearts believe. Some love of Death
Seized all their being and hurl'd them against the World;
And mocking all intelligence they fell.

Such full abandonment possessed their spirit
That they contemned all prizes ever Man won
All works accomplisht, lives by men achieved.
And vied with the Creator to make Death
Impossibly the glory of all the glories.

Were they in love with Failure from the first?
Because there is no new thing in Success
For praise to the high gods? Nor reckoned once
If there be flaws in failure, or if tears
Should o'er their broken bodies be expended.

The Holy Master of men found naught in prowess
And so was lowly—and little to rejoice in
Among the reputable, so He poured
On reprobates His molten gold of friendship
And wooed the Crucifixion heaven adores.

O, what tame worship could such a Rebel brook?
Claims He not some defiance for His meed
Of things held fixt and legal and secured,
Passionate avowals that none else dare approve,
And hearts that cannot deign to be victorious?

Colossal dignities and decorations
Are not for heroes. There is no soul can live
That will not spurn the Universe, and Salvation,
Here and hereafter, and even the life of the soul
Till all be emptied and it lie with the Conquered.

W. H. HAMILTON

This poem is reprinted by permission of J. M. Dent and Sons from their *Anthology of Scots Poems.*

'For the foolishness of God is wiser than men. . . .'
PAUL, in 1 *Corinthians, ch. i, v.* 25

'We are fools for Christ's sake. . . .'
PAUL, in 1 *Corinthians, ch. iv, v.* 10

CONTENTS

7

ILLUSTRATIONS

AUTHOR'S PREFACE

Those who have read my first book, *Tibetan Journey*, will find much of *God's Fool* quite different both in content and style. In the former I was less concerned with matters of political and spiritual interest, chiefly because my friend, Geoffrey Bull, had been captured in Tibet and was in a Chinese Communist prison. Another reason—and one which I should have thought was obvious, but which did not appear to be so from the reaction in some quarters!—was that a travel book did not provide a satisfactory medium for disquisitions on politics and theology.

Now that Geoffrey Bull has been released, and all that we ever knew and thought and accomplished has been made known to the Chinese Communists through their diabolical methods of interrogation (see *When Iron Gates Yield*, by Geoffrey T. Bull; Hodder and Stoughton), a record of the events leading up to that desperate dash for India across an unknown part of Tibet described in *Tibetan Journey*, can be given.

In many respects the matter in this book will be found to be very controversial, but I wish to impress upon those who read it that it is in no polemical spirit of destructive criticism that I write. I have set forth anachronisms and Scriptural irreconcilables as I encountered them, primarily because I could not accept the spirit of compromise and defeatism as compatible with the character of God and they were in very great danger of turning me aside into frustration and unbelief, an experience only too tragically common to my generation; and, also, I wanted to place on record that in all my experiences, while man and his ingenuity might be, God and His word were not too small for any circumstance.

Author's Preface

In my preface to *Tibetan Journey* I suggest that the experiences recorded there constitute my 'initial challenge to my generation'. In *God's Fool* I deepen and extend that challenge to include a whole new set of circumstances.

I would like to take this opportunity to thank Clarence Hjelmervik and Gordon Bell for the use of some of their photographs to illustrate this book, and also my wife, my brother and others for the help which they gave in the preparation of the manuscript.

Some of the quotations from Scripture in this book are taken from J. N. Darby's *New Translation*, others from Weymouth's *New Testament in Modern Speech* or Moffatt's *New Translation*.

GEORGE N. PATTERSON, F.R.S.G.S.

Kalimpong, India

Chapter One

THE PROBLEM

I am a man with a passion for God. Yet on looking back over my life from the vantage point of twenty-nine years of it I found myself oddly surprised at the little one is really influenced in a crisis by what one knows or does not know of God.

As I sat there in that remote valley in Tibet where no white man had ever been, fifteen thousand feet above sea-level on the roof of the world, I thought of all the factors that had gone into bringing me to this point—of the challenge and defiance of the very laws that govern the lives of men on this circling planet, with the key to the secret of life; and yet because I had been asked to do something that I could not believe possible, because it conflicted with my opinions, involving the destiny of nations, the lives of millions, the security of my own beliefs and ideas, I sat there uncertain, torn by indecision. Confident of success because of the knowledge of God that I had gained in several years' experience, and certain of failure because of my ignorance of what the future held.

From where I sat on a rocky promontory high up on the mountain, overlooking the river and village spread out on the valley floor, I could see Loshay, my Tibetan servant, grooming my horse for tomorrow's race, I could see blind old Drolma sitting outside the door of her son's house enjoying the heat of the sun through her greasy sheepskin gown, I could see the boys of the village filing away behind Jigme Pangdatshang, their leader's son, rifles over their shoulders, as they went out for a day's hunting. Only an occasional sound seeped through the silence—a high-pitched voice, the bray of a mule, a far-off, mysterious crack from the uninhabited forests—but apart from that I might be dreaming in front of a painting. The sky an unsullied, unvarying blue, broken only by the giant snow-peaked ranges that surround the valley. Peace and beauty and God.

Yet I had been asked to leave—had been commanded to leave. If I remained the peace and beauty might still surround me but it would leave my soul, for God would not be there. There could be no doubt that it was God who last night had ordered me to go. I had even got up in the sub-zero temperature and listened to Geoff's breathing in the darkness, looked at the dim reflection on Loshay's face from the dying red embers of the fire, to assure myself that I was not dreaming, and then, shivering in the icy atmosphere, zipped myself into my double-layer sleeping bag, and lain and stared into the darkness as I tried to comprehend what had been asked of me.

When the voice had spoken to me the first time I had thought that Geoff was calling me and sat up suddenly, to find that Geoff was asleep and the two servants, wrapped in their gowns beside the fire, likewise. There was no one else besides Geoff to call me 'George', and so I had settled down to sleep again, certain that I must have been dreaming, when the voice spoke out of the darkness again, 'George'. There could be no doubt about it that time, and also there could be no doubt about its not being Geoff's voice, for his breathing was deep and regular and had never faltered, and this voice came from the darkness at the foot of the bed. I sat up again, looking towards the direction from which the sound had come, and with crystal-like clarity remembered the incident of the child Samuel when God had spoken to him.

'Speak, Lord, for Thy servant heareth,' I repeated quietly.

The room seemed to lighten before me, and then the voice spoke again. 'I have brought you to this place as I promised but this is not the end of my promise, there are still greater things ahead. I told you that I would send you to Tibet and other countries of Asia to communicate to those who have had no opportunity of hearing all that you have learned of me, and that no one would be able to stop you from accomplishing my purpose for you as long as you obeyed my voice. I have brought you to Tibet through every obstacle, but this is still only a small part of the work I have yet for you to do. Not only Kham, or Tibet, or Central Asia, but the whole world must know that I am still the God of Abraham and Moses, David and Elijah, the God and Father of the Lord Jesus Christ. What you have done so far is nothing compared to what I have still for you to do. The way in which I have led you has brought you into possession of unique knowledge. You are the only person with the knowledge of the Chinese Communist plans to take over Tibet and the other countries of Asia; no one else knows, no one even suspects that China is making for India. Therefore you will go to India with the knowledge you have gained and I will use you to stop the Communist advance and frustrate the Communist plans for the conquest of Asia. For *I* have sent *you* there, and no man nor nation can withstand me. I only require that you should be obedient to my every word. There is no living without dying, there is no dying without living.'

I had argued with every argument I could find, first against the idea of a 'vision', for I hated it with all my Scottish realism and hard-headedness; and then, when that remained constant and unassailable, against the implications contained in the visitation. It was not the ridiculous nor the fantastic in the vision that troubled me, but the necessity it implied for participating in 'politics', the *bête noire* of every missionary. The problem finally resolved itself into the simple decision—was I prepared to obey God against generally accepted, and even my own, beliefs? To follow blindly in a complete abandonment of submission to the Divine Will, or trammel the Divine power with accepted shibboleths of human opinion? The significance of life depended on the answer I gave to that so I dared not make a hasty decision. The destiny of nations, even the lives of millions of people, must not be allowed to influence that decision in any way, for it was the glory and purpose of God that was at stake.

As I sat there, remote from every influence but that of God, I must decide whether I should go forward with my faith in company with God alone, or retreat into a splintered belief that would for ever after lacerate my peace of mind and soul in the know-ledge that I bowed to the force of circumstances, or any other euphemism that might be coined for the power of the Communists in their conflict with God. To turn aside now would be a confession of failure, irrespective of what sophistry might be used to explain away the circumstances to others. Did I go forward with God into a fantastic unknown, in a life lived to intoxicating fullness in a growing knowledge of Him and sense of His constant presence and power and purpose, or did I remain with 'no Highway more, no track, all being blind', with a suburban complacency of mind but an eternal despair of emptiness in my soul? Was this to be the end of a twelve-years' adventure for an eternal prize? Twelve years. . . .

Chapter Two

THE STRUGGLE

'Just you listen to me, my lad,' the doctor exploded angrily. 'You should be a jolly grateful young man that you're living at all. Eight months ago, by all normal reckoning, you ought to have died, and yet here you are still; but I can assure you that if you go on to the operating table in this frame of mind you'll certainly never come off it alive. We must have your co-operation and in your condition, if you haven't the will to live, then you'll die and that's all there is to it! You're the one who preaches that God has a purpose in every person's life, but I'm telling you now that if ever anyone has been spared for a purpose it's you. Three times in your life already I have given up hope of saving your life, and three times only a miracle has saved you. And for what? To die from an operation on your leg because you're tired of suffering? Just you snap out of it if ever you want anyone to believe your contention that there is a purpose in life. Put your mind to it and I'll have you on your feet playing football or climbing your precious mountains as much as you like—or just don't bother and finish yourself off. The choice lies with you.' And pulling on his motor-cycling gloves savagely, he stalked out of the room.

I lay gazing at the ceiling, jarred out of the woolly apathy that had packaged me for the past few months. The only interest that I had left was in the rise and fall of the agony which swept me. I used up all the energy I possessed to fight off the waves of pain while my leg was being dressed by the nurse, sweat starting from my taut body and soaking my pyjamas, and then lay in an exhausted haze until the next time for dressings. Eight months before I had come home from work complaining of a pain in my leg and some sickness, and this had raced into septicaemia and a delirium of pain, to be followed by two unsuccessful operations. Now they wanted to operate again, probably unsuccessfully as before, more pain, and so it would go on, I thought bitterly. Why should I fight for a life that had only a focus of pain? 'Because you believe there is a purpose to it,' the answer came back immediately. But how firm was that conviction? Now that I was stripped of the intellectual pleasure of the mental gymnastics involved in comparing what others had experienced and taught and written, and faced the problem squarely for myself, I found myself tottering on the verge of unbelief.

Theoretically I did believe that behind every life was a purpose. Theoretically I believed it was possible for a person to discover that purpose and divine *raison d'être*. But now, as I searched my soul following on the doctor's words, I had to confess that experimentally I knew little or nothing about it. Ruthlessly, and with a growing fear, I searched all my experience for something on which to base my belief, and found only a little, very little, out of a mass of reading, discussion and activity, on which I could lay hold. The eighteen years of my life so far had been lived in conformity to a blindly accepted traditional pattern.

I had religious parents, and attended as many church services as possible in the group amongst which I had grown up, known as 'Plymouth Brethren'. Every Sunday morning I attended the communion service, or 'breaking of bread meeting' as it was called; every Sunday afternoon the 'ministry meeting' for exposition of the Scriptures, followed by a Sunday School class; then the 'gospel service' for non-Christians in the evening, both in the open air outside and afterwards inside the hall. On Wednesday night there was a prayer meeting, and Saturday afternoons were spent visiting outlying villages, preaching and distributing gospel leaflets. On Saturday nights there were other meetings for exposition of the Scripture, and 'conferences' every few weeks throughout the district when some prominent speakers would expound some profound Scriptural theme for an hour each. Then there

were regular visits to the homes of friends where the various
Bible doctrines would be talked over at length in informal discussion. A week packed with religious activity but now, on cold
analysis, seen to be devoid of any assurance of purpose or any
object. It did it all not because of any conscious conviction of
demand on God's part that I should do it but because it was the
done thing amongst the Christians of my particular group; or, as
they phrased it, because it was 'the sign of a good testimony and
an interest in the things of God'.

Now it all appeared artificial, empty, devoid of significance,
removed from life; wide-open to the Marxist allegation of being
unrealistic, an opiate, not interpretable in terms of everyday life.
Was my *raison d'être*, therefore, merely to acquire sufficient ability
in the handling of the Bible in order that I might reach the platforms of the many Brethren churches, or 'assemblies', throughout
the country, and from there to communicate that knowledge to
apathetic 'sermon-tasters' like myself, and all the time to know
the gnawing doubt that what I was preaching was theory and not
actual experience? Yet what other course was there? The denominations, as such, were closed to me since I could see no justification
for their existence from the Scriptures; and the only type of
church gathering for which there was any Scriptural justification
was that expounded by so-called Plymouth Brethren, but which
was being denied in practice by them through an unauthorized
nineteenth-century traditionalism and legalism that were more
pernicious than any admitted sectarianism. The true Church—the
'ecclesia' of Scripture—the habitation of God among men—was
a fellowship of *persons* standing in a definite relationship to God
on the basis of the redeeming work of His Son, Jesus Christ, and
the purifying work of the Holy Spirit indwelling these persons,
with the responsibility and the sufficiency of its maintenance rest-
ing entirely in the Godhead, and it required no unauthorized contribution from the opinions of men.

The process which began with the institution of the monarchi-
cal episcopate by Ignatius, and the so-called episcopal succession
of Irenaeus, particularly as it was interpreted to mean the tactual

transmission of apostolic authority, had reached its logical conclusion in the neo-Catholic Roman idea of tradition when canon
law was taken from the care of theologians and handed over to
lawyers, who introduced the entirely new notion that 'canon law
is made by the bearers of ecclesiastical authority' and thus transformed the 'church' into a 'corporation' or institution. Christianity was no longer the church of Christ, ruled by Christ, but merely
a corporate institution ruled falsely in the name of Christ, until it
came to be thought ultimately that Christ could only work
through the medium of this churchly organization. It only required the passing of several centuries to develop the notion and
give it historical authority. The Tridentine Council had only to
place the 'sine scripto traditiones' on the same level as the Holy
Scriptures themselves and the latter, being 'completed' by this
new source of knowledge, were successfully eliminated as the
final court of appeal. And, finally, the 'codex juris canonici' of
1918, by which all matters connected with faith and morals in the
Church were subordinated to the Pope, rounded off the whole
concept.

It could be argued also, as far as that went, that from a strictly
historical point of view the claim of the Greek Orthodox Church
to be the true Catholic Church of ecclesiastical tradition, following on the first and major cleavage with the western neo-Catholic
Roman tradition, was perfectly legitimate. Greek Orthodoxy did
not arise as a result of a revolutionary movement, but, on the
contrary, from an undeviating loyalty to tradition, while the
Roman Church had diverged by revolutionary processes.

As far as the denominations in the West were concerned they
all could not help but acknowledge that they stood, as it were, on
the shoulders of the Roman Church. From a purely historical
point of view the Reformation and post-Reformation Churches
were the product of some fifteen hundred years of what was
largely the history of the Roman Church. The Reformation was
rather a cleaning up of the Church than a totally new beginning.

The only deviation from this traditional ecclesiastical pattern
was the appearance of groups from time to time who protested

against the disparity between the current religious structure and that outlined in Scripture, and who, in spite of the persecution, returned to the simplicity of the 'apostle's doctrine' and gathered together in groups observing only New Testament church principles. These would flourish rapidly for a time in their particular generation until gradually the purity of their original stand would be corrupted by permitting some human element to dominate instead of the spiritual. Some powerful personality would exploit some personal opinion or emphasis, and gradually the group would lose power and disappear from the historical scene in vague reports of religious eccentricity—to be followed in some later generation by the upsurge of another demand for pure conformity to New Testament principles.

The Plymouth Brethren movement was the nineteenth-century protest against a dead ecclesiasticism that could neither justify its existence from the Scriptures it claimed to acknowledge, nor defend itself against the rising tide of attacks by the neo-Catholic Movement led by the brilliant Cardinal Newman, and the rapidly multiplying schools of materialism and 'free thought'. Those early Brethren believed that in proportion as the Christian body ceased to be a spiritual structure in the primitive apostolic sense, the fine suppleness and freedom of fellowship, participation in privilege and discipline, proper to a spiritual structure, must give place more and more to the coarser character of an organized legal structure. If one thing could be added outside the inspired revelation of the whole truth contained in the Scriptures then, on the same premise, one hundred or one thousand other things could likewise be added—with no confidence in any. For if the power of the authority of the original revelation was insufficient how could any man-inspired addition carry with it any force?

The early days of the movement—which later came to be known as the 'Plymouth Brethren', although this was a misnomer and rejected completely by those who were associated in those groups—had been revolutionary and far-reaching in its impact on contemporary religious thought. An Episcopalian minister in the Church of Ireland, John Nelson Darby, with a brilliant record in

Classics and Law before entering the ministry, had become more and more disturbed by the anomalies practised in the Church which were in direct contradiction in many instances to what the Scriptures taught. The most disturbing factor of all, so far as he was concerned, was that those anomalies could not be set right without involving the collapse of the complete structure, particularly in those matters relating to Communion and Baptism. During the period of his difficulties he heard of a few people who met together in a room in Dublin to carry out the simple commands of Scripture with regard to these very matters, and he went along to investigate. He was so impressed by the integrity of their Scriptural approach that he gave up his clerical calling to associate with them. With some of the most brilliant minds of that generation—William Kelly, C. H. Mackintosh, Dr. Tregelles, Dr. A. T. Pierson, George Muller, B. W. Newton—and many others grown disillusioned and weary of organized religion, they founded groups of believers practising only New Testament principles of church gathering in Bristol, Plymouth and other towns throughout the country in a rapidly spreading movement.

At first an open freedom of fellowship with every believer was encouraged amongst them, but gradually, as in all similar movements in history, the corrupting human element began to creep in and certain people with their own personal emphases of doctrine began to exert undue influence, at first in their own local groups and then in a widening circle of others. From healthy controversy with those holding different emphases in doctrine it was only a step to arbitrarily excluding all those who would not agree or submit to some specific opinion, and to justifying this exclusion by maintaining that they were 'guarding the platform', or 'guarding the testimony of the local church', according to their particular phraseology. Irving, abandoning Cardinal Newman's theory of a continuous, universal, visible Christian society, taught a new Pentecost and a new Catholic and Apostolic Church and became the pioneer of modern tongue and healing movements and pentecostalism: Darby taught that the Church is in ruins and invited Christians to abandon sectarian churches and to reintegrate into a fellowship of non-sectarian churches—which soon became another distinctive sect: Muller taught that all good-living believers had a right to church fellowship irrespective of any other denominational connection. Then all these schools of thought subdivided into a multifarious collection of sects each tenaciously holding on to their own particular 'Scriptural teaching'.

I knew it all so well, the history of the great controversies as well as the petty squabbles. The occasions when one sensed the tenuous fingers of divine majesty reaching into human affairs and then the exasperations when some human littleness swept away the vision. I had known enough in the lives of my parents and of some others to warrant a belief in God and His interest in human affairs, and I had known enough in my experience with the majority of Christians to doubt the existence of God at all. It was not the mass of evidence contributing to my unbelief that troubled me now, but the fact that there *was* evidence, however little, for a belief in God, and I seemed to have so little personal experience of it compared with some of those whose lives I was acquainted with through reading. If there was a God was He really interested in every detail of my life? Did He really desire to control every action so that I might experience the ultimate good?

The words rose before me: 'Confide in Jehovah with all thy heart and lean not unto thine own intelligence; in all thy ways acknowledge Him and He will make plain thy paths.' If that were true, then I must accept the plain fact that what most professing Christians practised was wrong, that what I had been practising up till now was wrong. Apart from accepting Christ's sacrifice as being sufficient to atone for my sin before a holy and righteous God I had no experience of a daily confiding in Jehovah with all my heart, no experience of leaning on an intelligence other than my own, no experience of God directing my ways, no experience of my paths being plain. Was I a Christian at all, then?

As my faith shattered to pieces around me I at last came to a point where I need not retreat or prevaricate. While I had failed, as a follower of Christ, in not practising a day-by-day obedience to

His control, yet I had practised a day-by-day trust in the efficacy of His atonement for my sin before God. That, and the peace and assurance I had experienced flowing from it, no one could take from me. I had met God in Christ, and on that ground my faith was unshakeable. Had my faith in this been disturbed then there would have been only one course open to me in my present state of ruthless self-analysis, the way of scientific humanism which, for me, must end inevitably in Communism. So far only my religious beliefs had stood between me and an intellectual commitment to the Dialectical Materialism of the Communists. With the weakness of my beliefs shown up following on the doctor's angry words, in a world without assurance of divine purpose, I was left with the only alternative of the relativity of truth, one of a world of social animals conditioned by my environment, and must accept the implications of such.

The middle road of the Rationalism, or Liberalism, of the so-called Higher Critics held no appeal at all. Either there was a God who had revealed Himself and His purpose in Creation, with an explanation of any apparent contradiction in men and nature, or there was no God at all and it was simply a waste of time to look for Him or to invent Him. If the latter were true, then all that was required was not to 'wince or cry aloud in the fell clutch of circumstance', but although bloody yet remain unbowed and master of one's fate; trying to order the circumstances into the most coherent pattern possible until the grave swallowed the human entity. Given the premise of 'No God, no heaven, no judgment' the Lenin-Marx-Engels dialectic gave a comprehensible and satisfactory explanation of the circumstances which made up life. Yet I knew that Dialectical Materialism could not provide all the answers, and either avoided or ignored major problems which inevitably and inescapably arose from consideration of Darwin's Evolution of Nietzsche's Superman. In theory, Christ held all the answers as the revelation of God to man. In theory, Marx held some of the answers apart from God altogether. In an objective analysis, therefore, it was only fair to Christ to acknowledge the possibility that most of so-called Christendom was not Christian in the full sense of the principles He had laid down, and that that might well be the reason for the failure and lack of power in those who professed to be His followers.

Nor could there be any compromise, in spite of the comforting words spoken by Communists recently in their new policy of *la main tendue* to allay the suspicions of prospective members for the Party. Lenin's words were clear and unmistakable: 'Religion is the opium of the people. Religion is a kind of spiritual vodka in which the slaves of capital drown their human shape and their claims to any decent life.' Or again: 'Dialectical Materialism, the philosophy of Marxist-Leninism and the theoretical foundation of the Communist Party, is incompatible with religion. The world-outlook of the Party is based on scientific data, whereas religion contradicts science. As the Party bases its activity on a scientific foundation it is bound to oppose religion. The Komsomol has never regarded religion from a neutral angle. Anti-religious propaganda forms an integral part of Communist education. Religious superstition and prejudice are unscientific. That is why Komsomol members must not only be convinced atheists and opponents of all superstitions but must actively combat the spread of superstition and prejudice among youth.'

And I could never be a 'convinced atheist' and believe that religion was altogether a 'fallacy' judging from what I had gathered out of my own short experience already, even if there were many things that I still did not understand. I knew that Christ was indeed a living reality. That experience of Him brought my rocking, pain-shot world back into perspective again. He had made Himself known. Further, He had promised to be known in a daily, hourly relationship if I would but submit myself to Him. I had only to admit that I was wrong in the past in my futile dissipation of energy, 'doing things for God'—I had only to admit that He was still alive and supreme, and that the majority of Christians were guilty of ignoring His existence and supremacy—I had only to submit myself in a new abandonment of faith to His control, accepting His daily guidance as I had accepted His daily atonement—to know that purpose for which

I had been born, to know that peace which flowed from a consciousness of oneness with God in working out my destiny.

As I implacably analysed my position I came at last to the conclusion that there was only one thing to be done, only one way to settle the problem for myself—put the greater to the test and, if it failed, then adopt the lesser. Jesus Christ was manifestly greater than Karl Marx. Jesus Christ had claimed to be the Son of God, co-equal with God, the Creator. Karl Marx was only one of many with particular ideas on life who went in his turn, like all others, to death to remain there. God had said: 'Prove all things; hold fast the right.' So I need accept nothing that could not be proved to my full satisfaction.

The choice lay clear before me—full submission to God for whatever purpose he had in view for me, regardless of the opinions of men, or, in the event of my recovering from this operation without this incentive, a life without God and without meaning save that of immediate expediency. In short, to be a fool by man's standards, or a fool by God's.

I chose to be God's fool.

Chapter Three

THE CAUSE

The operation was successful, and five weeks later I was up and walking about. I had gone on to the operating table determined to live, and then afterwards to devote myself to finding out and accomplishing whatever purpose God had in store for me. Everything from now on that was not expressly commanded by God I would reject. I would devote myself as never before to the study of the Scriptures, not so much that I might merely increase my knowledge of them as had been my object in the past, but rather that I might find the principles governing approach to and discerning of the mind of God, and thus be perfected as an instrument for His use in His time. Nor would I forsake my secular reading in all this, for it provided a healthy form of intellectual gymnastics, would keep my outlook and sympathies wide, and my mind active and aware of contemporary trends of thought. So much for the training of spirit and mind; there still remained the training of my body. Football, tennis, horse-riding, hiking and mountain-climbing should be sufficient to bring the body into a condition where it could be used in any circumstances and in any part of the world when God should so choose.

I was aware that all this had not constituted a 'call', however, that rather vague spiritual experience ostensibly granted to ministers and missionaries. I knew only too well the various definitions of a 'call', from the merely mercenary ones of an increased stipend and larger congregation to the absurdly mystical ones of emotional disturbance through platform bludgeoning or getting a significant Bible verse at an appropriate moment. My own particular spiritual experience had not indicated a religious calling—either to become a minister, or preacher, or missionary—any more than the infant Samuel's experience made him a priest or a prophet. Like Samuel, I took it simply to mean that I was now under obligation to place my life at the disposal and direction of God—'Speak, Lord, for thy servant heareth.'

It was natural, of course, that I should immediately think of 'becoming a missionary', for that seemed to be the generally accepted target for a life dedicated to God. As far as I knew there was no other outlet for a 'lay' person who wished to place himself fully under God's control. Yet I had received no command from God to go abroad, and the only comparable activity at home lay in the sphere of evangelist. Theoretically, an 'evangelist' was one who went to areas where there were no churches or 'meetings' of any kind, depending on God alone for maintenance and guidance as he made known the gospel of Jesus Christ in outlying places. But the increasing sectarianism and formalism of the past years had changed the evangelist's function; he now went from assembly to assembly to hold 'special campaigns' of a few weeks' duration in which the people who formed that particular assembly would rally round in a special effort to assist the evangelist, distributing gospel tracts round the houses in the district and holding open-air meetings. The evangelist would preach every night in the hall, sometimes visiting homes in the area to invite people to attend the hall and hear him preach, and then if any attended—and few did—and were converted—and fewer were—he would baptize them by immersion, and then pass on to another assembly for another campaign. It was true that there were a few, almost unheard of and little known, who were attempting to discharge the work in the New Testament sense of the term, but for the most part the majority of the evangelists seemed to feel that they must 'keep within the assemblies' to ensure their financial support, in the same way as the actor knows that his income depends on his 'keeping in the public eye'.

With my new determination to accept nothing save that which was expressly taught by God, I obviously could not aspire to such a 'calling', even if it were possible to break into the 'circuit'. To one without a command the Scriptural injunction was, 'Whatever the condition which the Lord has assigned to each individual —and whatever his condition when God called him—in that let him continue. This is what I enjoin in all the churches.' God had called me to serve Him, but until He indicated the next step I was under orders to remain as I was, as much as Joseph was when commanded, 'Be thou there until I bring thee word.'

My interest in mountain-climbing led me to read books on the subject by Eric Shipton, Frank Smythe and others, and to follow their expeditions in the Himalayan mountain ranges of Central Asia. It was while I was reading of Sven Hedin's expedition to Tibet in *Trans-Himalaya* that the voice of God spoke again in clear direction—'This is where you will go to preach of Me.'

I thought I was prepared for any eventuality but when the challenge came I was found wanting. My mind protested against the impossibility of the task. Yet God had spoken. There could be no doubt that Central Asia was my place in the purpose of God for whatever work He should choose, and Tibet the first step in that destiny. Tibet, the forbidden land, of which so little was known. Tibet, shut up to foreigners, even those with influential friends in high places. Tibet, a buffer state, isolated by the political agreement of three major powers—Britain, Russia and China. Tibet, in thrall to priests, jealous of their power and unscrupulous in their methods of preserving it. Tibet, the roof of the world, three-quarters of its territory over fifteen thousand feet high. Tibet, without roads or rails, without banks or post offices. Again I was faced with the choice of turning aside into uncertainty or plunging into a gamble with God. Inexorably the voice of God beat down my protests: 'There is nothing too hard for God . . . the nations are esteemed as a drop of the bucket. . . . He breaketh in pieces mighty men without inquiry and setteth others in their stead. . . . There is no authority except from God, and those that exist are set up by God . . . Jehovah, God of our fathers, art not thou God in the heavens, and rulest thou not over all the kingdoms of the nations? And in thy hand there is power and might and none can withstand thee. . . . Fear not nor be dismayed by reason of this great multitude; for the battle is not yours, but God's.' I stammered into silence before God.

It was sheer folly—but the foolishness of God was wiser than men; and Paul, who had become a fool for Christ's sake, had seen the foolishness of preaching Christ accomplish more than the wisdom of Socrates. I, too, had been called to be God's fool.

Although there were several books available on Tibet, yet they seemed to convey singularly little information about the country. Religion and customs were exhaustively covered, but information about travel conditions was practically non-existent. Vast areas of thousands of miles were still blank on the map, with no information as to whether they were inhabited or not. Most of what was known was on the Indian, or western, side of Tibet. To the north lay Russia; to the east, China; to the south, Burma. The British Expeditionary Force under the command of Sir Francis Younghusband, and subsequent expeditions, official and otherwise, had nearly all gone into Tibet from the Indian side, but beyond Lhasa, which was twenty-one days' journey by mule caravan from the Indian border, little was known of the further five months' mule journey to the eastern, or Chinese, border.

The language books available, too, gave western dialects, such as Sir Charles Bell's *Colloquial Grammar and Primer* with its Lhasa background, and Jaschke's *Grammar* with its Ladakh background. On the Chinese side no books were available, and in any case a different dialect was used amongst the inhabitants of that area— wild and independent Tibetans of Kham, the largest province of Tibet. It was evident, then, that any attempt to enter would have to be from the Indian side, where the British Government was in power, and where English was the language medium through which Tibetan could be learned. However, the British Government in India was opposed to any foreigner entering Tibet, and its diplomatic policy was to keep Tibet isolated as a buffer state, so that even Sven Hedin, friend of Lord Curzon, at that time Viceroy of India, could not get official permission to enter.

The unexplored and unknown nature of the country presented

a major problem in methods of sustenance and supply. There were no banks so no money could be obtained; everything would have to be obtained by barter on the spot. There were no shops except in the few remote towns so no goods could be obtained; everything had to be carried. There was no information as to where exactly villages might be found so it might be that, when new food supplies were essential, there would be no inhabitants with whom to barter. Therefore, even given the premise that one could get into the country, the next problem was where to go, and how to exist when one got there.

To the person who believed in God, and who had the Bible for a textbook, the only problem, of course, was the veracity and extent of that belief. I was faced with the inescapable evidence of the fall of Jericho to the people of God, and the entry to Canaan by the people of God, accomplished through obedience to God's commands, in the assurance that He had ordained these things to happen. I was faced with the fact of the remarkable provision of food and water and clothing for the host of Israel, from the delivery from Egypt until, forty years later, the entering into Canaan. I was faced with the evidence of Elijah's solitary defence against Ahab the king, and the prophet's stopping of the rain, through his prayer, for three and a half years, as the punishment for idolatry and apostasy. I was faced with the fact that God had sustained Elijah for these same three and a half years of famine by directing him to a particular brook and feeding him through particular ravens, as well as through the hospitality of a particular widow, with a meagre but miraculously never-ending supply. The principle involved in the successful overthrow of circumstances on behalf of God was simple and comprehensible: 'I have commanded the ravens to feed thee *there*. . . . I have commanded the widow woman to feed thee *there*. . . ." To be in the proper place— whether country, valley, brook, home or company—to which God had directed, was to see the purposes of God accomplished by his preparation, because God had willed it so.

It was a principle that had activated all the servants of God from the beginning of time, absolute obedience to every detail of the commands of God. For speaking as God's servant when God had not told him, Moses was only permitted to see the Promised Land from afar off but not allowed to enter it. For not going forward when God commanded it, and for being afraid of the strength of the opposition, a generation of Israelites died in the wilderness without ever entering the Promised Land. For retaining some of the goods of the Amalekite enemies when God had commanded that all should be destroyed, Saul was deprived of his kingdom and saw it given to David. But when men allowed God to direct affairs in them and through them, no matter how impossible of fulfilment they appeared, He always justified their obedience victoriously and gloriously. Such a dependence and allegiance was necessary to safeguard His own glory. The greater the obstacles the less likely were human beings to overcome them, and so the greater glory there was to God in manifesting His power.

To get into Tibet, then, which appeared so impossible an obstacle, and where so many others had failed, meant a complete dependence on God to guide and provide. Many others had gone forth professing the same dependence, but had fallen prey to the weaknesses of human organization and ingenuity, and had consequently fallen short of the objective. There had been nothing wrong with the lives of these others who had tried and failed, but obviously, since there was failure, there must have been something wrong somewhere, for God could not be wrong—and in a choice between saying that all men were wrong or that God was wrong, I decided on the former. Evidently the fault lay not in the *lives* of those who had failed but in the *methods* used.

Brought up as they were in an atmosphere of denominationalism of one kind or another, their whole outlook was coloured by organization. The example of Christ and the early apostles in evangelizing was either forgotten or ignored, the example of direct control and command of the Holy Spirit to speak or withhold from speaking, to move or to stand still. Perhaps they had forgotten that Christ Himself, the Son of God, had said: 'I cannot do anything of myself. . . . I do not seek my will but the will of

Cluster of Tibetan prayer flags, ripped to shreds by howling winds, on top of a mountain near Kangting.

him that has sent me. . . . The works which the Father has given me that I should complete them, the works themselves which I do, bear witness concerning me that the Father has sent me. . . . I have not spoken from myself, but the Father who sent me has himself given me commandment what I should say and what I should speak. . . . As the Father sent me forth, I also send you. . . .'
It was obvious that God alone would control and direct His servants in evangelizing the world. A 'feeling of responsibility' for 'the perishing heathen', or the producing of 'good ideas' to encompass their salvation, was nothing in itself. God required no help from His creatures in forming an 'Asiatic Missionary Society', or the 'Church of Christ in Asia'. He had said, '*I* will build *my* church,' and that was sufficient.

There had been missions within the Roman Catholic Church, and also groups such as the Moravian community, but, in their modern form, missionary societies appeared to have sprung from a peculiar source. They could be traced back to Wilberforce's 'Clapham Sect', a voluntary society formed of his friends to produce reforms in Parliament, including the abolition of slavery, by gaining the support of the public. The rapid development of capitalism through an expanding industrialization, and a growing social consciousness, led to the formation of more and more philanthropic societies on the same voluntary pattern, with business men giving of their time and ability and forming themselves into something on the pattern of a capitalist company, to find the best ways of bringing their 'spiritual' ideas—as opposed to Wilberforce's 'political' ideas—before the public, and soliciting their support for their particular religious cause. On the basis of the support gained in this way, another missionary would be sent out to whatever field particularly interested the 'Board of Directors'.

In the spiritual revolution of the nineteenth century a radical change had been introduced when George Muller of Bristol ran his famous orphanage without soliciting public support, and devoted his energies to praying to God to provide in whatever way He saw fit all that was required to meet the daily needs of over two thousand children. This followed the 'novel' example of Anthony Norris Groves who abandoned a lucrative dental practice to travel to Persia and India to preach, moving step by step as God commanded him, and without a 'Home Board' behind him to send out money as required, depending entirely on God to provide through whatever channels He saw fit to use. Robert Morrison and Hudson Taylor to China, the famous Cambridge Seven, including the England cricketer, C. T. Studd, to China, India and Africa, indicated a fresh return to the old apostolic methods, with the world once more on the brink of being shaken by a dynamic gospel.

However, as before, this individual dependence on God for guidance and provision to meet whatever situation arose in whatever surroundings was undermined by human reasoning and the inevitable organization, and those who had themselves gone out in full dependence on God alone, and known His support, evidently began to feel that this same principle did not apply to *all* servants of God, for they gradually modified their stand and compromised with 'common sense' by forming 'Faith Missions' on the same pattern as the previous religio-capitalist 'Board' system, whose function it was to propagate the ideas and works of their particular group associates. There was no direct soliciting, but they adopted the principle of keeping the work and the workers before the public eye, stressing the missionaries' needs and the Christian public's responsibility in meeting that need, and indirectly soliciting by the regular issue of missionary 'prayer-letters', the formation of 'prayer-partner groups' and the gradual expansion of the size and circulation of missionary magazines, depending on the wealth of the particular society. The result was that it was no longer necessary for the 'ordinary' Christian member of the public to listen to God for instructions as to how to disburse his money, but he simply had to select from this wealth of publications whatever 'good scheme' he particularly felt merited some encouragement.

These were the methods, then, used by modern denominational, non-denominational, and inter-denominational groups in advancing foreign missionary work—methods that fell woefully

short of, and often bore no relation to, Scriptural principles—
methods that had their roots in human ingenuity, and were
utterly inadequate to provide the answer to the problems raised
by the evangelization of Tibet or any other country. If I were to
acknowledge the authority of any of the popular modern Missionary Societies or Boards, I should have to apply as a candidate,
go to a Bible School for instruction in Scriptural teaching and
missionary methods, and then, if accepted by that particular Missionary Society, should be assigned to an area selected by them
(unless my choice of field happened to coincide with the Board's
own opinion). There were too many human factors to consider in
such a course, and, contrary to the common contention that 'two
heads are better than one', or that a group of people, or Board,
were less likely to mistake God's will than an individual, there
were too many flaws in practice.

The missionary emphasis of the Plymouth Brethren had started
with the work of Anthony Norris Groves and continued to blos-
som in the Scriptural manner for some time, but gradually they
too forsook the simple principles of Scripture—the responsibility
of the servant to God alone, and the autonomy of the local
church in identifying itself with its own member going abroad as
a missionary—and soon several people got together and decided
to collate various items of news from Brethren missionaries working abroad and issued these items in the form of pamphlets to the
various assemblies, in order to encourage interest and prayer.
This function developed rapidly and soon the people concerned
became the 'forwarding agency' for moneys contributed by Christians who did not know the addresses of certain missionaries
abroad. In time, too, these people acquired the authority to inter-
view 'candidates' sponsored by the Brethren assemblies throughout the country, before they were sent abroad, for their approval
or 'commendation'. If they approved of a candidate his name was
included on a 'prayer-list', and his activities reported regularly in
a magazine devoted to the work of Brethren missionaries; if they
did not approve, while they could not prevent him from being
sent abroad with the full approval of his local assembly, they

would not include his name on the 'prayer-list' as a 'commended worker', and in consequence he would be deprived of the best-known channel of financial support from the assemblies.

The only difference that I could see between this 'system' and any other was that, once commended by the local assembly and approved by the 'Brethren Council', the candidate did not appear to be subject to interference or control from then on—he was then an independent unit, responsible to God alone. However, what was to happen when the last bank was reached, the past post office passed? Of what use then was any assured financial support through organized channels of any kind?

Was the God of Elijah, who had miraculously supplied him with food by the ravens, merely a God who had supplied only for that particular time in history? Or was He equally able to supply —miraculously, if need be—any modern servant in similar circumstances? The generally accepted attitude amongst 'Evangelicals' was—in theory, if not in practice—that they believed God to be a miracle-working God to Moses, David, Elijah, Daniel, Christ and the apostles, but no longer so because there was little necessity to be so. It was obvious that He *could* be if He so desired, but they had little need for Him in this capacity—better if He were just prepared to add His blessing to their 'good ideas'.

There was one way to prove whether that power latent in Christianity was all that God said it was, and also to ground my own belief effectively for all that was to be accomplished in the future, and that was to put it to the test. If I was to be a fool for God let me know the ultimate folly of abandoned credulity, and have as my epitaph, if need be:

May they,
When the forts of folly fall,
Find my body near the wall.

'Be not therefore careful,' said God, 'saying, What shall we eat? or, What shall we drink? or, What shall we put on? for all these things the nations seek after; for your Heavenly Father knows that ye have need of all these things. But seek ye first the kingdom of God and his righteousness and all these things shall be added unto you.' Further, if God was to help me miraculously in Tibet, without a 'natural' source of supply, on the sole principle that I was in the place commanded by God, according to His will, then obviously the same principle applied equally in Britain and I ought to be able to test this miraculous sustaining power there. Consequently, I decided to give away the money I had accumulated over the years, leave myself without any, tell no one of my position so that there could be no question of trickery or duplicity, and ask God for whatever was required for food, clothing, studies, etc. I should then be in an unassailable position to declare whether the God of the Lord Jesus Christ was a living God, sufficient, willing and able to reveal Himself to men, and provide for every need. No need for organization of any kind, denominations or missionary societies, if He were able to sustain all things, as He had promised, by His mighty power.

I told no one of my spiritual experiences, or the spiritual crisis through which I had passed, and this was made easy for me through having to change jobs during that period. Up till the time of my illness I had been a fitter in a local foundry but an uncle suggested that I should now go to work as a machine operator in the munitions section of a large engineering works near by. Rumours of war were gathering, and already working hours in the factory had been extended to twelve hours per day. When war was finally declared on Germany top production was insisted upon, and we were put on to fortnightly spells of day and night shifts, twelve hours a day for seven days a week.

This left very little opportunity for leisure as I had to leave home shortly after five in the morning and did not return again until nearly seven at night. The hard work, too, brought on its own mental and physical fatigue so that I could not concentrate on study as I had been doing. By the time I was twenty-one I had been promoted to foreman, supervising seven hundred men and women in shell production, working even longer hours with the increased responsibility, and was completely exhausted when I reached home. I fought against the constant desire for sleep, and if I did fall asleep over my books I would go to bed and rise in the early hours of the morning to study for an hour or two before going out to work. On several occasions I tried to get out of the rut and volunteered for service with the Forces, where I thought I should have at least some time to call my own, but in vain.

Just when I thought that I could stand no more I was suddenly given a temporary transfer to another job as a test driver of Army vehicles, while the factory was being reorganized on new production lines. It still involved a twelve-hour working day but was day-shift only, and with most Sundays free. Further, the test track was at a sea-side town, Portobello, on the east coast of Scotland, and in the clear, bracing air I began to feel more active and alive again, and turned with a renewed interest to my studies.

The Brethren assembly in Portobello was composed of some eighty people, who met in a small room above a billiard hall, and in addition to the usual types of meetings they held a weekly 'Bible Reading'. This was a conversational type of gathering where one brother would 'open up' a passage of Scripture by reading through it and pointing out the main outlines of the subject under discussion. After that the other brethren were free to add their contribution, in a verse-by-verse debate, supporting any viewpoint by referring to relevant portions in other parts of the Bible, others being ready to agree or disagree, according to their individual knowledge of the Scriptures.

It was my first introduction to this type of meeting, and I was thrilled with the opportunities it afforded for thrashing out controversial subjects from Scripture. There was no question here of a man standing up and giving a prepared sermon for thirty minutes, perhaps containing all sorts of false premises and questionable conclusions, then sitting down and there the matter closed. Here everything that was said had to be possible of support from Scripture, and while a particular viewpoint might be 'nice' or 'appreciated' its true value lay in the weight of Scriptural evidence to support it.

It was a company that exhibited many apparent idiosyncrasies. For example, they would not permit an organ or any other musical instrument to be used in the assembly. The reasons for this were varied and interesting, from the argument that it was Jubal, the descendant of the accursed murderer Cain, who was the 'father of all such as handled the harp and organ', to the argument that nothing should be permitted to enter the assembly that had not first of all 'passed through the waters of baptism'. This astounding theory was adduced from the Old Testament incident where Hiram floated all the trees down the river before they were built into the Temple. The middle-of-the-road position was that God had not seen fit to give any instructions about the use of instruments in the assembly, and so there was no authority for an organ being there at all.

The opposite school argued that Lamech, the first poet in Scripture, was the father of Jubal, and therefore also descended from Cain, and yet hymns were permissible. This was in turn buttressed by the evidence from the Old Testament that, while God had given David no instructions with regard to musical instruments for the Temple, yet David, the 'man after God's own heart', not only put them there, but also put himself to the effort of inventing new musical instruments; and God allowed it, for His glory rested in the Holy of Holies. The middle-of-the-road position for those in favour of music was that, if God had not given instructions regarding the use of instruments in the assembly, neither had He specifically forbidden their use, and therefore either view was permissible according to preference.

They were a group of very fine, genuine believers from various strata of society, but predominantly miners and fishermen. Known amongst other Brethren assembles as the 'Tight' school of thought, because of their strict interpretation of and adherence to Scripture, they refused to allow anyone to 'break bread' (take part in Communion) until they had been baptized by immersion; or, if the applicant for Communion was a visitor, he or she had to produce a 'letter of commendation' from another accredited assembly, since it was held that, while every assembly was autonomous, the 'testimony' in general should be guarded against infiltration by 'grievous wolves' who might creep in unawares and spread 'false doctrine' and thereby destroy the 'liberty in Christ Jesus'. The preachers who came along were also carefully 'sifted', so that only those of a like-minded 'tight' or strict school of thought would be invited to minister the Word of God. This ensured a consistency of attitude and practice among the believers, and was termed by them, 'being faithful to the testimony'.

The mining and fishing element were a deeply devout community, and on visiting each other's homes the talk would most of the time centre in 'the Word', and that in no spirit of sanctimoniousness or cant. Shortly after entering the home Bibles would be brought out and an impromptu 'Bible-reading' would begin that would continue for hours, out of a deep and genuine desire to know more of God. Scriptural principles and precepts were sought out, weighed and discussed in meaning of word and context, until everyone had grasped the truth concerned, young and old alike. The responsibility to God and to men was considered, along with the responsibility of the local assembly (the local manifestations of the 'ecclesia') to God and to men; and the spiritual discipline outlined in Scripture and absorbed in such gatherings was exercised impartially to keep the 'church' pure. They were men and women quietly going about their daily work but whose intensity of devotion to God and desire after the knowledge of His Word exceeded even the proverbial fanaticism of the Communist to Marx and the Communist Manifesto. But there the comparison fell through, because they took no interest in the social, cultural or intellectual problems surrounding them, and even categorically taught that these were outside the legitimate interest of the true Christian. It was not that they took no interest in their neighbour's need, for they recognized a spiritual responsibility in this that often led to material and financial assistance which exceeded anything advocated by doctrinaire Socialists and Communists.

It was amongst such people then, for all the weakness and unacceptability of some of their interpretations and assertions, that the Bible began to reveal fascinating new possibilities. 'Prophetical' and 'typical' studies presented hours of research and instruction in the progressive revelation of the mind of God to men, from the beginning of creation to their relationship with Him in in the eternity to come. The establishing and functioning of the 'ecclesia', the true Church according to the New Testament, became a practical possibility in such a fellowship of believers, who, regardless of clergy, race, colour or social status, would allow the Holy Spirit to exercise any person in individual or corporate obedience to the Word of God, in the maintaining and edifying of the whole structure, while at the same time allowing every individual to pursue whatever calling was his social responsibility. In this way, the whole structure of society would become permeated with the principles of the kingdom of God, and the 'church' be enabled to fulfil its real and eternal purpose—'to announce, among the nations, the glad tidings of the unsearchable riches of the Christ, and to enlighten all with the knowledge of what is the administration of the mystery hidden throughout the ages in God, who has created all things, in order that now to the principalities and authorities in the heavenlies, might be made known through the church the all-various wisdom of God, according to the purpose of the ages, which he purposed in Christ Jesus our Lord'.

The faith was simple and sufficient, the vision compelling and magnificent. It had shaken the world before men had corrupted it and it became vitiated through compromise; it could shake the world again.

Chapter Four

THE GAMBLE

My final decision was precipitated as a result of a conversation with two friends. I had been discussing the usual problem of whether the Scriptures were the God-inspired and complete revelation of the mind of God for men with a clever university student friend, when we were joined by another student who was introduced as 'a staunch Church of Scotland man, who would show that it was possible to be a Christian without accepting absolute authority for Scripture'.

We began with 'Sin' and the 'Fall of Man', and, still arguing, went out to a nearby restaurant for tea. The customers at the adjoining tables were amused and interested, listening to the three-cornered battle—the agnostic, claiming not to believe anything unless capable of proof; the cautious, church-going, 'nominal' Christian; and the fanatical fool.

'There is one way in which any argument you may produce can be floored,' I said finally—'and that is by the scientifically approved one of experiment. Take the word of God as we find it in the Bible out of the wraps of theory and expose it to trial in as many ways as possible, and, according to the principles on which our scholastic and scientific studies are built, you will be able—after a sufficient amount of experiment by trial and error, and by observation and deduction from all the data obtained—either to confirm it or, if you still refuse to accept it, concede that you forsake your own "scientific" position. In other words,' I added, drawing my wallet from my pocket, 'I say there is a God, and that this God has revealed Himself and His purposes for men, in and through His word, the collection of books we know as the

Bible, or Scriptures, and that all truth for men and life is contained there, the key to it being with Jesus Christ, who must be acknowledged as the Son of God, who came from God as the final revelation to men of His will for their redemption from inherited and practised sin. If the absolute divine lordship of Christ is recognized and acknowledged in a day-by-day submission to His control, then all the words of God regarding man's present and future destiny will be fulfilled to the letter, the seal of the future inheritance being in the present revelation of God through the Holy Spirit indwelling the believer. Now, I have some money here,' and I emptied the contents of the wallet on to the tablecloth, and counted—'two pounds, seven shillings altogether. The rest of the money I have is in the bank and in bonds. Well, I'll give away all that's in the bank and in bonds, and keep only this two pounds, seven shillings. I'm due to finish work soon and start medical studies in London in September, so that I won't be earning any money then, and will therefore have no resources or means of support. I only have some knowledge of God, have a belief that I am in His will in going to London for this medical course, and have the Holy Spirit as my means of communicating with Him.

'I make you a promise. I will not tell a single person, other than you two, what I intend doing so that this will be between the three of us and God. I will not tell my parents, nor let it be known to any church or missionary body. I won't dress differently, nor alter my style of living so as to suggest by implication that I am short of money, nor adopt any of the well-known and rather invidious means of drawing attention to my needs. To the interested observer, I will simply be someone who is going to study medicine at his own expense, with no apparent needs, so that people will not feel any compassion or the need to help in the usual way. Only you two will know that I no longer have any resources, and that anything I require will have to be supplied by God. If I have to ask a single person for help, I promise you I will return home, and never again mention the sufficiency of God or my belief in Him.'

The Gamble

There were words of protest at the unnecessary extremism of this step, but the matter rested there on parting. I went home and, after prayer, drew up a list of people to whom I felt that God would have me give my money—some in difficult circumstances at home, some working as missionaries abroad—until I was left with the two pounds, seven shillings, and only next week's wages to come. This would take me as far as Baldock in Hertfordshire, where I had arranged to meet a friend who had a fruit farm there but who spent most of his time preaching in the surrounding villages, before beginning my studies in London.

I decided not to lay aside any money for my tuition fees, on the same principle of 'taking no thought for the morrow'. To set anything aside for 'a rainy day', or 'just in case something cropped up', seemed to me to belittle the ability of God to provide, and was not 'faith' in its real sense. Since God had not promised me a 'tomorrow', then if God had given me more money that I required for 'to-day' it must obviously follow that the surplus of money was for someone who required it that day, if God so directed. When God knew that I required money for fees or food or clothing or for any other reason, He could just as easily supply it through any other spiritually sensitive or God-conscious channel on the same principle. There could be no compromise if victory was to be assured in the battle ahead to the glory of God. Pure revelation demanded a pure faith. What was it Browning had said?—

> *Pure faith, indeed—you know not what you ask!*
> *Naked belief in God the Omnipotent,*
> *Omniscient, Omnipresent, sears too much*
> *The sense of conscious creatures to be borne;*
> *It were the seeing Him; no flesh shall dare.*

But it was just *that* faith that God demanded, and to which every follower must aspire.

On leaving my job, I had intended entering university to study medicine, but God indicated that the seven-year course required for a degree was too long, and was not within the scope of His

44

purposes for me in the future. A knowledge of medicine for my own use in unexplored areas, and the ability to help any with whom I might come into contact, would be sufficient, and I learned that such a course was available at the Missionary School of Medicine in London, from a young fellow who had just returned from taking that course and whom I met in a mutual friend's house. I applied and was accepted for a year's concentrated study of Anatomy, Physiology, Medicine, Dentistry, Surgery and the use of anaesthetics, beginning in September 1945.

The school had been bombed during the war, and no hostel facilities were available, so that all students were responsible for finding their own lodgings. It was right in the centre of London, off Southampton Row, which meant that it was very difficult to find suitable board and logings near at hand, and some distance would have to be travelled every day to and from the school. I had no notion of where I might stay, and London was a strange city, but, just before I left Hertfordshire, a friend gave me his brother's address in London, and also the name of another friend. I went to both of these people on the day of my arrival but neither of them had any room to spare. However, one of them introduced me to a neighbour, and I was fixed up in a Mr. Gibbs's home in Hackney for the duration of my stay in London.

The money for my trip to London had been miraculously provided at the last minute. David Haxton, my friend with the fruit farm, came to me just before I left Baldock and informed me that the Lord had instructed him to give me £5. Some of the other Christians had also come at different times, and in different ways had said much the same thing: 'This is a gift from the Lord' . . . 'We would like you to have this as from the Lord' . . . 'I feel that God would have me give you this'—and had in this way provided me with over £20, covering my fare and school fees. I had given them no indication of my personal circumstances, and to all outward appearances showed no signs of being in need, and these were country folks, many of them not at all comfortably off.

It was a glorious and unforgettable experience to rise morning by morning, sometimes with only sufficient money to pay my bus fare to the centre of the city, and then perhaps find a letter addressed to 'G. Patterson, Esq., c/o Missionary School of Medicine, London', containing some gift, sometimes from people I had never seen, or never heard of, or from a sender, who preferred to remain anonymous, only 'The Lord had told them'. The landlady was due to be paid every Saturday morning after breakfast—and there were occasions when I had to wait until the last minute before God provided the week's rent money. There was the time when the normal postal delivery was past, and the postman gone, without any sign of my week's rent turning up, and a registered letter was delivered by special delivery, before I had finished breakfast. Always what I needed was provided in time, but rarely in the way which I would have anticipated. The channel of supply was not confined to the post office either. Once I put my hand in my overcoat pocket, left hanging on a peg, after spending the last of my money on a restaurant meal and found a £1 note that had certainly not been there when I entered. In a multitude of ways, without ever having to inform a single person and without any church or organization supporting me, I received all that was necessary to pay for lodgings and tuition in a strange city.

Except on one occasion. I had finished a term and arranged to return home to Scotland for the vacation, but God had only supplied me with £3. This meant that if I bought a ticket to go home, I could not pay my landlady, and if I paid my landlady, I could not pay my railway fare home. There was really no choice, from the Scriptural standpoint, for I had just lived for a week at the landlady's expense and was therefore morally bound to use what God had given me for that purpose. I had no justification from Scripture for postponing payment, for any attempt to do so would be a confession of failure in faith and a violation of principle. Nor could such a course be reconciled with the conclusions of experience, for very often it had seemed to me that it was too late for God possibly to supply—only to find my needs met at the very last moment. Now I had all day in front of me before my train left Euston Station for Scotland.

The Gamble

I paid the landlady and left for the end-of-term examination at school, telling her that I would not return as I was leaving for Scotland that night. The day was unproductive as far as my requirements were concerned, no letter or Good Samaritan appearing. As evening drew near I became fascinated by the gamble against human odds, and throwing everything on God I paid the supper bill for myself and two fellow students, just before the train was due to leave. I had known God to supply on one occasion when I was standing in a bus queue without my fare, and a friend had drawn up in his car, thrust an envelope containing £5 into my hand and driven off with only a wave of his hand. It had happened before: it could happen again. But it did not.

I walked up to the booking office at Euston Station and no messenger from God appeared. I looked at the time on the clock and saw that the train was due to leave almost immediately, and knew that I had to go forward and carry this to its limit or admit failure. I counted my money, and found that I could take a ticket as far as Crewe, which then left me only some loose change, amounting to just over three shillings—and stepping forward, I bought the ticket to Crewe.

I fell asleep shortly after leaving Euston and was wakened by the ticket inspector as the train drew into Crewe. I felt so fogged with sleep, and so weary after my strenuous weeks of study, that my first thought was to give the inspector my name and address and ask to be allowed to pay later. But this course was obviously only an easy way out of the situation and it seemed to me that my whole life was so bound up in the decision that I had to pursue the principle of faith in God to its conclusion irrespective of what was involved, so I let the thought go, albeit grudgingly, and stepped on to the cold bare platform, into the dispiriting atmosphere that seems to belong peculiarly to large railway junctions at midnight. I had a cup of tea and a sandwich at the snack bar, then left the steaming warmth of the place for the cold darkness of the road. I did not know what lay in front of me. I only knew that if necessary I would walk all the way to Scotland before passing judgement on God.

The Gamble

I walked on through the night, stopping only for a short sleep under a hedge, until the cold wakened me and compelled me to move on again. I was on the outskirts of some town when a lamp was suddenly shone in my face, and a voice said: "Hullo! What are you doing here at this time of the morning?"

When my eyes became accustomed to the light I saw that the voice belonged to a policeman, who was scowling at me suspiciously. 'Walking,' I replied laconically, faintly irritated at the officious tones in my present state of fatigue.

'I can see that,' growled the policemen. 'Where to?'

'Scotland,' I returned, ambiguously.

'Let me see your identity card," the policeman said abruptly. I pulled out my wallet, and handed over the card without a word. 'Hmmmm . . . George N. Patterson, Laurieston, Falkirk; Wellington Street, Portobello; Montague Road, London; you get around, don't you?' he said dryly. 'What do you do for a living?'

For a moment I was tempted to make a facetious reply, but instead restrained myself and said: 'Yes I do. Student.'

'And what are you doing here'—he was obviously about to say again, 'at this time of the morning?' when he thought better of it and left the question in mid air.

'Walking to Scotland. I've got no money, you see,' I volunteered gravely. To be under suspicion from the law as a servant of God was a new and not totally unpleasing experience.

The policeman evidently thought his leg was being pulled for he swung the torch to inspect the whole of my person and obviously noted the polished brown shoes, well-pressed trousers, sound waterproof with the silk scarf knotted at the throat and carved walking stick, for he said heavily: 'Oh, yes. You'd better come along with me.'

We walked in silence for some time until, as we approached the centre of the town, which the signposts declared to be a place called Middleton, we could see each other more clearly in the lamplights and in the grey light of early morning. The policeman began to ask a few more questions, guardedly at first, then as he received unusual, though civil enough, replies as to my activities and beliefs he seemed to forget his earlier suspicions and talked freely. He was in deep waters when it came to talking about God, but valiantly volunteered the information that his grandfather was from Scotland and a very religious gentleman. Evidently he must have changed his opinion about my character for no more was said about 'coming along with him', presumably to the police station for interrogation, and he went so far as to offer his company as far as the main road out of Middleton, where he informed me there would be the possibility of a lift in a lorry travelling north to Warrington.

After leaving the policeman I walked on without getting a lift and, nearing a railway station, decided to go and inquire the price of a ticket to Warrington, remembering that my friend, David Haxton, had moved to there from Baldock, and I would be sure of a bed there at least—which seemed to me my most pressing need at that moment. The ticket cost two-and-sixpence and I sank on to the carriage seat beside the workmen with relief.

I arrived in Warrington about eight o'clock to find the Haxtons preparing to leave for a day in Manchester where David was to speak at a Youth Rally at night. I had a quick breakfast and went off with them and, when we arrived in Manchester, agreed to go on with David Haxton, to stay overnight with a friend and take part of the responsibility for preaching on the Sunday. When I was leaving the hall after having preached, a young fellow came up and handed me an envelope—containing two pounds. I returned to Warrington to stay the night, and left early next morning to walk to Preston from where I took the train to Scotland. When I arrived home my mother took one look at me and wept.

'Have you been walking from London?' she cried, and when I nodded cheerfully, 'I knew it, I knew it. But what was wrong? Didn't you have your train fare?' I shook my head negatively, and she continued: 'But what was wrong? How was it you had no money?'

I had never told my parents of my decision to give away all my money, as I had promised my two friends, so that she could not understand why I should have to walk because of a lack of money.

Then she added, surprisingly: 'That was all my fault. Someone gave me £5 to give to you but I didn't bother to send it on to you for I thought you wouldn't need it before you came home. Then Mr. Easson came out with another £5 to give you, and I began to wonder why folks should suddenly want to give you money, but then didn't think anything more about it. When you didn't come on Saturday morning I phoned your landlady and when she said you had gone home suddenly thought then somehow that you might have no money, although I couldn't understand how that could be when you had plenty before you left home.'

I explained then the circumstances and my reasoning, and told them they must never feel that they had a special parental responsibility for 'helping' me, for that would only serve to confuse the whole issue. They themselves were too well aware of the spiritual principles involved to demur, although, after the recent experience, they might spend some very anxious moments. I pointed out, too, that they were not really responsible for any blockage of supply, for obviously God who had supplied ten pounds to my mother could have supplied five pounds to me through some other channel if that had been His intention. God's purpose must have included that test of faith for me, to see how far I was prepared to go without questioning God—and included also, in His purpose, was the conversation with the policeman, the address to the meeting outside Manchester, and the other meetings that I had agreed to take with David Haxton in a fortnight's time on my return.

I needed that test of faith, too, for on returning to the medical school I was faced with what appeared to be an insurmountable obstacle. For the second time I received intimation that I was to be called up for service with the Forces. I had already received one set of papers, and had lodged a protest against any further 'war service'. When I appeared for my medical examination I was told that I had no other option than to go into the Forces, as there was no possible ground of appeal in my circumstances. I asked for the appropriate forms that should be completed to register a protest with higher authorities, and finally was given a conscientious objector's form as being the nearest to what I required. I had completed the form, pointing out that I was not a conscientious objector, having been engaged in munitions production for six years already, but that I was objecting to service now for two reasons. Firstly, I had served my country as an obedient citizen night and day for six years in the capacity for which the Government thought me best fitted; had I been accepted for service with the Forces then I would now be free to continue whatever work I desired. Secondly, God had now given me another task to do, and my allegiance to the commands of God was above my allegiance to my country in rendering unto God the things that were God's and unto Caesar the things that were Caesar's. When the two conflicted then 'obey God rather than men' was the divine command.

After completing that form I had heard nothing further until the arrival of this new letter, summoning me for yet another medical examination. I reported my request, and then lodged another protest within twenty-four hours, according to the provisions laid down. This time there was a response and I was ordered to appear before the local tribunal for conscientious objectors.

Just before leaving for the tribunal I received a telegram from my father containing the good counsel to 'walk humbly, be wise as serpents, and as harmless as doves'. Good counsel it was, but very difficult to follow in the face of the bullying tactics of the Judge-Jeffreys-type Chairman, a poor advertisement for the renowned integrity of British justice. He seemed to take a sadistic delight in pondering over each case, then dismissing it as sarcastically and contemptuously as possible. When one nervous young fellow fainted under cross-examination, he sneeringly ordered him to be removed and brought back when he recovered, and coldly called out the next name: 'George N. Patterson'.

I walked forward slowly to the well of the court, my eyes on the three men above and in front of me, struck by the incongruity of their quiet laughter as they discussed something between themselves. It had come to this, then, that contemptible little parish bullies were authorized to sit in judgement on a man's dearest beliefs and arbitrate on his destiny. Unable to see that their own moral cowardice was greater than the supposed physical cowardice which they so obviously attributed to their victims, they were as blatantly biased in judgement and as perverted in spirit as it was possible for any human being to be—and yet they were authorized to decide the sphere of my activities for the next few years of my life. It was monstrous. Men so conspicuously given over to calculated injustice were evidently opposed to divine principles and would naturally give judgement against me. But I would never accept their decision. I would fight it through to the end. It was not just a question of miscarriage of justice, or a battle of wits between the individual and the State, it was a question of the existence of a personal God and His revealed destiny to a man who believed in Him.

The dry, pseudo-impartial voice read out my name and history and the grounds of my protest, and then went on to build up a damning case against my 'conscientious objection', citing my willingness to participate in the manufacture of munitions as proof of its folly. Such were the 'heads I win, tails you lose' tactics so beloved of many such tribunals. Perhaps I should have interrupted earlier; perhaps it was a tactical error to let that cynical voice swell out in mounting triumph in a flood of oratory, and then, when the last rhetorical nail was ostensibly driven home in a satisfied tone, to make its owner look ridiculous after such an effort by saying only that I agreed, I was not a conscientious objector, indeed I had specifically stated that, together with my real objections on the paper now in front of the chairman. It was the end. There was a little word-play on the old legal loaded questions: 'What would you do if someone struck your sister?' 'Doesn't the Bible say that the powers-that-be are ordained of God?' etcetera. All completely irrelevant, but apparently necessary for their self-justification in the verdict already reached in their own minds.

'Your plea for exemption is dismissed, but you will be permitted non-combatant service,' finished the chairman.

The Gamble

It was the final twist in this travesty. 'I do not want non-combatant service,' I replied steadily, 'and I appeal against your decision.' I left the court and went into a side room where a clerk gave me a form of appeal to the London Appellate Tribunal, which I completed and posted right away.

Some time later I received a summons to appear before the Appellate Tribunal in a different part of London. Strangely enough, the court-room was smaller and the proceedings more informal, which was the opposite to what I had anticipated. Again there were three men, a chairman and two colleagues, but this time such courtesy and sympathetic consideration were shown as could not have been exceeded. The chairman listened to me thoughtfully, putting in an occasional question, and then, when I had finished, said he would like to ask only one more question: 'In the event of your application for exemption being rejected by this tribunal will you accept that decision as final, or will you refuse to go to the Forces and go to prison instead?'

'I will never go into the Forces, for the reasons I have given,' I answered, politely but firmly. 'If it means prison then I am willing to accept this.'

'But you will be of no service to your God there,' the chairman pointed out, reasonably enough.

'Nor will I be of service to my country,' I replied, 'but I will have been faithful to my God; and I feel that I have already done all the service that could reasonably be asked of me by my country.'

The chairman spoke in a low voice with his colleagues for a few minutes, and then made his statement. 'I am afraid it is beyond the authority of this tribunal to establish a precedent in this matter, and so we must reject your appeal. The decision of the local tribunal must stand.'

I was stunned. I had been so sure that God would step in miraculously to prevent this, and only that morning I had been reading of the three young Hebrew captives who had defied the might of Nebuchadnezzar and the Babylonian Empire: ' . . . If it be so, our God whom we serve is able to deliver us from the burning fiery furnace, and he will deliver us out of thine hand, O king; but if not, be it known unto thee, O king, that we will not serve thy gods, nor worship the golden image which thou hast set up. . . .'

And now it appeared that it was the second of these alternatives that was to happen. The modern Nebuchadnezzars and their golden images, totalitarianism and the State, could no more be bowed down to than their ancient counterparts, even if it meant the burning fiery furnace or its counterpart. Perhaps I might be forgiven by friends if I compromised principles through pressure of such circumstances, but if I aspired to be the representative of God in an alien environment then I must never allow expediency or convenience to govern my life. Mine must be the divine bondage that was more desirable than human freedom.

I left the court and made my way towards Westminster Abbey, a favourite spot when I wanted peace and quiet in which to think and make a decision. There was no one there when I arrived, and I walked down the centre aisle to a seat near the front, the sound of my heel-taps ringing sharply in the quietness. I did not notice the time pass as I reviewed my life, and sifted my actions and beliefs, but gradually it was borne in upon me that the organist was playing a Bach Prelude, and I lifted my head to let my spirit rise with the soaring thunder of the organ's bourdon note. When the recital finished I felt washed of all doubt, and rising to my feet I passed into the aisle again on my way out, when I suddenly stopped. There on the floor at my feet was the inscribed plaque to David Livingstone: 'Other sheep have I which are not of this fold . . . them also I must bring.' I left the Abbey, and the sound of the traffic outside was like the Bach Prelude in my ears.

I returned the form, permitting me non-combatant service, again pointing out that I was not objecting to combatant service but to all service, and then carried on as before with my studies, every day expecting to find my call-up papers in the post. I had been told that I would probably receive them in about ten days, but the days moved into weeks, and the weeks into months, and still the only word that I received was an official form from some

Government department asking me to state what my studies were and what were the marks obtained at the last examinations. I had almost completed the medical course when I received call-up papers again. I reported as before for medical examination, and explained again that I was not prepared to serve in the Forces, and was in turn assured that I would receive the final call-up papers in ten days.

I concluded that if faith is 'the assurance of things hoped for, the conviction of things not seen', I must carry on as if no obstacles existed to the accomplishing of the will of God, and now that the medical course was finished and the examinations passed I must make preparations to leave the country—which meant starting by booking my passage out.

A few months previously I had met a young fellow, Geoffrey Bull, at that time awaiting demobilization from the Non-Combatant Corps, who also intended going to Tibet. I had made his acquaintance in an unusual way. When I had distributed my capital the previous year I had sent some money to a missionary working in India. I had had no knowledge of the details of the work there, but in replying the missionary had said that he was working in the Tibetan language amongst the Tibetan people. I had no idea that a Brethren missionary was working amongst Tibetans and a correspondence developed between us, in the course of which the missionary mentioned another young man interested in Tibet, and gave his name, Geoffrey Bull, and his address.

I wrote to Geoff, and we had managed to meet once or twice during his leaves, when we found that we had much in common in faith and vision. Geoff expected to be demobbed before the end of 1946, and hoped to leave for India as soon as possible after that. It was assumed by both of us that we should go to India, as that was the only approach we knew from our reading, and, moreover, our friend was on the Indian-Tibetan border. Poring over a map in London on one occasion we traced our projected route through Kalimpong in North India, the beginning of the trade route through Tibet to China.

The Gamble

So it came as an overwhelming surprise when one day, while at prayer, God said to me: 'You will go to Tibet via China.'

It did not make sense. I knew no one in China. There was very little information available of expeditions on the Sino-Tibetan border. There were no language books on the dialect spoken there, and any language studies would have to be done through the medium of Chinese, which would have to be learned first, before a start could be made on Tibetan. There was nothing reasonable about it from the human standpoint, and the whole notion seemed foolish. Yet I was certain that God had commanded it, and obedience to divine command must be the governing principle if any activity was to be successful.

I wrote to Geoff of my experience and decision, and the next morning I received a letter from him informing me that he could not go via India as God had commanded him to go by China. Our letters had crossed in the post! The hand of God was with us, directing our steps. We should go by China like Abraham of old, 'not knowing whither'.

I went to book my passage to China through a travel agency in London. It was a late afternoon in a misty London, with streets beginning to fill with late shoppers and hurrying workers. Everything seemed strikingly vivid and clear—the hurrying anonymous faces, the rushing traffic, the lights springing on one by one in the dusk—and yet it all seemed unreal. For the passage taking me to a strange land and a strange destiny, which would involve an expenditure of thousands of pounds before we were through, as well as the rejection of universally accepted principles, was to cost £120—and I was alone, in the middle of a strange city, without enough money to pay for a bus ride home! I had only 2½d. in my pocket and had to walk to High Holborn before I was able to take a bus to my lodgings in Hackney.

It was stimulating to walk with God in a daily gamble, when all around were evidences of a frustrated hunger after an empty, transient excitement to relieve the colourless monotony of a meaningless existence. Life—abundant life—was waiting to be grasped and it was being rejected in favour of the mechanics of a

The Gamble

mere existence. So much Francis Thompson must have felt when, sitting on the Embankment and thinking of the kingdom of God, he wrote:

> *O world invisible, we view thee,*
> *O world intangible, we touch thee,*
> *O world unknowable, we know thee,*
> *Inapprehensible, we clutch thee!*
>
> *Does the fish soar to find the ocean,*
> *The eagle plunge to find the air—*
> *That we ask of the stars in motion*
> *If they have rumour of thee there?*
>
> *Not where the wheeling systems darken,*
> *And our benumbed conceiving soars!—*
> *The drift of pinions, would we hearken,*
> *Beats at our clay-shuttered doors.*
>
> *The angels keep their ancient places;—*
> *Turn but a stone, and start a wing!*
> *'Tis ye, 'tis your estrangèd faces,*
> *That miss the many-splendoured thing.*
>
> *But (when so sad thou canst not sadder)*
> *Cry;—and upon thy so sore loss*
> *Shall shine the traffic of Jacob's ladder,*
> *Pitched between Heaven and Charing Cross.*
>
> *Yea, in the night my Soul, my daughter,*
> *Cry,—clinging Heaven by the hems;*
> *And lo, Christ walking on the water*
> *Not of Gennesareth, but Thames!*

Chapter Five

THE DEPARTURE

I returned to Scotland to make preparations for departure, confident that there was nothing of the vision given to me that God would not accomplish. Even the arrival of another set of medical call-up papers did not disturb me, and again I lodged a protest when I left the recruiting centre.

With my year's experience of God's sufficiency in London behind me to buttress my distrust of human ingenuity in divine things, I was reluctant to appear before any 'Council of Brethren' in Glasgow, the accepted procedure for Brethren missionary candidates. I would have the commendation of the elders in my own assembly according to Scripture, and that was all that was needed. But Mr. Easson, an old and respected friend, one of the chief men among the Brethren in mid-Scotland, persuaded me to recognize the 'order', insisting that there was no compromise of principle involved in attending the meeting of brethren, who were interested only in the spiritual nature of my call. I forbore to point out that I knew of several occasions when the brethren had ignored the spiritual nature of a call for very natural reasons—including one from Mr. Easson's own assembly. However, I concluded that there could be no harm in going anyway, and very hesitantly completed a questionnaire which purported to be necessary for official Government purposes before anyone was allowed to leave the country, and I appeared before the council accompanied by Mr. Easson and another friend, James Black.

The meeting was held in a block of offices in St. Enoch's Square, Glasgow, and took rather the form of a board meeting. About a dozen business men, representing various assemblies, were seated around a large table. The 'company directors' setting was offset considerably by a very friendly and congenial atmosphere. I was offered a chair at the foot of the table, facing the others, and was asked if I would like to give an account of my 'call'.

When I had recounted my spiritual experiences leading to my conviction of going to Tibet, several of the brethren then asked me questions:

'Have you a good ear for music? That is very important in language study.'

'Have you any experience in building? You may have to build a house or a hall.'

'Have you ever led any souls to the Lord? If you cannot do this in Britain, you can hardly expect to do it abroad.'

One of them leaned forward. 'Mr. Patterson, I should like to ask you a question, if I may. I notice from the questionnaire here that you have been in a famous engineering works, engaged on munitions production—in a good position, too. I am in engineering myself, and I know that you must have been very well paid, yet you state here regarding your present resources, "None". Now if you are going to receive the Lord's money in future, it is essential that you be a good steward, and in view of this, I should like you to explain your reasons for answering "None".'

I told them briefly of the disbursement of my capital, and the reasons for it. There was a hesitant silence, and then one of them said: 'But Mr. Patterson, wouldn't it have been much wiser to keep the money and not throw it about recklessly, even for such good motives? After all, you have an expensive passage to pay for, and a lot of expensive kit to buy before you go abroad. Perhaps the Lord gave you the money for that very purpose. Now you still have to find it elsewhere.'

'The God who supplied it then is the God who can supply it now,' I answered. 'I would have had to begin "living my faith" some time—and now I have the experience *before* I go abroad, and the confidence that God can supply in any circumstances.'

Nothing more was said on the matter, although several of the business men continued to look dubious. Bob Easson and James Black had a few words to say on my behalf, and then I was assured that I should have the commendation of the 'Brethren' and go forth with their prayers.

'Can you come and speak at the meeting in Camelon next Sunday?' asked Bob Easson afterwards, 'and then come and have tea with us? I have one or two things I want to say to you.'

My subject at Camelon had been 'The Church', and after a short discussion at tea on whether or not 'The Church' was the 'Bride' referred to in Scripture, Mr. Easson came to the point.

'I want tae gi'e you a word o' warning,' he began bluntly. 'When young fellows leave tae work on the foreign field, they very often have a guid grasp o' Scriptural principles—in theory; but, when they get there, their letters begin to get more and more concerned wi' the high cost o' living oot there, and the high standard o' living back here. Ye had better decide before ye go, whaur your support is goin' tae come from. Dinna depend on the "Brethren" at Bath, or at Glasgow, or even on your ain assembly; be like Elijah, and depend on God alone. Elijah wisna disappointed, and neither will you be.'

I smiled at the old man, to whom I owed so much, and for whom I had the greatest respect and affection.

'Well, whit are ye smilin' at? It's nothin' tae laugh aboot. You young men seem tae forget that the Scripture says, "Young men be strong"—no' "Young men be headstrong"!'

'I'm just smiling at the idea of being dependent on any organization or assembly for support,' I said, 'when for the past year I have managed to live without them.'

The old man scowled at me from under grey-tufted brows and then growled uncertainly: 'Whit dae ye mean? I heard whit ye said at Glasgow, but didnae rightly follow what was goin' on. Whit did ye say happened tae a' the money ye had?'

'I gave it away, as God instructed me,' I replied. 'I wanted to be like Elijah you're talking about, and depend on God,' I added gravely, but still smiling.

'Dae ye mean tae tell me ye went tae London wi' nae money in your pocket, and lived for a year that way?' the old man asked incredulously.

'I went to London with two pounds seven shillings in my pocket,' I corrected lightly, 'and lived for eighteen months that way.'

'Why did ye no' tell your assembly—or tell me, so that I could have telt the other assemblies?' he demanded.

'Because I wanted to be like Elijah, and it would have been contrary to Scripture for me to do that; and secondly, because God didn't tell me to work that way; thirdly, I wanted to find out if Elijah's God was still the same today. There are plenty of people who say He is, you know,' I added gently, 'but there aren't many who really believe it.'

The old man was speechless for a few moments, and when he looked up, I noticed there were tears in his eyes. 'And did ye get a' ye needed?' he asked quietly.

'On every occasion except one.' And I recounted the incident. 'And, in addition, my fare and all my kit are paid for,' I concluded.

'Ah, weel,' the old man growled accusingly, apropos of his own thoughts, 'ye were aye ower weel-dressed onywey. We'll ha'e a word o' prayer afore ye go.'

A few weeks later I received word from the travel agents that a passage had been booked for me on the S.S. *Stratheden* due to sail on March 5th from Southampton, and was pitched into the rush of last-minute preparations.

I informed the Ministry of Labour and National Service that I had been allotted a passage to China and would they please inform me what steps I should take about leaving the country as an official exit permit was necessary. I received the reply:

'Dear Sir,

'NATIONAL SERVICE ACTS

'I have to refer to your letter of the 11th inst., the contents of which we have noted.

'Would you be good enough to inform the Ministry whenever

the Shipping Company notify you of the exact date on which you will sail for China. The position regarding your liability to be called up for Military Service remains as stated in our letter of 21st August 1946.

'Yours, etc.'

I took it to mean that if I were not called up before the ship sailed I could go right ahead and leave the country. I had little doubt that the inexplicable permission had been ordered of God. A possible explanation I heard from my father. It appeared that, about the time of the London Appellate Tribunal, my father had written to the Home Secretary telling him of my position with regard to the demands of National Service, and my desire to go abroad as a missionary. He had added:

'. . . Having read the Prime Minister's speech at the recent General Assembly, in which he stressed the paramount spiritual need of the present time, I make this request for the gracious exercise of your personal official intervention to secure his exemption to permit the furtherance of his calling. Confident of your consideration and sympathy.

'Yours, etc.'

Whatever the explanation, the sovereign influence of God was necessary in the lives of certain people, and I was more certain than ever that the God who knew no obstacles in the past could be safely trusted with the future. In the meantime, Geoff had met some missionaries from China and they had invited Geoff and me to stay with them in Central China until we had sufficient language to travel further west into Tibet. They estimated that at least three years' study would be necessary to lay a language foundation by means of which we could travel, and through which any satisfactory approach to the Tibetan language could be made. It seemed a reasonable assumption, and it also afforded time for God to move in any manner needed to open our way into Tibet itself. We had also heard, in the meantime, of another young fellow, Gordon Bell, who felt that he was called to work in Tibet, and who expected to finish his medical studies in a few months when he would join us in China, prior to moving into Tibet.

The Departure

The ship steamed out of Southampton in the drizzly grey dawn of 5th March 1947, and five hours later I was sea-sick. Gibraltar was close at hand before I began to take an interest in my surroundings again.

I had met Geoff on board, and we occupied a cabin which had been turned into a large dormitory. The ship had been used as a troop carrier during the war and had not yet been reconverted for civilian use, and so was carrying all the passengers in one class. There were about one hundred missionaries on board, either new recruits or 'old hands' returning to their districts now that the war was over, out of a total of some thousand adults and two hundred and fifty children—so there was plenty of 'activity' in hymn-singing, children's services, gospel meetings and Bible-readings.

It was my first experience of the contempt in which the missionary was held by his 'pagan' fellow-countrymen abroad, and I was astonished by it. At home I had seen, and in a measure had become accustomed to, the stigma attached to Christianity, particularly Evangelical Christianity, but then it was an accepted maxim of our generation that enthusiasm in any form was *infra dig.*, and in religion especially definitely *de trop*. Yet at home there was in some respects a quality of good-natured tolerance about the superciliousness. Here on board ship the contempt was marked and bitter, to the point even of unbearable disgust. It was a puzzling attitude for there seemed to be no reasonableness about it, unless it lay in some sort of guilt complex. The lives of many of those who despised the missionaries consisted of a selfish round of pleasure-seeking, from deck games in the morning to propping up the bar in the evening, and according to their own tales their lives at their various destinations were made up of the same daily round, with a period of regrettable but compulsory association with the natives in order to be able to earn sufficient money to be able to continue the process. They had nothing at all to give, and little time to spare even for the care of their own children on board, and yet they despised those whose lives consisted of giving, many of whom were their intellectual and social superiors

63

and who could have held positions higher than many of their critics would ever hold.

It was ironical to think that those same parroting products of a perverted materialist concept of life, inherited directly or indirectly from Darwin, had forgotten or were in ignorance of the admiration that that same supposed father of materialism had for the missionary. In his classic account of *The Voyage of the Beagle*, in writing of Tahiti and the attacks made on missionaries by English critics, Darwin had said: 'Such reasoners never compare the present state with that of the island only twenty years ago; not even with that of Europe at this day; they expect the missionaries to effect that which the Apostles failed to do. . . . They forget the human sacrifices, a system of profligacy unparalleled in any other part of the world, infanticide, bloody wars, destruction of women and children—all these have been abolished. For a voyager to forget these things is base ingratitude; for should he chance to be at the point of shipwreck on some unknown coast, he will most devoutly pray that the lesson of the missionary may have extended thus far. But it is useless to argue with such reasoners; I believe that, disappointed in not finding the field of licentiousness quite so open as formerly, they will not give credit to a morality which they do not wish to practise, or to a religion that they undervalue, if not despise.' But since the time of Darwin, George Bernard Shaw and Somerset Maugham had popularized the caricature of the missionary to bestow on society an intellectual benison for its contempt.

I was aware, too, of the sanctimoniousness and barely concealed superciliousness of the 'professional' Christian, be he priest, missionary, minister, or soul-winner, whose personal obnoxiousness aroused antagonism, and who, with the dedicated smile cloaking his or her own self-esteem, succeeded in confusing the offensiveness of the Christian with the offence of the Cross. Products of an unthinking but militant traditionalism they solved the problems of the Universe to their own satisfaction with a Bible School Handbook of answers and a tolerant smile. The incongruities and puerilities of both parties would have been amusing to analyse had there not been such tragic underlying connotations to the yawning gulf.

Port Said came as a relief after ten days at sea, with its shouting, gesticulating 'bumboatmen', acquisitive shopkeepers and large Simon Artz store; but the most lasting impression would always be the unclean memory of the persistent, whispering vendors of Spanish fly and nude photographs, who followed us everywhere.

It was in Ceylon that the East first began to entwine itself around my senses. Our arrival on shore started a rush of natives offering their services as guides, rickshaw-pullers and pimps. My chief impression was the study in contrasts. A large, gleaming limousine would pass a slowly plodding, bullock-drawn, bamboo cart; a native in flowing white robe would pass with a friend in faultlessly cut western lounge suit; women in beautiful saris would pass almost naked sisters begging in the gutters; dirty, mysterious-looking shops would front one side of a street while on the other would be an exquisite palace of gleaming white stone, surrounded by trees, bushes, shrubs and flowers of every shade of green and every variety of colour. The temple was an imposing building of ornate architecture, and with a feeling of emptiness about it. The meeting hall for Christian believers was simply built, of white stone, with large windows opening on all sides to a well-kept green lawn, surrounded by tall, graceful palm trees and intensely green shrubs with white, red and pink blossoms; inside the hall it was cool from whirling fans and warm with friendliness.

Perhaps it was the colourful intensity of contrasts on the island, or perhaps it was the strange tropical storm that raged all about the ship when we returned on board, when a howling wind screamed and tore at the rigging and lightning blazed and ran across the heavens while the sea itself remained perfectly calm— whatever it was, the fancy-dress party that night was strangely tawdry and insipid.

Singapore might well have been an English harbour but for the heat. Some missionary friends were awaiting the arrival of the ship, and took Geoff and me off on a sight-seeing tour. It was a swiftly changing kaleidoscope. A large street with Chinese shopfronts opening right on to the roadside; barrows and stalls, with goods of every description, scattered about the street; the shouts and shrieks of the passengers as they struggled on or off the tightly packed bus before the driver moved off again; washing hanging like victory flags from every window, and stretched right across the streets; the strident hooting of the driver's horn as he tore along the crowded road, scattering pedestrians to right and left; the expression on Geoff's face as the bus swayed drunkenly from side to side, and coolie after coolie seemed to disappear under the wheels; lorries appearing suddenly from nowhere with shouting, gesticulating drivers; rickshaw-men wandering right in front of the wildly careering bus; native children darting out in front with flashing, white-toothed grins and shrill calls—and still the bus raced on.

The ship entered Hong Kong at night. About two hundred yards away the hills rose sheer out of the water, and Hong Kong spread itself in a million flickering coloured lights from the foot to almost as far as the summit of one of the mountains. It was too late to do more than visit the main street of Kowloon, on the mainland of China, and look in the very modern shop windows and repulse the advances of the very modern Chinese prostitutes. It was our first contact with this ancient, cultured people.

The post-war influx of missionary society recruits, with the preponderance of young women among them, armed with the popular religious clichés and stock answers to the problems of evangelizing the heathen, would amuse rather than impress these members of a nation that considered other younger civilizations barbarians. Even on board ship, we had been asked by many of these finished Mission products what we hoped to accomplish 'alone', without the backing of a 'Mission', and that by people who were members of so-called 'Faith' missions—asserting militantly their belief that 'all things are possible, only believe'!—oblivious to the contradictions offered by their own position. We had even been invited to join one of these Missions to gain the 'advantages' of the organizational machinery, while our contribution, it was suggested, would be to marry two of the single young women of the Mission, and thus help to double the number of workers on the Tibetan border. For it was the accepted policy of most missions not to send single women missionaries to the West China border of Tibet, and since something like 80 per cent of missionary candidates were women, it meant that the few married or unmarried males they had were required to keep the depleted inland mission stations going, to the neglect of the border stations.

This phenomenon of the disconcerting preponderance of young women in the context of missionary societies was easily explained, but not so easily controlled or remedied. Very few among the various denominations of Christendom would hold to the contention that a woman should be allowed to preach, fewer still that she could be an 'apostle'. Yet the word 'missionary' was simply derived from the Latin verb *mittere*, 'to send'; which was the equivalent of the Greek *apostolos*, 'one sent forth'.

The creation of 'Missionary Societies' altered the Scriptural meaning of the word 'missionary' or apostle, so that instead of meaning a messenger of God sent to accomplish a special work in the spiritual context of the Church, it came to mean any member of a missionary society, regardless of vocation or task, with an often vague spiritual experience termed a 'call'. This change of meaning and emphasis was further facilitated by the 'institutional' work of the missions when pure evangelism gradually took second place to medical, educational and orphanage work, a sphere in which women could participate widely, so that a teacher or a nurse instead of being simply a teacher or a nurse serving abroad in the same capacity and with the same appellation as at home could become a 'missionary'. To a generation of emancipated women who had little outlet for their energies within the structure of the churches at home, what with a graduate clergy, a vitiated gospel, a disillusioned and indifferent public, and few male converts, the Missionary Society was admirably constructed to fill the vocational gap for spinster ladies who had a desire to serve God. But the rapid expansion of the work of missions, the infiltration of women from institutional to evangelical work, was beginning to create confusion in administration, for it meant that more and more women were taking over charge of mission stations in all the aspects of missionary activity, and, in the ratio of numerical recruiting, must eventually take over the major administrative posts on the mission field—a situation difficult to explain to the Chinese, and to Bible-instructed people at home.

Missionary magazines were already full of reproaches such as: 'Where are the young men?' and gentle gibes like: 'Lord, don't send me, send my sister'; seeking to adjust the scale of recruiting and restore a measure of balance to the whole. It was the old story of human ingenuity failing to be ingenious enough to anticipate the problems arising out of divine commitment, and the return to a patching expediency to meet adverse circumstances as they arose, an attempt to bolster the shaky structure on which the reputations and work of so many respected people depended, which was careless in the meanwhile of what happened to the reputation of God in the process. Gradually the responsibility was being shifted from those who were at fault in beginning the structure to those who were put to such shifts to keep it from toppling.

Not that there were not some very fine young women to make the suggestion of marriage within a mission a considerable temptation for two young men, for, while there were many whose 'call' had perhaps arisen out of the conflict of adverse circumstances, or even, perhaps unconsciously, out of the need for sublimation, yet there were many who were spiritual, intelligent, balanced and attractive. My own experience during the war years had been enlightening and instructive, when I had the job of supervising the work of all types of women from the 'quiet and capable' to the 'ornamental and sophisticated', but I had never come across any who came into the category of being appointed by God for me. Nor had I met any on board ship either, and I was not prepared to accept anything less.

However, in the welter of mixed opinions, Mr. Thompson, a field director of the China Inland Mission, was very friendly and helpful, and—despite our youthful obstreperousness and rashness!—told us that we could stay at any of the C.I.M. stations on our journey westwards. He also informed us that the C.I.M. had several members on the Tibetan border, among them a certain George Kraft, who spoke Tibetan very well and would be only too willing to help in any way he could in any venture towards Tibet.

That all seemed very remote on board a ship just approaching Shanghai, and the problems presented by that city itself loomed large enough to discourage any further speculation. We had been told that the C.I.M. headquarters in Shanghai were full to overflowing and that there was no hope of finding accommodation there. We knew no one to contact in the city, but, on the other hand, we had become acquainted with a fellow voyager, Miss Hulbert, an elderly Brethren missionary, who, having spent several years in China, could speak the language, which was a great help in the circumstances; although this in turn was outweighed by conditions in the city, such as she had never experienced. Refugees who had travelled to West China during the Japanese invasion were returning, together with refugees from the Communist-occupied north, and the city was overcrowded with them. There was tremendous currency inflation, and prices of food and necessary commodities were prohibitive at the rapidly devaluated scales—a pound being worth some 39,400 Chinese dollars.

Yet the deepening yellow of the sea at the mouth of the Yangtze set us tingling with excitement as we remembered that its journey began in the mountains of Tibet, more than two thousand miles away.

Chapter Six

THE DISILLUSIONMENT

The waterfront sky-line of Shanghai was imposing and impressive, but the clamouring coolies, apart from their dress, might have belonged to any port *en route*. Miss Hulbert came to us as we leaned over the rail, an open letter in her hand and a smile on her face. It was a note from a Mr. Conrad Baehr to say that he was waiting on the quayside with a 2½-ton truck to take our luggage, and that he had managed to acquire accommodation for us in Shanghai.

He gave a description of himself as 'tall, with blue suit, grey hat, and a crooked nose', and as we scanned the crowd on the quayside we could pick out his tall figure, waving in return as he saw us waving. He was waiting with another missionary, a Mr. Jordan, when we finally disembarked to go through the Customs formalities, and all-round introductions were made. Con Baehr was from a Brethren assembly in New Jersey, U.S.A., and had been in China for twelve years. Mr. Jordan was from a Brethren assembly in England and had been a missionary in North China for about thirty years. Then there was Miss Hulbert, a Miss Whitby, a new recruit accompanying her, Geoff and myself. Con, with typical American hustle, took control of the chaotic Customs shed situation and somehow in the indescribable din and confusion managed to persuade a reluctant but bribe-conscious Customs official to exert himself to inspect our baggage, at the same time keeping an eye on the shouting, tugging, arguing coolies, and finally getting everything and everyone assembled in the truck.

Con had fixed up accommodation in a former Methodist

70

The Disillusionment

Mission Home which had been converted into a block of flats, and which had been re-converted into a series of dormitories to meet the demands of the present overcrowding. Miss Hulbert and Miss Whitby shared a room with eight other women, while Geoff and I shared with nine men. We slept in camp beds, washed in cold water, had nowhere to put our clothes, and ate poorly cooked food—at a cost of 33,000 dollars per day. It was only an introduction to the soaring cost of living in China; 40,000 dollars for coolie hire to lift our luggage about twenty yards, 12,000 dollars for a simple meal, 4,000 dollars for a hair-cut, 1,500 dollars for a cup of tea—yet the shops were well stocked and well lit, and the streets jammed with gleaming, streamlined cars. It was only in the shadows that one fell over the dead bodies, wrapped in old sacking, waiting to be picked up by the early morning refuse truck.

With such conditions prevailing many were seeking to get out of Shanghai as quickly as possible, but this was not so easily accomplished. The railway between Shanghai and Nanking was not completed, the roads were in a deplorable condition, very little transport was available, the ships plying on the Yangtze were few and far between, and what few there were were heavily booked. Corruption in every branch of official administration was rampant, and bribes were openly given and openly received to ensure ship reservations. Yet, walking into the shipping office with Con Baehr at 11 a.m., we walked out again at 11.30 a.m. with four reservations in our pockets. It was only when we were breathing easily after the struggle that it dawned on us that all four reservations were for the one cabin!

It was impossible to do anything about it: 'Take the cabin reservations or no passage,' we were told—and Con's advice was to go ahead. It was four days' river trip to Kiukiang, the port at which we were to disembark, and it was just as likely that in the demand for reservations, if we postponed the trip now, the ladies might well find themselves sharing with some Chinese men later. However, Con could not resist a sly dig at English propriety and suggested that we put the onus of deciding on the ladies themselves. Consequently, when we returned to the apartments he announced triumphantly: 'Say, what do you know? We've got four reservations for Saturday!' The ladies were thrilled, and expressed themselves accordingly. 'The only thing is', Con continued, with a troubled frown, 'that they are all in the same cabin. How do you feel about travelling in that way?' He looked doubtfully at Miss Hulbert.

She immediately protested: 'Oh, that's impossible—we cannot all travel for four days together in the same cabin. What would the Chinese think?' She was one of the old school of missionaries and was horrified at the thought.

Con then began a long dissertation on modern China, on the length of reservation lists, and the prohibitive cost of living in Shanghai. He capped it all by saying that he would be leaving shortly, too, so that he would not be in a position to help if they chose to remain.

Miss Hulbert capitulated reluctantly, filled with misgivings and forebodings, whereupon Con cheerfully announced: 'That's good —I bought the tickets anyhow! I *thought* you'd take them!'

We had to go on board late afternoon to sail with the night tide, and when we arrived, the ship—a small river steamer—was already crammed with people who were staking out claims to sections of deck space and more and more were arriving every minute. Gesticulating, chanting coolies were rushing about all over the place with cargo and luggage of all descriptions. Vendors of fruit, vegetables and food were hawking their wares noisily amongst the passengers in high-pitched voices. And in the midst of it all, in a small cabin about 9 feet long and 6 feet wide, Con Baehr sang in a beautiful baritone:

> *King of my life, I crown Thee now;*
> *Thine shall the glory be;*
> *Lest I forget Thy thorn-crowned brow,*
> *Lead me to Calvary.*

He commended the four of us quietly to God in prayer, and then left.

The Disillusionment

We looked round the small cabin, and then at each other. Only one person could stand up at a time, for the personal baggage was piled up in the only space in the cabin, at the foot of the bunks near the porthole. The bunks, two on either side, one below and one above, were short and narrow, obviously constructed for the slightly built Chinese. Finally it was decided that Geoff and I should occupy the two top bunks, where we should be responsible for switching off the lights, and the ladies would occupy the two lower bunks. The two men would not rise in the morning until the two ladies were ready.

Every square foot of deck space and even corridor space was occupied by Chinese travellers, and it required considerable ability to negotiate the odd spaces between bodies and limbs to reach the lavatory or the dining-room. Exercise of any kind was impossible so that our only view of China during four days' travel was a large yellow section of the Yangtze River and a small section of distant colourless paddy fields seen through the small porthole.

As we drew into the jetty at Kiukiang, we could see several foreigners who had come down to meet us, including Mr. Bert Phillips of Nanchang, with whom we were to live while in Central China, and Mr. James, missionary at Kiukiang, in whose home we should be staying until we could leave for Nanchang.

Kiukiang was the centre of the age-old porcelain industry of China, where the best porcelain was still available and where almost every other shop was a china shop of some description. Nanchang, the capital of Kiangsi Province, was about 120 miles away. Both places had come to be well known through being centres of Communist uprising in China, which in turn spread to Hunan, Haifung, Lukfung and Canton, the Communists suffering heavy losses all the way at the hands of the Kuomingtang, or Nationalist, Party of Chiang Kai-Shek. It took the Nationalist Party almost five years, from 1930 to 1935, to drive the Communists out of Kiangsi, in a bitter, protracted blockade, with sporadic guerrilla fighting, and during these years the civilian population suffered untold hardship until finally the Communists, under their leaders Mao Tse-tung, Chu Teh and Chou En-lai, began their famous 8,000 miles 'Long March' to Northern China.

Communism in these parts had failed to establish itself as a working form of government, for it impoverished the areas over which it had control by land confiscation and redistribution, while at the same time conscripting man-power from the rural areas for military service. Yet only twelve years later the victorious Nationalists were on the edge of economic collapse themselves as the result of corruption and nepotism, and the Communists were advancing rapidly from the north, where they had, in the meantime, managed to accumulate an army of half a million men, and a 'People's Militia' of over two millions, along with an extensive administration system in Hopei, Shantung and Suiyuan, amongst other places.

The reason for this rapid recovery and expansion of the Communists, and, simultaneously, the moral and political deterioration of the Nationalists, was to be found in the Second World War, just ended. When the Japanese invaded Manchuria, Chiang Kai-Shek was reluctant to enter into a full-scale war against them until full military preparations had been made, but his hand was forced when he was kidnapped by a former overlord of Manchuria who was collaborating with the Communists.

Russia had finally interceded on Chiang's behalf by negotiating with the Communist Chou En-lai, on condition that Chiang would lead China to war against Japan. Russia's policy of saving Chiang's life was a brilliant move, for by sparing the one leader around whom the Chinese people and Government would rally, it enabled China to hold out alone against Japanese forces from 1937 to 1941, while at the same time furthering Russian plans for destroying Japanese power in the Far East.

Japanese occupation of the coastal provinces meant that the main sources of Chinese revenue were lost to China, and the Government tried to make good the deficit in the Budget by issuing banknotes to an extent that produced inflation on an astronomical scale. Food supplies for an army of nearly three million men had to be requisitioned from the landowners and peasants of South-West China, comprising the provinces of Szechuan, Yunnan and Kweichow, so that the burden on the people became unbearable.

As the value of the dollar notes, or 'yuan', decreased daily, everyone except the very wealthy gradually came within the orbit of suffering, especially the Civil Service and the intellectual classes. These, seeing their leaders indulging in misappropriation, bribery and nepotism, resorted to supplementing their own meagre incomes by the same means, until the whole administrative system of the Government was riddled with the corruption. American Aid, at that time on a colossal scale, merely served to accelerate the tempo, for no adequate supervision over the distribution of the money was provided, and many Chinese officials, from the top downwards, took the liberty of helping themselves to what they could.

Chiang Kai-Shek, reputedly a Christian, permitted national corruption to go on, although he himself did not participate in it. Others in high places were deeply implicated, however, and he had surrounded himself with sycophants who would provide no opposition to any of his ideas—and one of his ideas was that Chinese economy could never collapse because it was a rural economy.

These were the conditions obtaining in China and reflected in the everyday life of Kiukiang, and it was an ironical comment on the situation that we should have to pay 275,000 dollars for the hire of a truck that had been given free to China under American Aid.

There was only room for two people in the driver's cabin and so I volunteered to take first spell of riding on top of the luggage in the rear, while Geoff and Bert Phillips sat in front beside the driver. Miss Hulbert and Miss Whitby were remaining in Kiukiang for the time being. The 'road' was only a wide path, deeply pitted with ruts and holes, running between the rice paddy fields, and throwing up suffocating clouds of reddish dust. The driver knew nothing of the technique of driving and kept the truck going in top gear all the time, up and down gradients, however steep, until the engine stalled. It was inevitable that eventually there should be a breakdown. It was also inevitable that the driver should have no tools with him with which to effect any repairs.

'This is China,' said Bert Phillips, resignedly.

However, some time later another truck unexpectedly appeared—the only vehicle we had seen since leaving Kiukiang, apart from a wheel-barrow containing a tied and squealing pig on the way to market—and we managed to borrow a screwdriver and a pair of pliers from the driver. The truck passed on into the distance, and the experience of the period I had spent test-driving during the war paid its dividends, for the Chinese driver had no idea where to begin to look for the trouble. Finally, the engine was coaxed into life again and we all piled in once more. Every few miles the driver succeeded in stalling the engine, or in incapaciting it in some way or other, which meant another overhaul and check of various parts, until, in a particularly lonely spot, slithering through clinging mud in a deluge of rain, it finally gave up with an ominously conclusive cough. Stripped to singlet and trousers in the downpour I dismantled the carburetter and petrol pump with the screwdriver and pliers, cleaned plugs and points, and by the feeble light of a flickering torch assembled it and instructed the driver, through Bert Phillips, to proceed the rest of the way slowly in third gear. After that we kept going until ten o'clock when we reached a small village and decided to eat. We also decided to stay there for the night, for we were in the heart of bandit country and several robberies and murders had taken place in that area recently. There was no accommodation available so Geoff, Bert and I all bunked down on the top of a packing case in the truck, 5 feet long and 3 feet wide.

We limped into Nanchang about 2 p.m. the next day, having taken twenty-eight hours to travel a hundred and twenty miles, ruined flannels and a sports jacket, broken two trunks and my favourite walking stick, lost Geoff's hat—and paid 275,000 dollars for the privilege of doing so.

Nanchang was the capital of Kiangsi Province in Central China, and in 1947 still showed signs of the heavy fighting that had taken place there recently. It was in Nanchang that one of the many instances of Chiang Kai-Shek's personal bravery was reported. Chiang, as Commander-in-Chief of the Northern Expeditionary Force of the Nationalist Army, was engaged in fighting with the army of Sung Chuan-Fang, then Governor of the five provinces of Kiangsi, Chekiang, Kiangsu, Fukien and Anhwei, who was himself directing operations from a ship anchored in the Yangtze off Kiukiang. It was reported that Chiang had been killed in action, but it was later learned that Chiang himself had led about a hundred men in an attempt to scale the city wall of Nanchang, when many of his men had been killed but he himself had survived.

As a city, Nanchang was not imposing or prepossessing; one long, wide main street, the surface of which was split and ragged, with other unsurfaced, uncared-for streets tapering off to the lanes and slums of the city's outskirts.

The homes and compound belonging to the Brethren missionaries were situated quite near to the centre of the city, and were approached by one of those narrow, stone-paved lanes. A narrow doorway in an otherwise blank high wall led from the lane into a wide and spacious compound. Behind a row of smaller, one-storied houses, where were the homes of the servants, there was a large garden, and beyond and to the side, two large two-storied houses. The Phillipses lived in one house, and Geoff and I were to share the other house with two young missionaries just out from Britain, George Hanlon from Scotland and Geoff Scott from England. A large building on the left was the 'Fu-yin-tang', or, Gospel Hall.

It was my first experience of the 'compound', or 'paternalist', system practised by missionaries, and it came home to me with a jolt as the weeks passed to realize that this system was the one practised by nearly all missionaries. Several times during missionary talks at home a tenuous thread of doubt had crept into my mind about the methods used, but the impeccable phraseology of the speakers, their sound knowledge of 'Scriptural principles', their unassailable evidence on the screen of large assemblies, had served to lull the suspicions aroused.

Now there was no tenuous doubt, but cold, concrete, factual evidence not only before my eyes but openly discussed all around me by missionaries. It was even suggested to me by one of them that I ought not to take photographs of the missionary's large, commodious house as people at home would not 'understand' and 'might get the wrong impression'.

The practice was, of course, only a question of policy among the denominational and inter-denominational missions, and was merely an inevitable development from the accepted premise of denominationalism. However, when practised as a system by those from Brethren assemblies it constituted a violation of the very principle on which they gathered together. The Word of God taught a missionary sent out from a local church only to preach the 'whole counsel of God', build up autonomous, self-supporting, self-propagating churches in whatever locality the Spirit of God might lead him to, and then pass on to some other place to continue the same work. Yet here were missionaries, sent out from assemblies which were established on these very principles, building houses, anticipating permanent residence in the locality, purchasing land, and even building halls at their own expense, thereby making the indispensable centre of the Christian community themselves, around whom every activity revolved and without whom it could not exist; living examples of a 'one-man ministry' against which Brethren assemblies in Britain and elsewhere had supposedly taken their stand. Evangelists and colporteurs were hired to preach and distribute literature. The final unbelievable folly was committed when the deeds of their houses and halls were filed with a Company floated in Britain for that purpose. It was not only violation of Scriptural principle of the most flagrant kind—it was political suicide.

Yet these same missionaries violently campaigned against participation in politics of any description. Coming out from Britain under a capitalist system of procedure, setting up in a foreign country under an imperialist system of procedure—that is, where the missionary was responsible for the financial as well as the spiritual activities of his community, if not in a clergy-laity relationship then certainly in a superior-inferior relationship with the people of the country—instituting a western-conceived system of church-gathering and practice that spoke of 'cultural aggression', with the kinds of meeting, types of worship, and musical instruments and hymn-tunes all western-conceived and produced. All this with a rampant, militant Communism only a few hundred miles away and advancing rapidly. The tragedy did not lie in the missionaries' ignorance, nor in the short-sightedness of their practices, nor even in their complacent acceptance of a lifetime's sojourn in one place to carry out and perpetuate those practices; it lay in their subconscious conviction that the Chinese were intellectually incapable of fully understanding the Scriptures, and constitutionally incapable of putting them into practice.

It was not only a tragedy in their own lives, and in the lives of the Chinese who had come under their ministry and influence; they made it a tragedy in the lives of many young missionaries who came out to the 'foreign field' burning with zeal and vision. They came with a vision of a country filled with the knowledge of, and desire after, the things of God, and this gradually dwindled to the hope of a 'district' with a few assemblies under their care and jurisdiction, and the vision finally died in the ruthless assertion that the people of the country were not capable of being elders, or of exercising spiritual authority or discernment of any kind. The missionary was absolutely essential in the village or town or city or district, not only to instruct believers in 'the truth', but also to hold them together in some semblance of conformity to a Scriptural pattern.

And I had thought that God was All-Powerful, All-Sufficient, had provided all things to sustain whatever He had commanded, could overthrow governments and set up kingdoms, could take me to Tibet in the face of every obstacle! Yet now I was confronted with this from fellow Christians: 'You must not . . . you don't understand the difficulties . . . the people are different . . . you have a long Christian history behind you to condition your thinking . . .', etcetera. Oh yes, the missionaries believed, and preached, that God was All-Powerful, All-Sufficient, able to sustain whatever He had commanded, could overthrow governments and set up kingdoms, could take anyone anywhere. They believed all that—*but*. It was that 'but' which made all discussion on the subject so utterly unprofitable and exasperating.

'Do you believe that the principles of 1 Corinthians chapters 11–14 can be practised today?'

'Yes, *but* the Chinese background is one of superstition and idolatry while we have several centuries of Christian enlightenment behind us.'

'Yet the Thessalonians also turned from idols to serve the living and true God, and Paul, as far as we can gather from Scripture, only remained a few weeks amongst them and then moved elsewhere.'

'Yes, *but* the Thessalonians were an intellectual people and able to receive Paul's teaching—just look at the things he taught them.'

'What evidence have you to make you think that they were any more intellectual than the Chinese? And, anyway, doesn't Scripture say that "the natural man receiveth not the things of the Spirit of God"? No one can understand the things of God except the Spirit of God, and the Spirit is available to every believer, be he Thessalonian, Chinese or British.'

'Yes, *but* there is a sense in which they must be instructed in Divine truth, and instructed until they can take over spiritual authority for themselves.'

'And when does this transaction become effected? Missionary work has been going on in China for almost a hundred years on a large scale, and yet missionaries are still in the *same* districts, in the *same* houses, carrying on the *same* work. Are your Chinese Christians of the present day any more capable of "spiritual authority" than those of fifty years ago?'

'Yes, *but* there is always this question of "face". No Chinese will willingly be the cause of another's disgrace, but will do everything in his power to help the other "save his face". Why, don't you know that that gong you hear beating at regular intervals throughout the night is not to announce the time, but is a warning sounded by the watchman, on the authority of the magistrates, so that any thieves who may be in the area can have an opportunity to escape, and then, if they are caught, they have only themselves to blame for the consequent "loss of face" and cannot blame the watchman or the authorities? All this is part of the Chinese character which must be taken into account when we consider the principles laid down in Scripture. How could you in such circumstances expect them to administer discipline in the case of moral defection? The missionary, as a stranger from the West, can, and that is why it is necessary for him to remain in the one place and watch over the testimony.'

'So you don't think the Holy Spirit in a believer is able to overcome this, or any, defect in character, and produce that which is in direct accordance with His wishes?'

'Yes, *but* all these other things must be taken into consideration. Do you think *you* know better than all these godly missionaries who have spent a lifetime on the field? We all come out with ideas, but we have to learn to submit ourselves to the direction of those who have had years of experience, who know their Bible far better than you do, and who, incidentally, have got something to show for their beliefs.'

'Has any other way ever been tried—the apostolic way, for instance?'

'Yes, *but* it has produced nothing.'

'What do you mean by "nothing"?'

'Well, look at Mr. ——. He has spent about thirty years in China, wandering about from place to place, and what has he got to show for it?'

'What can he have to show for it when he doesn't believe in setting up a house, or building halls, or paying evangelists and colporteurs? The point is, are there any *believers*—as opposed to your "rice Christians"—in the places he has visited? Do they carry on according to the Scriptures, in simple dependence upon God?'

'Yes, he has no doubt been used of God in the conversion of souls and their instruction, *but* he has no *established* work to show for a lifetime's activity.'

F   81

'What do you mean by *established* work? An area agreed upon as the result of a thoroughly unscriptural division of the country by various missionary committees, and justified by the name "Comity of Missions"? Or a piece of land in that area on which a house or a hall is built, given the name of "assembly" and then attended by a group of "rice Christians", who are mostly house servants, or garden servants, or watchmen, or paid colporteurs, or paid evangelists—all dependent on the missionary's beneficence? A settled living and pastorate to pass on to the next young missionary who comes out to join him?'

'Oh well, if you don't agree with compounds, I don't know why you carry on staying in one. It's very much like biting the hand that feeds you.'

'In the first place, it isn't—for the house is no more yours than mine, given by the gifts of believers in assemblies at home. In the second place, if that's the way you feel about it, I would rather move out to a Chinese inn than forsake Scriptural principles. I have complete confidence in God that, even without sufficient language to order a meal, He can provide all that is necessary, if it is done in obedience to His commands. I certainly would not accept your theories, much less carry them out!'

'Oh you can't do that—what would the Chinese Christians think if they saw a division of opinion among the foreign missionaries? It would be very bad for the testimony.'

'Tell them the reason for it and point out the various Scriptures involved, and let them settle the matter for themselves for a change. It would be a far healthier attitude than this hypocritical, sycophantic, time-serving that passes for Christianity among them.'

'Well, we'll just wait and see what *you* can do. . . .'

Discussion seemed impossible and always petered out in the same petty way. There was no way out of the impasse, for the established missionaries could not envisage leaving their allotted areas, and violating the terms of 'comity' by entering areas which had been allocated to other missions. They could not contemplate the possibility of leaving the large, roomy, western-style house and settled living, for the dubious Chinese inns or rented Chinese houses on a temporary basis. How could they leave the whole carefully thought-out, meticulously planned system for a simple dependence on God alone? It would mean the end of missions, the end of family life, the end of secure, ordered existence, the end of an assured life-job. They could not see that it would be only the beginning of a mighty work of God.

The only alternative would be to fight to preserve it, to resist any attempt to destroy it, and to adhere quite consistently to the principles on which they were operating, justifying the strange practices by using the accepted phraseology and platitudes in their own minds—a sort of spiritualized 'double-think' and 'double-talk', and getting by on a reputation for sound knowledge of the Scriptures.

Many of them had come out filled with enthusiasm to evangelize and build like the early apostles, but they were met by the solid and formidable weight of opinion and tradition of senior missionaries, and finally, faced with certain unpopularity and all that that could involve, they succumbed to the futility and bewilderment of it all. Some of the senior missionaries with reputations as 'sincere, godly men' were bound to pass on this traditional point of view to the novice. And, quite apart from this, his own practical sense would suggest to the novice that he would have no place to live in if he did not agree to live in a 'compound' house, and take over the responsibility of running and perpetuating the very system with which he might disagree in principle.

There was also the risk that he would have no one to help him with the important primary arrangements regarding language lessons, or even, in the last analysis, that he might find himself isolated by the very force of his own convictions. Nobody who had come out to take part in this work would care to find himself in a minority of one. He would begin to ask himself whether the position he was getting himself into was not due to his inability to work in harmony with his fellows, his dogmatic scriptural ideas and his general all-round unsuitability for the work of a missionary. This last doubt was the most deadly of all, of course, for the young missionary, full of new zeal and vision, might not greatly care whether or not he lived in a mud hut, nor in his early faith trouble much about the lack of sympathetic helpers in a foreign land, but the thought that he might have to forfeit his calling because of unsuitability would be too terrible to bear.

Then again who at home would understand *him*—a fresh young recruit—if he set himself up against reputable men, who had 'spent a lifetime in the field', who could be heard expounding the Scriptures ably from conference platforms when they were at home, and who were acclaimed as missionary 'statesmen' for their glowing accounts of their missionary work? And so many such bowed before the inevitable, and the paternalist-compound system and other incongruities were perpetuated.

When I spoke out against a state of affairs with which I could not agree, my passionate denunciations and 'revolutionary' suggestions were met by the complacent assurance that I would eventually change my mind and come to see how mistaken I was, in the same way as others who had held like beliefs. But I held two advantages that were virtually unassailable. One was the obvious utter ruin of the work in Kiangsi following on the Japanese and Second World Wars, and one was the fact that I had the confidence of some of the assemblies at home with which I had come into contact before coming to China.

The argument that the old school, the paternalist-compound school of missionaries, had something to show for their efforts could not be substantiated in Kiangsi at least, for the whole area was an empty shambles as far as a living Christian testimony was concerned, even at that time. The missionaries returning after the war found not only empty mission houses, but also empty mission halls, the so-called believers having melted away when the source of their employment, the missionaries, went home, and the very missionaries who were now arguing the advantages of the paternalist-compound system were those who had had to go out week by week on their return to China to look for the erstwhile Christians who had formed the local 'assemblies'. Here and there a family might be found standing steadfast, but of one virile, functioning New Testament assembly—never a trace. The situation was farcical in the extreme, but tragic in the context of lives spent, money wasted, and imminent judgement at the hands of the Communists. A meagre handful to show for the labour of a century when the support of the missionary was removed. Almost any theory would be better than the evidence produced in support of that one.

Yet all the preparations were going ahead to rebuild houses, rebuild halls, look for the former 'Christians' and carry on as before, and the methods used to ensure the continuance were the old, old ones of: 'You'll do as we think best.' These methods had fallen down as far as I was concerned, for I would not accept any theories of this kind, and even if I had to withdraw from the field, I warned, I would declare from every platform and to every assembly back home how strongly I disapproved of the paternalist-compound system. I had been well enough known in Central and Eastern Scotland before I left for the believers there to be aware that I knew what constituted a New Testament church, so that I felt I would have their support, and this encouraged me to believe in myself and to feel that I was not unfitted for the work of a missionary.

It was a tremendous strain, however, since I stood almost alone as far as I knew. Geoff did not consider the issues so important, and George Hanlon and Geoff Scott, the other new missionaries, while agreeing in theory, could only look forward to working in that area within the structure of compounds already built, in fellowship with senior missionaries who held these ideas, so that there was no alternative but to fit in. However, when Geoff Bull realized that we might have to stay in Kiangsi, in order that we might take over one of the mission stations, he, too, came into the battle. There was obviously a calm assumption that we would not be able to go any further towards Tibet because of the existing agreement of the Comity of Missions which recognized N.W. Kiangsi as a 'Brethren area', and Sikang, in West China, as a 'China Inland Mission area' with some others. For Geoff the gravity of the issue was finally settled when the senior missionaries sat down to allocate houses and work among approximately twenty mission stations in N.W. Kiangsi for some twenty new recruits *who had not yet left their own countries*—and Geoff knew of one at least who wanted to go further west to work amongst the tribespeople. Geoff, normally quiet, gracious, humble, and vaguely abstracted, became an inflexible opponent of the paternalist-compound system—and even contemplated measures that were too extreme for me!

It was ironical that the major obstacles to accomplishing God's great purpose for us in Tibet should come from the operation of a system created in all good intention by the servants of God, and particularly from those servants who vehemently rejected the very idea of a denominational system at all and whose message was founded on that belief. It had always been so, however, from the very beginning; God's purposes were for ever being thwarted by His own self-confessed servants. No enemy of God could stop any work of God, but some servant of God would come forward with a 'good idea', and either it would be accepted, or some disagreement would be caused on account of it, and so the work of God would be hindered.

God told His people, Israel, to walk into Canaan. He gave it to them as their own land, promising that wherever they placed the soles of their feet would be theirs, but some of them thought it would be a 'good idea' to send men to spy out the land first, just to see what it looked like. They returned to say that the cities were strong, and the inhabitants giants, there were too many difficulties in the way, and they began to argue amongst themselves as to the 'advisability' of going forward, in spite of the promises of God. The dissident voices won the day, and as a result God said that only two amongst them all, Joshua and Caleb, who had also seen the land but had advised going forward according to the command and promise of God, would ever enter the land. The rest died in the wilderness.

Very well, then! The God who took Joshua and Caleb through successfully, because they followed his commands as a dog follows its master, could bring us through as well. The God who could overthrow governments could also overthrow systems. And, in any case, the writing was on the wall as far as any system was concerned—particularly a western-conceived system of expansion, with all the trappings of bourgeois imperialism, such as compound-missionary work—because of the implacable advance of the Communists.

No organized religion would last for long, no western denomination supported by money from the West would be tolerated. No foreign missionary would be allowed to teach 'bourgeois claptrap', as religious superstition was described by the Communists, to the Chinese people—and without the missionary, without the money from the West, without the paid Chinese pastor or evangelist or colporteur receiving his regular stipend through the missionary, who would be the focal point of Communist accusation as a 'counter-revolutionary'—without all these the whole system must collapse, and only the true believers remain.

I could well understand how Communism might be used as a whip in the hands of God to scourge His disobedient servants, as a judgement on them for well-meaning malversation of the Scriptures to the detriment of the glory of His name, as a purge to cleanse out the self-deceived—all that was keeping the 'pure' from shining forth in testimony to His Son as 'Christian'. But the accomplishing of this end meant inevitably a clash between the will of God for us and the beliefs and plans of the Communists for world domination, particularly in China and Central Asia. At some point in the future these forces must meet, and there could be no retreat; the conflict must end in the utter annihilation of the one or the other, for it was implicit in their opposing beliefs.

In the meantime we studied the language and preached. Since the war students had been crowding into the universities, and as there was an acute shortage of Chinese textbooks on all subjects, English was a compulsory subject, to enable the Chinese students to use English textbooks. They clamoured to be taught English, and crowded into Bible classes and meetings of any kind conducted in English. It was an explosive field of opportunity for any interested party, for new China had thrown off the ancient idol-worship, was contemptuous of the Confucian precepts, was impatient with the involved trammellings of Buddhism and Taoism, and hungering after something new. Missionaries tried to meet the overwhelming demand with supplies of Bibles, gospels and religious literature, but there were too few among them to illustrate the dynamic faith and burning vision that was needed to fill the vacuum.

The Communists, on the other hand, anticipated the hunger, and smuggled thousands of young men to Moscow to receive training in Communism, to translate the collected works of Marx, Engels, Lenin and Stalin, and pour millions of copies into China over the Siberian railway—and followed up the theories with an example of fanatically abandoned devotion and zeal in the cause.

There could be no doubt about the issue between a vitiated Christianity and a dynamic Communism, whether in China or elsewhere. The top-heavy structure that went by the name of Christianity must collapse, and only equally dynamic, Christ-centred Christians remain. They were the true Church as God had expressed it, the fellowship of Holy Spirit-indwelt believers, the true Christians, the real Christianity, in communion with God and each other, through the work of Christ and the Spirit, requiring no organization, no ordination of clergy, to ensure its existence and continuance, but maintained virile and unconquerable by the Holy Spirit as the result of Spirit-bestowed gifts, which incomparably exceeded the forces of materialism. Communism could no more harm this than could Roman Imperialism in the first century of its manifestation. Therefore, get souls! Souls fused with this fire, kindled from the flame of one's own fanaticism, that they in turn might set others alight until this fire swept the country, the continent, the world!

We preached—in the hall, in the streets, in the university, in the schools—and time after time the message went home to some soul. Mr. Kao, Mr. Wang, Mr. Chang, Mr. Liu—the number of young Christian converts grew steadily without thought of

Author, on right, while still in China, with Chinese teacher, and Geoffrey Bull, his companion who was captured by Communists in Tibet and only recently released.

monetary gain or personal advantage, until we could start a Bible-study class in our own room.

A very gifted Chinese preacher had begun attending the local church and he asked if he might attend the study classes. He was a valuable acquisition for he was teaching in the nearby Bible school of another mission. A striking feature about him, setting him apart from other Chinese 'Christian' workers, was that he would accept no payment for his services in the Bible school, maintaining that he was God's servant, and not the servant of a mission, and that he wished to depend on God alone to supply his needs. He could then be free to move elsewhere whenever God should so dictate.

For the first time in our experience, light began to shine in the dark testimony of Christian activity in China. Here was a man who was the living antithesis to all that the missionaries maintained and practised, for he had no 'system' behind him to supply his needs. A lonely apostle in China. It appeared that he was in Nanchang with another friend who had not been too happy about associating himself with the local assembly, because there was unconfessed sin amongst the Chinese members. The light in the darkness began to blaze! A Chinese believer, depending on God alone miraculously to supply his needs, while he preached and built up the groups of converts into New Testament churches, was miracle enough in itself, in view of all that the senior missionaries had maintained about their shortcomings, but that the Chinese believer should also point out that his fellow-countrymen were living in sin and therefore endangering the testimony to the glory of God, and that he should refuse to take part in it until the offenders were suitably disciplined, swept away for ever the intolerable theories of the paternalist-compound school, and gloriously vindicated the power of God and His Word.

'But why didn't your friend go to the missionary and tell him the position?' I asked the Chinese preacher, 'and then the matter could have been brought before the assembly. After all, the matter must be made known before it can be judged.'

'But he did go to the missionary,' he replied, 'and the missionary did not think that anything could be done.'

And so the assembly was deprived of the teaching of men who could have revivified it, and that was maintained which John Nelson Darby described in a translation of Ephesians chapter 4— 'that teaching which is in the sleight of men, in unprincipled cunning, with a view to systematized error'. The Chinese, who, according to the old school, could not grasp the fundamental principles of Scripture, could sit with us and discuss the Scriptures from the Hebrew and Greek originals, talking familiarly of the return to New Testament principles in the early days of the Brethren in Britain, debating the difference of opinion between the leaders of that period, and could select a book from my bookcase by one of the ablest expositors from the West and point out a grave weakness in the argument submitted.

It was our first introduction to those who were known as 'the Little Flock' in China. Several years before a Chinese Christian, a brilliant scholar, called Watchman Nee, while studying the Scriptures saw the truth concerning the Church and subsequently wrote a book on the subject, the English translation of which was entitled *Concerning Our Missions*. It was a simple outline of the pure apostolic principles of church gathering and activity but it started a movement away from missions and denominations, which swelled to tremendous proportions as the numbers of converts and teachers multiplied.

We had heard of the phenomenal rise of this movement in the Eastern Provinces of China from other missionaries, but they usually dismissed it with disapproval, and often with contempt, for many and varied reasons. The 'Little Flock' were holy rollers —they went into trances—they prayed for the gift of tongues— they believed in permitting women to pray and speak—they believed that not all Christians would go to heaven when Christ returned—they were 'exclusive', very rigid in deciding whom they would receive into their fellowship and communion—they insisted on baptism by immersion—they believed that Christians should not save money as the Lord's return was imminent—they were anti-foreigner—they were divisive—and so on. The list was impressive if only for its contradictions and possibilities. Only one

missionary of those whom Geoff and I had met had a good word
to say for the Little Flock, the same missionary who had been
denounced by his fellows for 'thirty years of wandering with nothing to show for it'!

Yet here were two Chinese believers who could have com-
petently occupied any conference platform in Britain with the
leading expositors there, and in 80 per cent of the cases would
have shown up more creditably. There was an oddly familiar ring
about the accusations, a faint echo from apostolic times, the disapproval of reactionary conservatism throughout the centuries,
the frightened complaint of hierarchical sectarianism which sensed
a threat to its own security.

As far as Geoff and I were concerned the die was cast. This was
to be the sphere of our fellowship in China. These groups, whose
excesses in many places were admitted but were due merely to
ignorance and lack of teaching, were products of the Spirit of
God working in simple believers. It was the responsibility of those
who were more enlightened in the Scriptures to teach these others
until they were brought into a more deeply instructed conformity
to the Scriptures. They were open and willing to receive any servant of God who would teach them, hungry for teaching, but it
would have to be the word of God that was taught and not men's
opinions.

If these were faults they were minor indeed compared with
those to be found among the missionaries. As I saw it, such missionaries were either unable or unwilling to see that their methods
violated the principles on which their very existence as Scriptural
testimonies depended. If anything was to remain for God as a
concrete testimony, whether the Communists took over or not,
it could only be found in these same virile, healthy, autonomous
groups now spreading so rapidly through China.

These groups also indicated a way in which the artificial barriers of 'Comity' could be broken down, for here was a movement that could spread everywhere, and was spreading, without
the need to recognize mission or denominational agreements regarding territorial boundaries of activity. Since these groups were

based on Scriptural principles Geoff and I could be confident that, as the early churches received the apostles and then sent them on with their blessing to the next objective, so would we be free to minister without hindrance among these modern New Testament churches and, in turn, be helped on to our Tibetan objective.

Chapter Seven

THE VISION

While we had anticipated a stay of three years in China, God was already preparing us for an early departure. We were confronted on all sides by the impossibility and inadvisability of such a venture with our three months' knowledge of the language and no fixed place on the Tibetan border to which to go, but our combined assurance that this was the will of God for us led us to spend more and more time in prayer in order to be absolutely certain that our movements and our wills were under the direct control of God and not swayed by the 'common sense' advice of the missionaries.

Out of this waiting upon God came the directions for me to begin inquiries regarding all that would be involved in travelling westwards through China to Tibet, while Geoff continued his studies of the Chinese language. In the meantime, the summer heat had grown intolerable on the plains, and all the foreign missionaries were preparing to make the annual visit to the mountains of Kuling, the hill station in North Kiangsi.

The journey to Kuling was through Kiukiang, by the same road over which we had come a few months previously. This time we covered the distance at breakneck speed, without a breakdown, in under ten hours. We had to travel in convoy, for there had been a series of robberies and murders, and only two weeks before nine women had been kidnapped from one truck. Armed soldiers were escorting every vehicle, and it was only safe to travel together in a group. There were seven or eight trucks and buses that day, and we left Nanchang at the tail-end of the convoy. The 'road' was inches thick in dust and with this rising in clouds from our own vehicle, and the clouds thrown up by the vehicles ahead, we were soon covered from head to foot in an ever-increasing red film. The driver soon decided that he had had enough and when the road widened at any point he accelerated recklessly and, keeping his finger on the horn, forced the others one by one to let him pass, until he reached the head of the convoy and comparative freedom from suffocation by dust.

Kuling was 3,500 feet up in the mountains, rising from the plains near Kiukiang. Trucks and buses came as far as the foot of the mountain but could go no farther, as the road degenerated into a narrow winding path. Women were taken up the steep climb in bamboo *hua-gans*, two long poles with a seat slung between, carried on the shoulders of four coolies. The luggage was carried on the backs of individual coolies, secured by ropes round their shoulders, and no weight seemed to be too much for them. One steel trunk required the combined strength of Geoff and myself to take it from our bedroom to the truck, yet one old coolie, who must have been nearly sixty, got underneath it and carried it all the way up to Kuling without laying it down, while Geoff and I were limp with perspiration and exhaustion merely walking up clad in shirts and shorts, carrying walking sticks and fans!

While the houses and shops forming the hill-station were at 3,500 feet, the mountains comprising the range rose to nearer 5,000 feet. I had always imagined that the peculiar shape of mountains in Chinese paintings was due to the fact that Chinese artists set little value on perspective, and so the shapes of mountains seemed as unreal as the shapes of bridges or human forms, as far as photographic likeness was concerned. But now I was struck with the distinct similarity between the contours of the mountains and the paintings of them—not that the Chinese artists 'held the mirror up to Nature', by any means, but the impression was very definitely there. The peaks rose up, sharply defined, and then fell away in a like manner on the other side. Small trees, shrubs and grass grew right up to the summit, which detracted from the sense of height conveyed by the smaller, but more savage and barren, mountains of the Scottish Highlands.

The Vision

A famous beauty spot was reached through the Nanking Pass, several miles outside Kuling, called Poyang Ridge. This was a point on the range which overlooked the famous Poyang Lake, and from here the green-clad mountains rose on either side and faded into the hazy distance, while straight in front, as far as the eye could see, was the almost perfectly level floor of the plains. Two long fingers of land jutted out into the lake from the north, or left, side, and broke up what might otherwise have been a monotonous stretch of water; the mountains dropped straight down at this point, so that it appeared as if one might step off the ledge and drop right into one of the little thatched houses, with the thin spirals of rising smoke, dotted about on the plains far below.

On the occasion that I visited the place with some friends, we remained to watch the sun set and the moon rise. The sun died away in the west in a blaze of gold, red and purple, reaching from the far rim of water, in intermediate, intermingling shades impossible to describe, to the clouds above our heads. Then as dusk fell, there appeared the red ball of the moon over the edge of the lake on the far horizon. In an hour or two, the lake was like a brazen sea ringed by a silver band; as far as the eye could see, the moon clothed the earth in a shimmering mantle of black velvet, silver and gold. Above, the clouds moved slowly, in sombre majesty, their undersides heavy with darkness and their edges gleaming with the magical reflected radiance of that distant orb.

It seemed incredible that men—who believed that the Architect who designed this Universe and the millions of universes beyond, the Artist who, night by night, painted scenes of unsurpassable beauty on the heavenly canvas, who took pains to present finished perfection in the design of the firmament, in the activity of the formicary, in the shape of the rose-petal that falls to the ground— should not believe that He is able to order the lives of men without their assistance. Yet, a few days later I sat in the company of missionaries, who had just gazed on these same scenes, as they discussed questions regarding the upkeep of mission property, the possibility of raising some money by claiming war damages from

95

the Chinese Government in respect of halls and houses damaged
while they were away, the problems arising out of the arrival of
new missionaries and the shortage of houses for them after they
had learned the language. It would appear that their God was
more like the Baal of Ahab's prophets than the Jehovah of Elijah,
in that he often took a holiday, to return only on occasions to
ratify the decisions they had taken in his absence.

The contradiction had built up until it became too much for
Geoff to contain. When asked to address a meeting of missionaries, he took as his theme some verses from 2 Cor. x:

'For we dare not class ourselves or compare ourselves with
some who commend themselves; but these, measuring themselves
by themselves, and comparing themselves with themselves, are
not intelligent. Now, *we* will not boast out of measure, but
according to the measure of the rule which the God of measure
has apportioned to us, to reach to you also. For we do not, as not
reaching to you, overstretch ourselves (for we have come to you
also in the glad tidings of the Christ) not boasting out of measure
in other people's labours, but having hope, your faith increasing,
to be enlarged among you, according to our rule; yet more abun-
dantly, to announce the glad tidings to that which is beyond you,
not to be boasting in another's rule of things made ready to hand.'

'. . . We dare not class ourselves or compare ourselves with
some who commend themselves . . . measuring themselves by
themselves . . . are not intelligent . . . do not understand. . . . We
will not boast out of measure, but according to the measure of the
rule which the God of measure has apportioned to us. . . .'

The two types of God's servants—those who 'measured themselves by themselves', by a measure of their own making, and
those whose measure was apportioned to them by the 'God of
measure'.

The *God of Measure*—who gave unto everyone who believed
on Him 'grace according to the measure of the gift of Christ';
whose desire was to bring them all 'into the unity of the faith and
of the knowledge of the Son of God, at the full-grown man, *at the
measure of the stature of the fullness of the Christ*'; whose ideal was

that all 'holding the truth in love may grow up to Him in all things, who is the Head, the Christ, from whom the whole body (the Church) fitted together, and connected by every joint of supply, *according to the working in its measure of each one part*, works for itself the increase of the body to its self-building-up in love'.

The *God of Measure*—who measured out the waters in the hollow of His hand, and meted out the heavens with His span, and grasped the dust of the earth in a measure, and weighed the mountains in a balance, and the hills with scales; who directed the Spirit of God, and as His Counsellor, taught Him, with whom He took counsel, and who gave Him intelligence and instructed Him in the path of judgement and taught Him knowledge, and showed Him the way of understanding; by whom the nations are esteemed as a drop in a bucket, and as the fine dust on the scales. Behold He taketh up the isles as an atom; and Lebanon is not sufficient to burn, nor the beasts thereof sufficient for a burnt-offering. All the nations are as nothing before Him; they are esteemed by Him less than a cipher, and vanity.

The *God of Measure*—measuring out the Universe, measuring out the Tabernacle, measuring out the Temple, measuring out the Church, measuring out grace, measuring out knowledge, measuring out gifts, measuring out work.

There lay the secret of success—in each one apprehending that for which he had been apprehended by Christ Jesus, the measure appointed to him by God. There are distinctions of gifts, but the same Spirit; and there are distinctions of services, but the same Lord; and there are distinctions of operations, but the same God who operates all things in all. The Lord of the Harvest would thrust out labourers into whatever part of the harvest field He saw needed them and only in that way would there be no confusion.

After such irrefutable declarations from Scripture, there could be no compromise with orthodoxy so-called (but rather heterodoxy, if one measured by Scriptural and not traditional standards). The decision regarding what was to be done in view of all the consequent controversy was made easier by God's insistence that we both move westwards to Tibet immediately.

The Vision

We still had no knowledge of how we were to travel, and where we should make for on the border of Tibet, nor even where the money was to come from to take us there. For China was outside the 'sterling area', and only a limited amount was permitted by the British Government as a quota for missionaries, and that had to come through a Government-recognized channel. In the case of Brethren missionaries this channel was through the offices of the editors of *Echoes of Service*, a magazine devoted to the activities of Brethren missionaries, in Bath, England. However, that was a very minor problem. If God was directing us westwards then He could supply in His own way, outside so-called 'official' channels, no matter how impossible that might appear.

Just at this time I went down with a sudden attack of violent sickness and headaches and was ordered a complete rest by the doctor, whose diagnosis was 'no organic disease, but suffering from strain through overwork over a long period'. The first few days of the rest were nightmares, for I seemed to collapse altogether when I had no reading, studying or activity to occupy my time, but after this had passed I felt better than I had done for years, and gradually I was permitted some light reading and activity again.

During my sickness and convalescence I had a curious experience. I was lying awake late one night, having slept most of the day, looking out of the window at the moonlight-bathed scene in front of me while I thought and prayed over the future, when the light seemed to grow steadily brighter until the whole window-frame was ablaze. Then slowly the shape of a burning candle appeared, the flame elongated and steady for some time, then disappearing as it formed itself into letters of fire—'Consuming and being consumed'. This passed, to be followed by a period of intense darkness filled with a chaotic confusion of sound and overwhelming pressure of imminent evil, then everything was calm again and in the lightening surroundings a Presence breathed assurance and slowly withdrew.

I had not been dreaming, for I was still wide awake and subconsciously noting the various articles of furniture in the moonlit

98

room, listening to the rise and fall of the cicadas' piercing whistle. I continued to lie awake until well into the night as I sought an explanation for the curious experience, particularly the cryptic message in the words, 'Consuming and being consumed', but finally I dropped off to sleep without being enlightened any further, my last waking thoughts sorting out words as I tried to crystallize the experience within the framework of a few lines of poetry which I shall not reproduce here.

For my convalescence I was given piles of magazines by various friends, and while reading through one of them one day I came across a report from a missionary working on the Sino-Tibetan border in Kangting, Sikang Province, in West China. This was the place where, as Mr. Thompson, the C.I.M. missionary on board ship, had mentioned, one of their members, George Kraft, was working. To crown it all, a letter arrived from Con Baehr to say that he had met an old school friend in Shanghai whom we might be interested to meet as she was working on the Tibetan border, a Pearl Kraft, wife of George Kraft of the C.I.M. She had come all the way from Kangting to Shanghai at that time to put her children in school, and after a short stay in Shanghai expected to return to the Tibetan border to join her husband.

It was a startling answer to prayer, and as soon as I was fit Geoff and I left Kuling for Shanghai to meet Pearl Kraft and have a talk with her. We met in the C.I.M. headquarters in Shanghai and learned from her that her husband was about to start a Tibetan language school in Kangting for some of the missionaries who were living there. She was quite sure that he would be delighted to teach us too. Regarding a place to stay, she would be glad to provide hospitality until we could find a place of our own, but it might be as well to see the leaders of the Mission while we were in Shanghai. We called on our friend Mr. Thompson, and another field director, and although they were at first a bit dubious about two 'free-lance' missionaries going into their territory, with all the possibilities that flow from teaching a different doctrine, they finally corroborated Pearl Kraft's warm welcome.

The way was now open for us to go when we liked. Pearl Kraft was leaving immediately as her passage up-river was already booked, and she advised us to proceed west as soon as possible, for from November onwards the level of the River Yangtze fell so low that river steamers could not travel upstream, and it was already October. While I waited for a reply from the shipping company Geoff decided that he would go on a preaching tour with Mr. Jordan, the senior missionary whom we had met in Shanghai and whose itinerant evangelism was work after our own hearts as we saw it in the Scriptures. It would provide valuable experience for Geoff, in travel experience and use of the language he had studied, while I would remain in Nanchang to handle any arrangements for travelling westwards to Tibet.

Meantime the Communists had swept on their victorious way and were now only one hundred and fifty miles away on the other side of the River Yangtze. Once they managed to cross the mighty river running from west to east through Central China, China was doomed. Already economic ruin was staring the Nationalist Government in the face, the lower denominations of the currency were completely valueless and the pound was worth 124,000 Chinese dollars and falling rapidly as the Communists advanced. It was possible to live only on the simplest scale, the price of food was so high. Every day that passed made the money we held more worthless, while at the same time bringing nearer the possibility of our being cut off from the west by the Communists. The money for our immediate necessities had been miraculously provided, for several missionaries, unknown to each other, had all approached us at different times and given us a sum of money—'told to do so by God'—and that at a time when every dollar was precious for their own needs. The seal of God's approval and blessing was on us in our decision and no fall of any government or rise of another could hinder us in the accomplishment of His purposes; rather, the fall of governments was necessary that He might be glorified. Britain, one of those who had most consistently closed Tibet to missionaries, had had to withdraw from its borders in giving independence to India. China, one of the other major powers responsible for shutting off Tibet, had also to fall before the inexorable purpose of God. The rise of another power in China that was apparently more militantly opposed to God was only significant in the present context as an instrument in the hand of God, as a hammer if need be, and meant as little so far as the future was concerned as any other power opposed to him. One good thing from the rise of Communism in China would be the clearing out of all missionaries, with their confusing Western practices, which had hopelessly cluttered up the Christian witness, and the consequent release of dynamic energy in a persecuted and purified Christian testimony standing on the Word of God alone.

But we must go forward, for God had commanded it. The rise and fall of governments, with the consequent economic crises, were to us due neither to control nor competition, nor inevitable cycles or spirals, but direct intervention by God in the affairs of men in a divine discipline on national conduct. Therefore, as such they must never be allowed to influence our decisions in any way, for in the mind and purpose of God they were only part of the workings of the same whole in which Geoff and I had our own particular part to play; they were not contradictory, they were complementary. Missionaries all around might be packing their cases and making preparations for leaving China as 'the only thing to do in the circumstances', but that was a confession of failure on the part of themselves—of their methods which were under judgement, of their faith which broke before Communism, and of their apprehension which admitted no vision but a blind present and an empty future.

Geoff returned about the beginning of November and we decided not to wait any longer for our friend Gordon Bell, but to proceed westwards immediately. Already reports were coming through that the Communists had reached the banks of the Yangtze and were shelling passing ships, one report giving the news of fifty-eight killed on one shelled ship. There was the usual round of feasts, presentations and speeches, and on Monday, November 10th, we bade Mr. and Mrs. Phillips good-bye for the next stage of our travels.

The Vision

The river journey from Kiukiang to Hankow, next port on the River Yangtze, took only one day, but we were held up in that city for a few days waiting for a passage through the famous Yangtze Gorges to Chungking. From Nanchang to Hankow had already cost us ten million dollars in expenses of one kind and another, and we had barely started. We finally managed to obtain berths on board the *Ming Lien*, one of the larger and better-appointed steamers plying between Shanghai and Chungking.

The Yangtze narrowed steadily as it became compressed into the slit channel of the Gorges, and opposite Hankow the water hissed past the sides of the small boats, or sampans, crowding the river's edge. Only a few days before the gang-plank leading from the shore to the ferry-boat had given way beneath the weight of the crowds pushing to get on, and over thirty people were thrown into the river. They were all drowned, of course, for no one would think of risking his own life to save another; such an act was regarded as folly, not heroism. The story was told of a foreigner on a similar occasion, who cried to a boatman to push out into the river so that he might rescue some of the struggling people and the boatman refused to go, even to help his own countrymen, until the foreigner had agreed on the price of the hire of the boat. The Yangtze claimed thousands of lives every year, hundreds of thousands in times of floods, so what were a few more out of season?

The mouth of the river near Shanghai was as wide as from Hull to Chatham in England, and navigable as far as Constantinople by the same reckoning, that is from Shanghai to beyond Chungking. Beyond that again it stretched for several hundred miles to its source in the mountains of Tibet. The rise and fall of the water due to the melting snow and rains varied as much as two hundred to two hundred and seventy-five feet in the Gorges. The shifting silt, uneven river-bed and jutting rocks, with the racing rapids, were reckoned unnavigable, and when a certain Englishman, Captain Plant, had suggested that regular steamer navigation through the Gorges was a practicable proposition he was laughed to scorn by the Chinese and English alike. However, he persisted in the face of ridicule and charted the channel, and proved his theory correct.

There were many small gorges and minor rapids but only three of them, the I-chang, Wushan and Kuie-fu, or Wind Box, Gorges were famous; and about the same number of really dangerous rapids. The I-chang Gorge began about five miles beyond the town of I-chang, first stop after Hankow. The ship cast off at early dawn, and the early morning mist and grey darkness showed only the hazy outlines of the hills surrounding the Gorge, when taking a sudden turn to the left, following the bend of the river, we were in the first of the Gorges. The Yangtze had become like any canal, but with banks formed by seven hundred to one thousand feet high mountains, and water which swirled past rapidly and dangerously. For ten miles the ship twisted and turned across the channel, following deep waters, and passing sleepy-eyed fishermen beginning to shake out their nets and push off their junks from the sides of the river.

The Chief Officer, seeing our interest, asked if we should like to watch the trip from the bridge of the steamer, and took us along to introduce us to the captain. The bridge was on the foredeck and enclosed on three sides by glass windows, giving a clear view of the river from any angle. Inside there were four pilots, besides the captain, two senior and two junior, but only one senior and one junior were on duty at one time. The senior pilot was an elderly Chinese with a face like carved teak, who leaned on the sill of an open window of the bridge and indicated the course to the steersman by slight movements of his fingers. His eyes never left the eddying, swirling surface of the water, and every few seconds brought a new movement of his hand. These pilots spent their lives on the river, working their way up from being on small sailing junks to owning their own junks; after many years, during which they became acquainted with the river in all its moods, they were accepted as recognized pilots.

About twelve miles farther on, the mountains gradually receded and we were out of the first Gorge into a more or less open stretch, with the river about four hundred yards wide. The force of the current was still so great, however, that the ship shuddered and swayed uneasily as it eased its way forward. Huge boulders and piles of rocks rose out of the river like an archaeologist's heap, and for several miles the river wound its way through this freakish scenery. As we approached the first rapids visibility was bad, rain having started and low, heavy clouds threatening to break overhead. The river had narrowed again and was racing like some Highland burn in spate, with small white-crested waves breaking in spume, eddying and swirling in occasional smooth, deceptive patches.

The pilot grunted, moved his finger, and the steamer turned obliquely to the right across the river, making straight for the opposite bank. Another movement of his finger and we were head-on to the first of the dangerous rapids. The water lashed and leaped away from the bow of the ship as we shuddered to a crawl, the hissing of the water and the beat of the engines making a fitting duet for the scene. Gradually the ship fought its way out of the rapids, the dramatic effect being somewhat spoiled by the sight of a single oarsman in a small sampan close to the river bank calmly making his way upstream. The ship continued to wind in a snake-like fashion across the river as it followed some unseen deep bed, and a junk, carried swiftly by the current downstream, swung across the bows in a dangerous slip. We eased over ever so slightly in order to give it room to manœuvre, and suddenly grounded on the sandy bottom. Full speed ahead was immediately signalled, and the ship churned over the danger area as the junk slipped past safely with only inches to spare.

The rocks were giving place again to sheer mountains rising in lofty splendour for a straight one thousand feet. Only about two hundred yards separated the yawning sides of the channel, and the captain commented on the dangerous character of the river at this point. A warning blast on the siren echoed and re-echoed among the peaks, warning down-coming river traffic that we were approaching Kung Liu T'an, another rapid. An S-bend in the river and we faced the solid, whipping mass of turbulent water, once more shuddering under the impact. Right in the centre of the river, dividing it into two tongues of foaming water, was a large, jagged, upthrust rock which seemed to bar all further progress. The old pilot moved away from the window and took over the wheel from the steersman, and with a turn faced the left bank for a little, then another turn and we headed straight towards the rock. Two hundred yards—one hundred and fifty—one hundred —fifty yards. The water foamed and tossed madly round the ship. Another turn and the ship slid past the length of the rock with about ten yards' clearance, and we were through into the Horse Lung Gorge. On the right appeared the small town of Miaoho, famous for its one thousand years old temple bell, and then a few miles farther up the gloomy gorge, still on the right side, Captain Plant's pagoda-like Memorial Tower, looking down on the Yangtze he defeated.

The Hsui T'an, the most important of all the rapids, was negotiated safely, with only a temporary grounding, exposing us for a brief minute to the fury of the water, and then we were through to a comparatively quiet few miles, passing the river town of Patunghsien, the notorious river crossing-point of bandits, at midday. Six miles beyond Patunghsien the second of the famous Yangtze Gorges, the Wushan Gorge, began and extended for over twenty-five miles. The river widened into a large bowl, and the ship followed an oblique course before entering a cleft in the mountains. At the right-hand side of the entrance, and about three hundred feet up, there was a small temple. This was only one of many to be seen all the way through the gorges. They were built by grateful junk captains as an offering to the gods for delivering them out of some danger at that particular point, and were intended to keep away the evil dragons that were supposed to lurk in the waters beneath, but they were at least useful as warning signals to incredulous and unbelieving infidels. We steamed safely past the point into the split in the two thousand feet mountains, which is like the work of some giant axe, and continued on our way forwards amidst the ferment of muddy, surly, swirling waters, smashing against the sides of the ship in ineffectual hatred. The channel wound its way through the gorge in a series of S-curves, and time after time the ship had to approach to within five yards of the sheer cliffs to find a way through. There followed a long stretch of river with the mountains forming a series of gigantic V's into the cloud-misted distance, mile after mile of sombre, sulky majesty. Towards evening the sky began to clear and the mountains revealed new shades of reds, browns and yellows to add to the indigo shadows in a breath-taking beauty.

The ship was to tie up for the night at a place called Wushanhsien, and Geoff and I decided to go ashore and stretch our legs. Wushanhsien was an old walled city with a maze of narrow streets, or rather lanes, lit by smoky, oil-burning lamps. It seemed so remote that we did not expect to find any foreigners there and more to exercise our Chinese than to satisfy our curiosity we inquired for the *fu-yin-tang*, or gospel-preaching hall, to be told that there was one, and we made our way in the direction indicated. When we arrived there we found two American ladies, one of whom had been there for twenty-five years, in a little Chinese house, and we had a simple meal of bread and cake with them by the light of a flickering oil lamp before returning to the ship.

The next morning was clear and sunny, and the open sides of the river were beautiful as they fell back on green fields and rose gradually to greeny-blue mountains in the distance. Ahead an apparently unbreachable range of mountains rose right across our pathway, about three thousand feet high. The morning air brought out the lovely autumnal shades of brown, green and yellow, and in the shadow above the Yangtze itself, just when it seemed we must hit the mountain, there appeared the gash that was the entrance to the Gorge. About one hundred and fifty yards in width, and narrowing to about one hundred yards in parts, the four miles of Kuie-fu, or Wind Box, Gorge was indescribable in its sublime majesty, the contrasting light and shade, the interplay of early morning colours, baffling description.

Late morning and we entered a beautiful basin surrounded by an amphitheatre of mountains. Over on the right, on a prominent point, the slender white finger of a pagoda pointed towards the unbroken blue of the sky, while just beyond nestled the walled city of Kuiefu. Several sampans pushed off to approach the ship and take off the few passengers disembarking there, and there was bedlam as the passengers tried to scramble on to the bobbing sampans from the ship, which was not stopping but only slowed down to a quiet glide.

We moored at Wanhsien that night and managed a meal of ham and eggs at the C.I.M. mission station, and the next morning left on the last stage of our journey to Chungking, the war-time capital of China. There was a C.I.M. missionary on board the ship and he was being met by friends at Chungking, so we were able to learn as soon as we tied up at the wharf that there was room for us in the C.I.M. headquarters there. Chengtu, our next objective, was about two hundred miles away, two days by dusty, jolting truck, so we were delighted when we learned that a plane was leaving in a few days and it could drop us there in just over an hour, and our luggage could follow later.

Only four days in Chungking, and yet in that time we met Ting Yo-han, or John Ting. Geoff and I had been asked to address the students of the China Theological Seminary, by the principal, Marcus Cheng, reckoned one of China's outstanding Christians. That same evening, as we were sitting in the C.I.M. sitting-room, a visitor was announced who wished to meet us, a Mr. Ting Yo-han. He was studying in a Spiritual Training College near by, and a friend from the China Theological Seminary had told him that two young foreigners on their way to Tibet had spoken at the seminary that morning. Then followed the remarkable part of his story.

Son of a wealthy, cultured family from Shanghai, he had been miraculously healed of an illness when young and had decided that his life must be used in the service of God, making Jesus Christ known to his own people, and then to those on the far borders, and then to those in Tibet. However, he was gifted with so much general all-round ability that his time was spent in everything but in passing examinations in Greek and Homiletics, so that he was advised to give up any idea of ever being an evangelist, an itinerant preacher of the gospel, and to join some mission as a technician instead; with his ability he would be able to service cars for missionaries, he knew several Chinese dialects and might act as interpreter for missionaries, or he could travel around China taking photographs for the visual-aid department of some society, or he might even go into radio broadcasting. The amount and types of advice were bewildering to one who simply wished to follow in the steps of Jesus Christ, without the help of missions or denominations of any kind, but the weight of opinion was so great and so categorically opposed to any thought of going to Tibet in this apostolic fashion that he decided that he must have some special word from God before he could move in any direction, and he set aside a day for prayer for that purpose. It was while he was praying for some word from God that his friend came into his room and told him of the two foreigners who were on their way to Tibet. It was the answer he needed. Would we mind if he and another friend, Mr. Hsu, joined us on our journey to the Tibetan border? They did not wish to join our mission, if we were members of one, but simply to go with us as companions in the preaching of the good news of Jesus Christ, trusting to God to supply whatever needs arose.

Geoff and I were even more thrilled when we heard John Ting preach several days later in Chengtu, after our arrival in that city. Some special meetings had been arranged by the C.I.M. missionaries, and on hearing of John's arrival he and his friend were asked to address the nightly gatherings in the church. Night after night John, quiet, stout, boyish for all his thirty-six years, preached to a growing congregation until the church could not hold the crowds of people, and every night saw more and more of his countrymen turning to follow the Master he so passionately loved and served. Mr. Hsu had had a more spectacular conversion than John: six times he had attempted to commit suicide because of his disappointment with life and had been stopped in one way or another, and he was on the point of hurling himself from a moving train when a lady gave him a Christian booklet which became the means of his salvation; but his preaching lacked the tremendous spiritual power that enveloped John when he spoke. Adultery, fornication, concubinage, idolatry, covetousness, hypocrisy, lying, evil speaking—the words of condemnation rolled from his lips in a steady flow, dividing inexorably between right and wrong, good and evil, in the lives of his fellow Chinese, and then telling them of a power that came from receiving Jesus Christ into their lives which never came or could come from Buddha or Confucius or Mencius, a power that helped them to put away sinful practices and live lives to the glory of God, with the consequent peace and joy that such a knowledge brings.

The meetings were still going on, with crowds of people attending and turning from their sin to God, when we decided that one of us must leave for Kangting immediately. We had only a little over one million dollars left between us, although there was another two million dollars in our luggage somewhere between Chungking and Chengtu, and all our letters were being forwarded straight to Kangting from Kiangsi. It was necessary, therefore, for one of us to go and find out what was waiting for us there. There was not sufficient money for both of us to go, but in any case it was necessary that one of us should stay in Chengtu until the position regarding Gordon's arrival was clarified. There should be some news of him among the letters in Kangting and if he were coming out soon then someone had better wait for him in Chengtu, rather than go on to Kangting and then have to make the long journey back again almost immediately. As Geoff wished to consolidate his studies in Chinese we agreed, after prayer, that he should stay on in Chengtu waiting for Gordon and then come on later with our two Chinese friends, while I would pack a haversack and take to the mountains for Kangting on the Tibetan border, travelling as light as possible to save time and money.

When the news reached the other inmates of the house it produced a surprising reaction—consternation, expostulations and dismay—for it meant that I should leave on the Tuesday morning, December 23rd, and consequently be somewhere in the mountains on Christmas Day. To the American, Canadian, Australian,

English and German missionaries there I appeared to be more be-
nighted than the blindest of heathen, and no amount of explanation on the pagan origin of the celebration could wholly con-
vince them of my genuineness as a Christian. Whoever heard of a
Christian who would not keep Christmas? Certainly there was no
proof that Christ ever was born on December 25th, but that was
quibbling over trifles. He must have had a birthday at some time
and if it happened to fall on the same day as the pagan festival of
Saturnalia then that was just a simple coincidence and of no importance. Santa Claus was a symbol, not an idol, and surely the
heathen would not think for a moment that missionaries, Christian missionaries, would worship an idol after all they preached
about the wrongs of idol-worship, nor confuse the tree and the
gifts, the decorations and the feasting, with their own supersti-
tious practices? Mr. Patterson had such peculiar ideas at times.
Would he please sign their autograph books? It would be such
fun to remember him afterwards at other Christmases.

Geoff, John and Hsu came to the bus station with me to see me
off on the first stage of my journey, to a place called Ya-an. It was
about three hundred *li* away (three *li* to one English mile) by
road, and one look at the bus made me resigned to a more difficult journey than the Kiukiang-Nanchang one. It was an old,
aluminium-bodied vehicle of ancient vintage, held together by
pieces of wire and string, and announcing in faded, dispirited
letters that it was able TO SEAT TWENTY PERSONS. From what I
could see in the mêlée there were about thirty-seven inside and
about another dozen clambering up the sides to sit on the baggage
tied precariously on top. 'These', said John, instructively and
cheerfully, 'are called *huangyu*, "yellow-fish", so called because
they travel more cheaply on top and they get covered in dust
from the road.' In order to provide more seating accommodation
wooden planks had been placed across the passage-way, but this
only meant that everyone was jammed tightly into a small space and
had to remain there in that position until de-bussed at their destination. One hundred miles like this! I had reckoned myself fortunate
with a seat at the window, but even this blessing began to fade

when less fortunately placed passengers noisily cleared their throats and expectorated dangerously through the window from a distance.

However, apart from one or two minor breakdowns, we managed to arrive in Ya-an by six o'clock that night. I had sent a telegram to some missionaries working there, a Dr. and Mrs. Crook, giving the possible time of my arrival, but they, out of long experience of Chinese transport, had wisely gone out to keep an engagement and left my supper ready to be eaten when I arrived. I went off to bed before they returned, and so did not meet them until breakfast the following morning.

When I suggested that I ought to be leaving as I had a long distance to cover that day, they immediately protested. I must stay over Christmas at least, if not longer; they rarely saw anyone in that part of the country and to walk out after two hours of conversation was too disappointing; I couldn't possibly make the journey over the mountains into Kangting alone, and no coolies would be available at such short notice. I had to remain adamant, though, for every day was precious in the circumstances, and Dr. Crook finally and reluctantly found me a coolie to carry my haversack. Tien Chuan, the first day's stage, was seventy *li* away, which meant a good day's walking, and Dr. Crook warned me of the coolies' habit of stopping several times on the way to smoke opium. The government had made it a capital offence to grow, peddle or smoke opium but it still went on on a large scale throughout the country, particularly in these remote regions in Sikang Province in West China where even the soldiers, officers and officials smoked and traded in the drug. A road of sorts had been built into Kangting during the war, but this had been allowed to fall into disrepair and was breached in innumerable places. It was rumoured that the Governor of Sikang Province, General Liu Wen Huie, had done this deliberately to ensure protection for himself from the Nationalist Government with whom he was becoming more and more *persona non grata* on account of his growing record of warlordism. Be that as it may, the road was in a parlous condition and no vehicles of any kind could travel on it, so that all loads to and from Kanting had to be carried in by coolies. The major portion of the tea for Tibet came this way, and as it was packed in long bales of eight bricks per bale, weighing about thirty pounds, it meant that each coolie carried a load of ten to seventeen bales of tea, a load of three hundred to five hundred pounds in weight. It was a heart-breaking, nerve-straining job, and with food even in normal times difficult to obtain the coolies sought to boost their failing strength by taking opium. They would carry their loads a short distance, and then stop for a quick smoke of opium at some den. This would give them sufficient boost to carry on with their load for another spell, until that too began to wear off and another smoke would be necessary. It was this that Dr. Crook warned me against, for to stop too often would mean being stranded somewhere along the trail in a lonely spot open to attack by robbers.

I left Ya-an about ten o'clock, and with the coolie moving in front at a steady lope, a sort of half-walk, half-run, we covered the ground steadily. The plains were already giving way to low-lying mountains, and the flat monotony of patchwork paddy fields stretching into the distance began to give way to intricate terracing where the peasants sought to utilize every bit of ground for their needs, and conserve the soil in simple, effective fashion. The earth in these parts was a peculiar reddish colour, and after a few miles of walking through the trail dust a thin, red film lay on clothes and eyebrows and hair, giving travellers and workers in the fields a bizarre appearance. About midday I ate a snack prepared by Mrs. Crook and washed it down with several bowls of Chinese tea, then prised the coolie away from his opium pipe to get on the road again.

We arrived at Tien Chuan about five o'clock, just pleasantly tired as the trip had been quite easy, and found an inn providing board and lodging for the night. The room contained two beds— three wooden planks to each bed—blankets, called *pu-kai*, and a sort of cottonwool-padded quilt of dubious age and origin with bugs ensconced obviously and comfortably in the seams. That was all. The coolie was given sixty thousand dollars for his day's work, and the inn-keeper one hundred and twenty thousand dollars for his night's hospitality, leaving six hundred and twenty thousand dollars to take me to Kangting.

The next day's trip was a notorious stretch of one hundred and twenty li, with only a few houses with no facilities about half-way. Travellers had to leave Tien Chuan before dawn, picking their way round boulders on a path beside the river in the grey mist of morning to reach the half-way mark before midday. The first stretch from Tien Chuan was comparatively easy, the trail winding upwards gradually, with occasional long flat stretches over which good time could be made, but beyond the half-way mark the trail suddenly swung upwards steeply and continued to climb all the way to the next village of Liang Lu Kou. Patches of snow began to appear on some of the shaded parts of the trail, and the air grew steadily colder. The coolie was stopping on an average at every twenty li to give himself a boost of opium, and as the day advanced I myself was glad of the respite offered, although it became more and more difficult to get the coolie away from his pipe and started again.

It was dark when we finally walked wearily into the huddle of houses known as Liang Lu Kou and found an inn. Tien Chuan had been palatial compared to this. The inn-keeper had to awaken a filthy old man from an opium sleep in a back room to provide us with 'beds', two bare slats of wood hardly sufficient to support the body lying sideways. However, I was so exhausted by the day's travel that I sank down gratefully on the hard boards and asked the inn-keeper for some hot water before he brought some food. My Christmas Day meals consisted of: breakfast, one bowl of rice and egg soup; lunch, four bowls of tea; tea, some water; dinner, rice, vegetables and a little stewed meat. The 'room' in the inn was less than six feet wide and about nine feet long, and lit by a minute fragment of cloth trailing in a spoonful of oil on a small red clay saucer. It appeared that the coolie was to be my room-mate for the night for he asked for his day's wages and then came back with a small lamp with a long glass funnel and a round-bowled, long-shafted pipe. Stretching himself out on his side he proceeded to take a reddish-brown substance from a piece of dirty paper and work it into a pill on the palm of his hand. This he finally placed in the bowl of his pipe and, cupping it in his hands over the top of the glass-funnelled lamp, he closed his eyes and inhaled deeply. The small light spluttered into darkness and the room seemed to hold only that slant-eyed, high-cheekboned, expressionless face suspended above the dying flame of the opium lamp. It was the last I remembered before I fell asleep.

I did not get away the next morning until after seven-thirty, and it was some time after that before the stiffness and soreness worked their way out of my legs. There had been a heavy fall of snow during the night and it made the going rather difficult. Ahead lay the beginning of the 'real' mountains of Central Asia, and we were already on the trail leading to a 10,000 feet pass. Water dripped steadily from huge 20–50 feet icicles suspended from the rocky outcroppings on the mountainsides, and streams gushed through only a narrow channel in their ice-locked crevices. Pine forests swept upwards in fantastic patterns of black and white where snow lay thickly on the foliage. Above the forests, on the face of the mountain in front of me, little black dots could be seen strung out in an irregular broken line, coolies with their loads of tea and other goods on their way to Kanting. By the time we came out of the snow-shrouded forests I was calling on the coolie to stop every twenty yards or so to ease my aching lungs. The last stretch to the summit of the pass was so steep that we had to climb holes cut into the snow and mountainside and ice, stopping every now and then to help each other over the more difficult parts. The road built and used by the troops was easier to negotiate but added many miles to the journey, so the coolies choose the more difficult and hazardous but shorter route to the top of the pass. Low-lying clouds hid what might have been an incomparable view from the summit, and after a few moments' rest in the piercing wind to recover my breath we began the descent on the other side. The contours of the mountains were such that the far side of the pass held no snow at all and after the freezing level had been passed everything became simply muddy.

First sight of the Tibetan mountains after crossing the watershed on the China-Tibetan border. The road, bottom right, leads into Kangting, two days' journey to the West.

The Vision

That day's stage finished at a place called Kan Hai Tze where we arrived at 4 p.m. We ate a simple Chinese meal of rice, vegetable and bean curd, surrounded by curious friendly coolies and curious, hungry dogs, pigs and hens. I had a walk round the village but there was nothing of interest to see, the place being the same colourless collection of dilapidated mud-and-bamboo structures with their grindingly poor, dispirited inhabitants and domestic livestock, found all over these parts. It was just as well I went to bed early for I was wakened before midnight by someone chanting a monotonous dirge and accompanying himself on a tambourine, clappers and a gong, which went on all night until dawn. It appeared from what I could gather by questioning the inn-keeper next morning that the gong-beater was driving away evil spirits. He must have succeeded, except for the one that possessed him, for every evil spirit in the vicinity must have fled that cacophony of sound.

For four hours we descended the other side of the pass down a winding path that was extremely difficult to walk on, so steep was it. The view all the time was magnificent, for the mountain faced across a fertile valley through which flowed a broad curving river. In the distance the spire of a large church, probably the Roman Catholic Cathedral, could be seen, and over to the right a large group of houses. This was Luting, the end of that day's stage. However, after a good deal of Chinese flour scones and tinned cheese, and finding that it was only a little after 1 o'clock, I decided to go on to the next village and leave myself less to travel the next day. It was only twenty-five li to a village called Wan Shih Ku and after giving the grumbling coolie, who wanted to stay in Luting, an extra tip and noting that I had only 175,000 dollars left—enough for one day—I crossed the swaying suspension bridge over the river and swung out smartly on the climbing, winding road, on the far side. We reached Wan Shih Ku by late afternoon, only slightly fatigued by the day's ninety-five li. Arriving in Wan Shih Ku ensured our definite arrival in Kangting the next day, so I shaved for the first time and washed for the second time in five days.

The Vision

The last sixty li to Kangting were through magnificent scenery all the way. The trail became more boulder-strewn and wound beside the river, which sometimes raged through a narrow rocky channel and sometimes swept majestically in a wide smooth curve beneath my feet. Occasionally a rope-fibre suspension bridge with wooden planks would precariously span it, or the roughly trimmed trunk of a tree across a tributary would enliven the tedium of straightforward walking. At 2 o'clock I turned the last bend in the mountains and the curved-roofed gateway of Kangting faced me a few hundred yards away. Snow lay in the hollows and was just melting on some parts of the streets when I arrived. I was surprised at the size and appearance of Kangting. I had expected a larger version of some of the dilapidated villages through which I had passed but found that well-built streets led away from the gateway into and through the town; solidly built wooden houses were evident everywhere and well-stocked shops seemed to be doing a thriving trade with picturesque Tibetan traders. I looked interestedly at these people from the land that I hoped to enter and liked immediately what I saw. Tall, strongly built men, with huge sheepskin-lined gowns worn carelessly over the shoulder, colourfully embroidered knee-high boots, fur hats tilted rakishly at the back of their heads; women with ankle-length gowns of sheepskin-lined coloured cloth, an apron of startling, contrasted colours, oiled black hair, braided with coloured silks and hanging down their backs in a long plait; men and women with faces strong, vivacious and quick to laugh.

The C.I.M. compound was in the middle of the town, on the other side of the river which ran right through the centre of the town from west to east. The town itself was built across the narrow floor of the valley and spread up the mountains hemming it in on either side. From one mountainside to the other was no more than three hundred yards and part of that was taken up by the leaping, rushing river, spanned by two roughly constructed wooden bridges. The mountains narrowed at the far, western end, leaving just enough room for the river and trail, so that Kangting lay in the narrow bowl of mountains overshadowed by

Kangting, wild border town between China and Tibet, and end of Central Asian Caravan routes. Taken from the steep mountain dominating town and facing north-west, with Roman Catholic cathedral in left foreground.

the towering peaks, backed by the snow-capped giants behind them.

A Sunday School was in progress when I arrived, so that I had time to wash and brush up before meeting the others. There were two families of C.I.M. missionaries working in Kangting at that time, George and Pearl Kraft, and Ed. and Marjory Beatty, with another widowed C.I.M. Worker, Mrs. Cunningham. Mrs. Cunningham was the oldest worker, having been in Kangting with her husband for over thirty years. He had travelled widely in Kham, as this eastern province of Tibet was called, and was well known for some of his botanical finds. He and his wife had been hosts to many expeditions in that area, including the Roosevelts' hunting-the-panda expedition, but on Mr. Cunningham's death his wife had ceased to be host in the mission and was replaced by another married couple. The new hosts were the Beattys, although the Krafts had priority through seniority. George and Pearl Kraft had been ten years in Kangting, studying Tibetan and working amongst the Tibetans, and before that five years studying the Chinese language. He was not a natural scholar: his six-foot-two-inch, two-hundred-pound frame was more suited to the athletics he had formerly indulged in before becoming a missionary, but by constant, unremitting study, fanned by his interest and love for Tibetans, he had acquired a wide knowledge and fluency in the language that established his reputation among foreigners and Tibetans alike. Ed Beatty was a Scotsman, as was Mrs. Cunningham, but Marjory Beatty and George and Pearl Kraft were all Americans. There were also some missionaries of other missions in Kangting at that time, adding up to a foreign community of some twelve or thirteen people.

After the introductions and usual exchange of news were over, I went off to my room to open the pile of mail that had accumulated for Geoff and me since we left Nanchang. The first was a cable from Gordon to say that he had sailed and would arrive in China late in January and thereafter travel to Kangting as soon as possible. The second was a letter containing a cheque for £18. The third a letter stating that further restrictions on the quota of money permitted to missionaries were being imposed. A few more from friends and family, and then one from America, from people unknown to either Geoff or myself, with a cheque for 75 American dollars. Thus God had provided all that would be necessary for Geoff in Chengtu and myself in Kangting for another time. Not only was there adventure in every circumstance of our lives, but the future was rich with exciting possibilities and eternity beyond an unsearchable inheritance. What was it Paul had said of his glimpse into Paradise? He heard sacred secrets which no human lips can report. Or again, on another occasion: 'There is a wisdom that we utter among the mature; a wisdom, however, not deriving from the present age nor from the leaders of the present age, whose power is on the wane. We speak God's wisdom in a mystery—that hidden wisdom, which, before the world began, God purposed for our glory; a wisdom which not one of the leaders of the present age has learnt; for if they had learnt it, they would not have crucified the Lord of glory. But we speak—to use the words of Scripture—of things which eye has not seen, nor ear heard, and which have not entered the heart of man: all that God has in readiness for them that love him. For to us God has revealed them, through the Spirit; for the Spirit searches everything, including the deeps of God. For who among men knows a man's thoughts, except the man's own spirit within him? In the same way also only God's Spirit is acquainted with God's thoughts.'

Chapter Eight

THE TASK

George Kraft arranged for me to have a language teacher, and almost immediately I was immersed in the disheartening complexities of the Tibetan language. The official language of the books was difficult enough (George Kraft reckoned Tibetan at least twice as difficult as Chinese, as it had taken him ten years to attain to the same fluency he had acquired in five years' study of Chinese), but having to study the Kham dialect without books and with a teacher who knew no English or Chinese, was a monumental task demanding all one's energies and all one's time. George warned me of the heart-breaking character of the language and also of the scores of failures among the many missionaries who came to work amongst the Tibetans. Full of vision and fire and ideas on their arrival, they soon weakened under the tremendous demands of study and the difficulty in making themselves understood among such a multiplicity of Tibetan dialects, and finally, defeated, they turned to Chinese or some other language and only contacted Tibetans when they handed them Bibles or booklets. Many of them had taken their mission's examination on paper, of course, but only a few had been able to preach an adequate sermon, and fewer still to carry on a conversation with the Tibetans. Only a handful out of all the scores working on the Tibetan borders, ostensibly waiting to enter Tibet 'when the door would open', would ever be able to travel any distance, for such travel required a knowledge of the language covering matters of trade, weather, trail conditions, as well as matters relating to the hire of animals, handling of servants and so on. George Kraft had been an examiner for several mission boards for some time and he was beginning to despair of ever finding anyone with sufficient 'stickability' to break the back of the language and then go on to master it in all its aspects. George himself still spent every morning in language study, every afternoon in visiting caravanserais, and almost every night in preaching in the church, and had very little time for those who were not equally sincere and devoted in purpose.

I had been putting in a steady ten hours a day of study for almost six weeks when the teacher requested a few days' holiday to celebrate the Tibetan, and Chinese, New Year; both observed the Lunar Calendar and New Year fell in the latter part of February. It was a welcome break and I decided to nose about the town and search out the meaning of the preparations and customs.

It appeared that any day after the sixteenth of the twelfth moon the members of a family gathered at the parental home, and sometimes also at each of the homes of the sons in turn, to eat the yearly feast. Several things had to be carefully avoided at this meal. No soup was taken lest it should bring wet weather whenever the one who had partaken of it went abroad during the following year. Conversation about the past or the future was avoided lest any subject should crop up which might spoil the harmony of the gathering, or cause trouble in the days to come. Afterwards, they 'fed the fruit trees' by placing rice in a notch cut in the bark; this was supposed to ensure a good crop of fruit during the next season.

In the latter half of the twelfth moon all cobwebs were carefully swept down to prevent the accumulation of hairy caterpillars. At this time the 'kitchen god' was absent, so that there would be no danger of his being annoyed by the flying dust.

On the evening of the twenty-third of the twelfth moon the officials and the official class worshipped the kitchen god; the people who were of an inferior class did not worship until the evening of the twenty-fourth. On the latter evening the kitchen god went up to heaven to report the deeds of men to the Immaculate Emperor, therefore he had to be propitiated before he started on his journey. Incense and a yellow paper 'report form' were burned before his shrine in the kitchen. The report consisted of a form with blank spaces for the names and remarks prepared and sold by the priests. During the twelfth moon the priests of the guilds and temples presented copies of these papers to wealthy families and received in return presents of money and rice. Non-vegetarian offerings consisted of pork or a cock, with cakes, salt, cereals, and a white toffee. In a vegetarian offering the meats were omitted. The toffee was supposed to effectively glue the god's jaws together and so prevent his speaking evil of the offerer. Tea and wine were also presented, and afterwards poured out before the shrine. At midnight on the last night of the year the god was welcomed back with incense and fire-crackers, and the door was then shut in order that the luck brought back by the god might be retained.

On the last day of the year the old door scrolls and lintel inscriptions were replaced by new ones. From the lintels were hung five fretted and gilded papers called 'joy-door-cash'. Merchants also stuck printed 'cash papers' along the edge of their shop signs or hung up bunches of evergreen cypress wrapped in the 'cash paper'. In this way the desire for continued prosperity was expressed. Among friends cards were exchanged to take leave of the year. People as a rule did not go to bed at all on the last night but stayed to guard the departing year. During these hours various small expedients were employed to bring luck or to avert misfortune. For example, an old sandal was dragged across the floor while members of the family beat it with sticks; this was called 'beating the rats' and was supposed to prevent rats breeding in the house. After the kitchen god had been welcomed back and the doors closed, all the household gods were worshipped. Towards morning merchants opened the doors and welcomed the 'gods of wealth', and the nearest 'god of the precinct' was worshipped, and in the open air obeisance was made to the 'Immaculate Emperor'.

In the morning *mien* (strings of flour like spaghetti or vermicelli) was prepared and eaten, as this required little cooking. After this meal the men dressed themselves in their finest clothes and visits were paid and New Year greetings exchanged, an ordinary bow from the waist being made to each other. When the door of a friend's house was shut, or if the house was only that of an ordinary acquaintance, a visiting card was stuck on the outside of the door. The young people crowded on to the streets enjoying themselves hugely with toys and sweets. The floor was not swept on New Year's Day lest the house should be infested by fleas during the year. Many other things also must be avoided. The sight of a broom would invite trouble in the future. The scales and 'steelyard' must be hidden or too many snakes would be seen during the summer. The refuse-bin induced the infliction of wrongs, and chickens with their pointed beaks would cause one to be sharp-tongued and quarrelsome. Dust and refuse must not be emptied out until after the fifth lest one's prosperity be emptied away with it.

The missionaries had arranged some special meetings to be held during the New Year celebrations but were still without a suitable preacher when John Ting arrived from Chengtu. The missionary work in Kangting had been difficult and disheartening from its inception forty years before (the Roman Catholics had been there nearly sixty years, and even managed to build the only cathedral of its kind in Asia); converts were difficult to find in the floating population that passed through Kangting from Tibet and China. Those who did come and stay in Kangting had either to provide for, or participate in, the excitement demanded by the pleasure-starved travellers from the mountain wastes of Central Asia, and so Kangting became a notorious centre of vice, with a reputation reaching all the way to, and even superseding, Shanghai. Opium was grown openly and widely throughout the province and was found in almost every house. The places that were not opium dens were brothels. Gambling for huge sums went on all day and all night, either in mah-jongg or in dice. The trigger-sensitive Tibetans were involved daily in drunken brawls and murders. It was a remote border town and the sky was the limit in anything. Little wonder then that very little impression had been made, and the little that had been done had been carried into obscurity by the constant movement of the population. There were only a few Chinese Christians in the church and most of them had come into the town from down-country. There was no Chinese of any ability who could preach and one of the missionaries would have had to do so if John had not arrived when he did.

John was hailed by the missionary community as a messenger of God, although for some weeks there had been considerable consternation and controversy over his 'free-lance' position. Would he split the church with a 'nationalistic' emphasis? Would he preach some new doctrine among his fellow Chinese and cause trouble? Would the missionaries have to 'support' him: as he obviously had no society backing him, would he not have to depend on the foreign missionaries for his finances? Further, was it not the case that he had failed to pass his examinations at Bible School and so was not an accredited evangelist and pastor? However, present necessity overrode fears of future complications and John, after praying about it, agreed to take the meetings.

The first night of the special meetings John and I prayed together before he left to preach in the church at the foot of the compound. I had not enough knowledge of Chinese to understand a full sermon but I agreed to remain in my room and help by prayer throughout the time John was preaching in the church. The meeting started at 7 p.m. and normally finished about eight o'clock, but nine o'clock passed and ten, and still no sign of John or any of the missionaries. At half-past ten Mrs. Cunningham appeared and told of the outstanding things that were happening in the church. John had preached powerfully on sin and judgement and salvation, and soon all over the hall men and women from that tough border town were weeping and crying to God for forgiveness. John calmly and with dignity refused to let the meeting get emotionally out of hand and warned the congregation that while some might weep their way to Christ, it was not a necessity for them all to do it, nor even a sign of genuine repentance. It was not enough to be sorry and then go back and do the same things again; there had to be a definite turning away from one's former sins and a new facing towards God and the things of God. This was the conversion that was necessary to enter the kingdom of heaven. When he had finished preaching there were so many inquirers and converts that every missionary had to deal with several each. Every night for a week, John carried on in the same way, ignoring the clock and preaching as the Spirit led him, and every night between twenty and thirty remained behind in a spirit of earnest inquiry, and all over the church men and women were to be seen on their knees in little groups. It was God at work in and through a simple believer who allowed Him to speak through him and use him in His own way without trammelling human limitations.

John's special meetings in Kangting finished with over fifty sincere converts who were prepared to leave all of their past life and follow Christ. Although the gospel meetings at night were past, John's real work was just beginning. The converts who had been introduced to Christ had to be instructed in the truths concerning His Kingdom and inheritance, and with peasants, coolies, soldiers, office-workers, servants and housewives among the company, it was difficult to find a time suitable to all. In the end John had them coming to his room in relays from half-past five in the morning until half-past ten at night.

It was here that complications began to arise and the inherent weakness of missions and denominations was exposed at its most vital point. Converts there were in plenty but what were they to be taught? John, as their spiritual father, out of his own experience taught them obedience to the Word of God and its sufficiency in all things pertaining to life and godliness. But the end of such teaching would be to make them self-sufficient, self-supporting and autonomous as a local company of believers and thus eliminate the necessity of the foreign missionaries' presence and the denominational structure taught and insisted upon by them. As the missionaries obviously could not preach that which was against themselves, and their very *raison d'être*, they took every opportunity to correct the 'error' taught by John by teaching the necessity of denominational observance according to their own particular persuasion and, consequently, confusion was the result. In trying to resolve the confusion the missionaries approached John and asked him to refrain from touching on any point of doctrinal difference lest they should lose the converts! The tragic farce of the whole situation was not so much that the converts were there only because of John's complete belief in and obedience to the Word of God in the first place, but that the points that he was asked to avoid were the fundamental Scriptural principles regarding baptism and communion. At the same time some of those same missionaries were already discussing plans for leaving Kangting and China in view of the rapid Communist advance. They would go, their imported western denominational structure would go, the Chinese would remain, the Word of God would remain; yet the step from traditional complexity to Scriptural simplicity was too great to visualize, let alone take.

John continued on his way in his simple greatness. Hours in prayer, hours in Bible study, hours in teaching. Not content with living in complete dependence on God to supply his every need he believed that he was responsible to 'tithe' that which was given him and return a tenth to the Lord's work in some other way than to supply his own need.

Night by night it was our custom for John and me to read and pray together till midnight. On one occasion while we sat and ate a simple Chinese meal that John had cooked he told me that the previous week he had had so little money that he omitted to lay aside his usual tenth. However, his conscience would give him no rest and troubled him so much that he finally gave away the tenth of what he had originally received from an anonymous friend, and that left him with nothing at all. At that time the cost of simple living was 250,000 dollars per day. Some time before a friend had asked him for the loan of some money, and now that he himself was penniless he felt like going and asking him for the repayment of the loan to help him over for the present. However, he was convinced that this would be a breach of faith in God, so instead he knelt down and poured out his circumstances to God in prayer and asked Him to provide. While he was still on his knees there was a knock on the door and he opened it to the postman and received a letter, and inside the letter was 300,000 dollars. Next day there was another letter, this time with a million dollars. And so day by day he walked his life with God.

Nor was there any trace of sanctimoniousness in him, either. No one ever enjoyed a joke better, and it was he who suggested gate-crashing the King of Jala's wedding festivities for his son.

The King of Jala had been ruler over a part of Kham, the largest province of Greater Tibet, before the ruthless Chinese general, Chao Erh Feng, beat down all opposition from Szechuan to Gyamda Dzong, within a few days from Lhasa, and Kham was re-christened Sikang and made a province of China. This had all happened forty years before, and within a year or two the Tibetans again drove the Chinese out of Tibet and left them with only small and ineffective garrisons in some of the area between the River Yangtze and Kangting, where they lorded it over the Tibetans who came into the towns to trade but went in fear and trembling of the Tibetans when they had to travel any distance outside them. However, the area was so vast and so remote from the rest of the world that the Chinese went confidently ahead with the establishing of their new Republic and President Yuan Shih Kai issued an order in 1912 that Tibet was to be considered a province of China. The King of Jala, like the King of Dege and King of Muli, had territory adjoining the Chinese border of Szechuan, and as the warlike Khamba tribesmen were for ever fighting among themselves and were outside the interest and jurisdiction of the Tibetan Government far away in Lhasa, it was relatively simple for the Chinese to dispossess the petty kings of their power by the constant threat of a Chinese Army sent to levy and collect tax.

At that time the King of Jala, a small, fat, ugly figure, was living in a Tibetan caravanserai near the outskirts of Kangting. He still tried to retain some shreds of his former dignity by having several servants escort him as a bodyguard when he walked through the town, but apart from the Tibetans from his own part of Kham who side-stepped and bowed low as he passed, doffing their hats

The King of Jala, left centre, with members of family, servants and priests worshipping exposed tapestry of Chenrezi.

and sucking in their breath so that the air he breathed might not be polluted with their own humble, offensive breaths, he went about unheralded and unsung. His son, a slim, white-faced stripling, who was always dressed in a Chinese gown, was to be married to the daughter of the Prince of Yutong, another tributary ruler.

Kangting intended making a gala occasion of the event and from early morning fire-crackers were set off in various parts of the town, and trumpets, deep-pitched and high, blended or competed with conch shells, to drive away the evil spirits. About mid-morning John and I joined the crowds who were making their way to the Jala caravanserai, laughing and chatting excitedly, and shouting as some friend was recognized in the crush. The crowd was so great that it was impossible to take a photograph, and yet as soon as the 'yee-hee' yell of galloping horsemen was heard the crowd seemed to part mysteriously to let them sweep magnificently through them to the gates of the caravanserai. It was amazing how no one was hurt.

We finally managed to make our way to the high wall surrounding the caravanserai, and by climbing on each other's shoulders and with help from some burly Tibetans we were able to secure an excellent vantage point on the wall near the gateway. Several armed Khambas were on guard there and the gate was kept almost closed, except for a small aperture, to keep out the milling crowds who demanded to see the magnificently dressed guests as they arrived and moved about the inner courtyard. Chinese in the simply cut but beautifully patterned gowns of brocade; Tibetan officials in their ankle-length gowns of rich brocade, caught at the waists with silk scarves of contrasting colours; swaggering Khamba traders with bulky sheepskin-lined gowns faced with brilliant brocades, caught up at the waist to the knees like a kilt so that their legs could move more freely as they walked or swung into the saddle, their rifles still slung over their shoulders, criss-crossed with their cartridge-belts and silver 'god-boxes', and their gold- and silver-inlaid swords thrust through their colourful cummerbunds; lamas in all their brilliant priestly maroons and

yellows. Above them all, on the veranda of a small house to the
right of the courtyard, were four monks, two playing on twelve-
feet-long trumpets and two on small two-feet trumpets, standing
unconcernedly and with grim-visaged concentration blasting
what remained of the atmosphere.

There were cries of interest from the crowd and then, coming
through them like a coffin-shaped boat on a sea of shoulders, was
the curtained sedan-chair containing the bride. The curtains were
of brilliant silks and brocades, the predominant colour red, signi-
fying happiness, and all topped by a golden ball flashing in the
bright morning sunlight. The gates were thrown wide open to
allow the chair-bearers to pass through and the crowd surged forward. While the guards struggled to force them back out again
and close the gates John pointed to the courtyard and we dropped
down behind the guards and disappeared among the thronging
guests.

Most of the people seemed to be gathered about the main door
of the house, and some were passing in and out from time to time.
After we had taken a few pictures we edged our way towards the
door and casually moved in as if we were among the guests. Just
inside the door three monks sat on beautifully embroidered carpets and, without lifting their eyes from their manuscripts spread
out on the floor at their feet, chantingly intoned some prayers.
Behind them a large altar had been formed on which were heaped
religious objects in silver and gold, offerings of water, food, fruit
and fire in front of several large golden images, and a host of
richly ornamented *trankas*, or religious scroll-paintings. Passing
these on the right we proceeded up some stairs on to the roof-
courtyard where the bride and bridegroom and main body of
guests were gathered. A large white tent, open at the sides, and
with intricate black embroidery on the roof, was pitched in the
centre of the courtyard, and under it the guests were sitting eating
sweetmeats, drinking tea and noisily playing mah-jongg. One
man moving among them seemed important enough to be one of
the parents so John went up to him and asked him courteously if
we might be allowed to take photographs, including one of the

The King of Jala, with members of his household, arriving for worship. Priests in right background, beyond King of Jala (in felt hat), are intoning the Buddhist scriptures. Servant on the left of the King of Jala is carrying ceremonial silk scarf and offering for the god Chenrezi.

esteemed relative himself. He might have been an esteemed relative but officially he was Master of Ceremonies, and after a great deal of embarrassed posturing his picture was taken, and then he offered to introduce us to the bride and bridegroom.

The bride was in a small bridal chamber, reclining on a raised dais, and surrounded by attendants and female friends. She was resplendent in heavily embroidered brocades and decked with jewels of various kinds on her neck, ears, wrists, fingers, and even in her hair. Whether it was the make-up she had applied so thickly or whether it was the strain of the proceedings, it was hard to say, but she was parchment-pale and her lips were a lipsticked-red wound in her face. The bridegroom, still dressed in Chinese fashion, was in another room playing mah-jongg with some of his friends. John took a few more photographs and then we left.

Kangting was full of these caravanserais where the Tibetan traders and muleteers put up during their brief stay in Kangting, while their caravans of yaks, mules and horses grazed on the mountainside outside the town. It was part of George Kraft's instruction that I should visit those caravanserais with him in the afternoons and listen while he talked to the Tibetans, or preached if they would listen. George's friendly manner and great strength appealed to the friendly, easy-going Tibetans who were quick to admire any ability in their skills, horse-riding, shooting, wrestling and tossing the bundles of hided tea on to a growing pile. The long, thirty-pound bales of tea that were carried in from Ya-an were split into two on their arrival in Kangting, and six half-bales were sewn together inside a piece of wet hide, making a bundle of about ninety pounds' weight, two bundles being an animal load of about one hundred and eighty pounds. These bundles were stacked from the ground upwards all around the walls of the caravanserais waiting for the caravans, and it was one of the Khamba customs to see who could build the highest pile from a standing position. The most powerful Khambas could pile as many as eighteen one on top of the other, the feat becoming more and more difficult as the top of the pile receded from them and the ninety-pound bundle had to be pitched high into the air, but

George had surpassed all their records by pitching twenty-one on to a pile. The story of the foreigner's prowess had got around, as stories did round camp-fires, and George was welcomed warmly to the fires to talk over feats of strength in his country, the strange customs of foreigners, and always, of course, his religion.

Every Tibetan talked about religion. While their priests were their mediators with the gods, and at least one male member of every family went into the priesthood, it still did not follow that the others paid no attention to religion. The stories told around camp-fires were nearly always of supernatural occurrences, in war and in peace, of mysterious things that happened at night, of the strange power of the priests. And during the day there was always a heap of stones with prayers carved on them, a cluster of flags with prayers printed on them, a spinning wheel with prayers packed inside it, moving lips with prayers falling from them, to remind them that religion was a very real thing.

So they were interested to hear what the foreigner had to say of his religion, and George would take out his Tibetan Bible, or a poster illustrating some story from the Bible, and tell them of Jesus Christ, the Son of God. It was on such an occasion, after he had finished speaking, that George then said his friend was also learning Tibetan and would explain the doctrine further, and turning to me he left me to face the curious stares of the interested Tibetans! It was a rough but effective initiation into Tibetan, for the Tibetans, while laughing heartily at my mistakes and difficulties, were quick to help in supplying the missing words. They also supplied other words that almost turned the thirty-year-old George Kraft grey overnight when he heard them and checked up on their meaning!

We were able to help medically as well; although at this time I did not wish to be side-tracked from language study, especially as there was a hospital in Kangting run by Roman Catholic sisters. However, there were occasions when the sick or injured for one reason or another could not or would not go to hospital, either through fear, suspicion, or superstition, and I had to use what medical skill I had. The dirty, ill-lit, smoky caravanserais covered many a sickening sight. A young woman lying among the straw, moaning, holding an arm that had been broken by the landlord who had beaten her for some minor offence, and had thrown her into the straw to lie forgotten, to recover or die as she pleased. Another woman with a festering hole in her face where her husband had cut off her nose as punishment for being with another man, although he himself was rarely out of the brothels. A little girl of ten with venereal sores through being abused; her mother, an opium addict, had twice sold her to different men to get some money to buy more opium. It was little enough that I could do in a town filled to the brim with such tragedies, but here and there someone could be eased in body for a little while at least, and life be made more bearable by the stumbling words of hope that I might bring.

I had been four months in Kangting when the news arrived that Geoff and Gordon had at last left Chengtu and were on their way into Kangting. In the beginning of our acquaintanceship I had found Geoff hard to understand, and his reluctance to come to a clear-cut decision hard to abide, but gradually I had come to admire the very qualities in him in which I myself was so lacking, and to see the wisdom of God in bringing two such opposites to work together. During our recent separation our correspondence had covered many matters, our appreciation of each other had deepened, and I looked forward with keen pleasure to meeting him again. Gordon I scarcely knew, but he had looked like someone who would improve on acquaintance.

On the day of their expected arrival in Kangting John and I went about ten miles down the trail to meet them, and sat on a huge boulder beside the broiling river to eat some sandwiches while we waited for them. I had taken my binoculars with me and was able to follow the winding trail for some distance down the valley, so that I was the first to notice the moving specks indicating a group of people coming towards us. A little later an *hua-gan* appeared round the bend. It was carrying a young woman missionary of the Worldwide Evangelistic Crusade (founded by the famous England cricketer, C. T. Studd). She was followed by

The Task

Gordon, then Geoff, then a Miss Phyllis Thompson of the China Inland Mission who was travelling to Kangting to write a book on the Mission's work in that area. Gordon had had a hectic journey across China by truck, and at one point the truck he was driving had fallen into a river and he had only just escaped with his life; the luggage he had with him had taken some punishment —among other things a typewriter and a small portable organ for me had got a thorough soaking. I thought wryly that this was an organ that could be accepted into some assemblies in Britain as it had been immersed like Hiram's trees for Solomon's Temple.

Geoff's four months in Chengtu had seen the founding of a New Testament church, through his preaching and the preaching of a devout Chinese business man, Samuel Tsang. There had been several conversions and then, with other believers who had joined them, they had formed themselves into a group practising only what was found in the Scriptures, to add to the many thousands more springing up all over China. He had been asked if he would consider a tour of all those groups in China, to teach them what we had learned of the Scriptures; and so already the 'impossible' vision of a few years before was beginning to be realized and China was opening up before us.

Now that Geoff and Gordon had arrived it was decided that the three of us should find a house of our own and run it for ourselves, as I now had sufficient Tibetan and Geoff sufficient Chinese. Prices for most things were astronomical, and it had taken one hundred million dollars to bring Geoff and Gordon, with their luggage, from Chengtu to Kangting; so that finding a house, running it, paying for teachers and preparing all that would be required to outfit an expedition into Tibetan territory, with such rapidly inflating currency, demanded a considerable effort of faith.

George and I were almost ready to leave on a short expedition into Kham when news of a house was brought to us. It was in the Tibetan quarter of the town and recently built, and therefore in comparatively good condition with only a few months' dirt to clean up. A fixed rent of three 'do' of rice was agreed on. There were eight rooms in the house, four upstairs, four downstairs, and Geoff and Gordon drew up a list of alterations to be made before moving in, which they would supervise while George and I were away travelling in Kham.

Miss Phyllis Thompson and a Miss Liu, a keen young Chinese Christian who could speak Tibetan and would travel with her as a companion, were also going with us for the first few days of the trip into Tibetan country to give Miss Thompson background and atmosphere for her proposed book. George was not too happy about the arrangement, though, for he felt that the Tibetans would put only one construction on two foreign women and two foreign men travelling together, and, later, when the two women would be left alone in the mountains, the possibilities were such as did not bear contemplating. However, the women were determined, so animals and supplies were ordered for them as well.

We left Kangting by the South Gate of the town on a beautiful morning in the middle of May. The horses were a bit frisky at first but quickly settled down to a steady walk, strung out in single file ahead of the slower-plodding pack-animals. Once outside the bowl of Kangting the trail wound steadily southwards and upwards for a time, and then turned towards the west over the mountains. Away to the south a snow-covered mountain range, topped by the serene 24,994 feet Minya Konka, reared majestically towards the sky; in some of the depressions the bluish surface of glaciers stood out against the pure white of drifted snow. Underfoot snow and ice lay in the shade, although the sun beat down warmly on our shoulders. Huge boulders filled a river on our right and churned it into a foaming fury. The lower slopes of the mountains all around were heavily wooded with a variety of deciduous and coniferous trees, with here and there a splash of colour from some wild flowers.

Four hours after leaving Kangting we reached the first day's stage, called Jedo. Although it was quite close to Kangting nearly all caravans stopped here on the first day instead of proceeding further, as it gave time and opportunity to redistribute awkward loads, or fix faulty thongs holding the loads on the animals. Jedo was only a small village of scattered wooden houses on either side of the trail at about 10,500 feet. It was very popular with the people of Kangting because of some hot sulphur springs another few hundred feet up the mountain, where the water was hot enough to make bathing pleasant even in Arctic temperatures.

We chose the largest and most promising 'house', and while the muleteers unloaded and unsaddled the animals we went in to inspect our quarters for the night. The whole house was only a rough structure of wooden planks nailed on to an uneasy framework of posts, and the rooms were divided from each other by inadequate partitions of the same kind. The rooms contained two bunks each—four wooden planks on a wooden trestle—and that was all. Miss Thompson and Miss Liu occupied a room on one side of us, while in the other about twenty Tibetan traders and muleteers and a Tibetan woman bedded down together. The kitchen was immediately underneath and volumes of smoke from the open stove passed through the wide cracks in the floor and kept us awake, long after the Tibetans had quietened into sleep, listening to the snarl and bark of the dogs outside.

Next day at noon we crossed the 14,500 feet Jedo pass on to the high Tibetan grasslands. The twisted, barren, stony stretch before the summit fell away behind and left us gazing at rolling, sun-bathed grasslands stretching away to dark, jagged mountains crowned by snow-peaked giant ranges. The trail wound through pleasant, tree-less valleys, and late afternoon brought us to Nawashi where we expected to remain for a few days. The mountains framing the valley were only about two thousand feet in height but the valley itself was about twelve thousand feet above sea-level, and the trail winding out of the valley rose steeply to the higher snow ranges beyond. A wide stream flowed through the saucer-shaped valley, and the luxurious grass was carpeted with gentians, primulas, asters and buttercups.

Nawashi was a typical Tibetan village, with the houses set far apart from each other and all built on more or less the same pattern. Seen from a distance the village looked like some sprawling feudal castle in medieval Britain, only on a smaller scale. The walls of each house were from eighteen inches to two feet thick, built solidly from stones and mud, the floors and flat roof being of smaller stones and mud to give a smoother finish. The roof had a low parapet, and often a built-up veranda or another small room on top, giving a battlemented and turreted appearance to the whole. A high stone-and-mud-built wall surrounded each house, forming a courtyard holding stacks of wood, stacks of drying dung, and tethered animals. The whole of the ground floor of the house was used as a stable for animals—yaks, horses, goats and pigs—the hens and dogs having the run of the house. Upstairs the family ate, slept and did everything else in one large room taking up the whole of the second floor, except for one or two small rooms, more like cupboards, holding multifarious odds and ends.

Lobsang, our host for the next few days, escorted us up the notched wooden log serving as a ladder from the ground-floor stable, and led us over to the carpeted dais near the narrow aperture that passed as both window and chimney. There was another small hole in the roof above the stove, but this too was inadequate and a heavy pall of blue-grey smoke hung everywhere, making our eyes water and smart. Instead of an open fireplace with triangular iron cross-piece holding the inevitable cauldron, there was a huge mud stove filling one corner of the room, the front of it ornamented with shells and broken china-ware inserted in patterns of religious significance. Three openings had been made in the mud structure, and round the edge of the openings three knobs of dried mud supported the precariously balanced cauldrons. Fuel was an occasional log of wood thrust through a lower hole in the front of the stove and handfuls of dried dung cakes.

In front of the carpeted dais several small, box-shaped tables had been placed end-to-end, and in one of them a saucer-shaped iron pan had been inserted which burned yak-dung with more smoke than heat. Some shelves had been nailed to the wall and these held an assortment of brass ladle-shaped scoops, some wooden bowls, a long wooden cylinder which was the churn for making butter tea, and a collection of Tibetan bric-à-brac. On the far side of the room there was another small room containing the household idols and religious paraphernalia, some old manuscripts, prayer-wheels, a handbell and thunderbolt, and Buddhist religious symbols on paper, and Lobsang said that the ladies were to sleep here. George and I were given the coal-cellar, and where there was no charcoal there were heaps of evil-smelling hides which we pushed aside to make room for our camp-beds. Of lavatory and bathroom facilities there were none, and while there was a delightful simplicity about this arrangement it was embarrassingly complicated at times. George and I spent an uncomfortable night beating off the attacks of rats, lice, fleas, bugs and other forms of life.

Next morning several patients had arrived while we were still at breakfast, news having got round already that the 'foreign doctor' had arrived. Most of them were only suffering from stomach complaints due to worms, but one little girl of about nine was brought forward with her arm in a horrible state of sepsis. She had been having treatment from the lamas for about four months, and from her finger-tips to above her elbow she was a mass of mud, dung, scabs, 'sacred paper' and pus. It was only after an hour's steady bathing in hot water, during which the child screamed all the time, that I discovered that the large whitish substance I had been trying to wash away, thinking it was coagulated paper pulp, was really about two inches of projecting suppurating bone. The whole arm was in such a horrible mess that immediate amputation was the only answer, but the father refused permission on the grounds that it was better for her to die whole, even if she were young, rather than enter into the next life lacking an arm. After a long argument her father agreed to take her to the hospital in Kangting to see if removal of the bone itself would help at all.

Afterwards George gave a short talk to those who had gathered on the Great Physician who not only came to heal bodies and sent His disciples to do the same but who could heal souls also. We went from house to house helping where we could, leaving a message behind to those who listened interestedly but who could not face up to all that was involved in being a follower of Christ. No polygamy, no polyandry, no promiscuity, no debt, no gambling, among other things, was too much to ask of them. What sort of life could they lead without these things? No killing, while their whole reputation was bound up in their family and tribal feuds? Why, they would be like lambs being led to the slaughter. Yet they saw nothing wrong with the paradox of the young calf lying downstairs, which had been slowly dying for the past few days, and which they would not kill to put out of its misery because their religion said that it was a sin to kill.

In one house we visited no one answered our yell, but as we could hear the sound of voices upstairs we entered the open door in true Tibetan fashion. While we climbed the stairs leading to the living quarters of the house the sound of droning voices grew louder, and on entering the low door of the room the sight that met our eyes was like some hellish exaggeration of the *Macbeth* witches' scene. Around the walls of the room were squatting ten old women and one old man chanting some incantation in a high-pitched monotone, and then dropping to a droning repetition of '*Om Mani Padme Hum*', their magic prayer-formula. Although their eyes were open they gazed unseeingly in front of them and paid no attention to us as we entered hesitantly and sat down on the floor beside them. They had put themselves into a trance by their incantations, and although their bodies moved rhythmically sideways, like pendulums, to the rhythm of their chant, they were not conscious of anything happening in that room at all. A room that was only lit by the dull uncertain light from the slits in the thick walls, showed dimly the long, loose, dirty robes of the wrinkled, drooling women and the vague outline of the filthy old man in the corner, all of them mechanically clicking the beads of their rosaries. The atmosphere was oppressive with the immanence of evil, clamouring for admittance into the innermost parts of their being. Spirits wandering in waste places seeking to be clothed.

I glanced at George and saw that his eyes were closed and his lips moving in prayer, but whether it was silent prayer was impossible to tell in the incessant din of that confined space. I joined George in prayer, praying as I had never prayed before, that the powers of hell would be set at naught in that place, for this was indeed a conflict of spiritual powers in heavenly places. This was only a reflection of the elemental battle going on in the universe all the time of which Paul wrote: 'Ours is not a conflict with mere flesh and blood, but with the despotisms, the empires, the forces that control and govern this dark world—the spiritual hosts of evil arrayed against us in the heavenly warfare.' This was what we were in reality facing every day of our lives although seldom was it revealed so nakedly. We had to conquer here or for ever hold our peace. The voices rose and beat against the ear-drums in a maddening, increasing tempo. 'Greater is He that is in you than he that is in them': the words leapt to my mind and my voice rose with theirs as I hurled myself on God for help to overcome in some way. And suddenly the tempo dropped for a second and in that gap George was forward on one knee in the centre of the floor.

'You are praying to God, aren't you?'

'Ray' (Yes). The words came with difficulty after a pause, as one or two tried to catch up the rhythm again.

'So are we, but our God——' and George was away on the good news of Jesus Christ and the deliverance He brought, words pouring from him in a torrent so that there was no opportunity for them to begin again on their hellish incantations. It seemed incredible that the room, which a few moments before had been like some antechamber of hell, should be now gripped by the Spirit of God, yet it was so. Not a sound was made and only George's voice, speaking as he had never spoken before, swept the silence with all the authority of the Word of God.

He finished, and automatically the old man began again: '*Om Mani Padme Hum*,' but his voice faltered and died away. The power was broken, prayer had been answered, faith honoured and God glorified before men and angels. The women started bustling about making tea, and as we ate and drank together conversation returned to normal subjects, and so we left them eating and talking as if nothing of moment had happened in their lives at all. The significance of the supernatural to them was not that it was something to lead them to the feet of God, but something to blindly use or be used by to stave off misfortune in their everyday lives.

Phyllis Thompson and Miss Liu had lived in a Tibetan village, seen Tibetan life, had even slept in a Tibetan tent with three nomads, one wife, four daughters and several young calves, and they were ready to leave for Kangting. Just to complete the atmosphere as they left thick clouds gathered and snow began to fall heavily.

It snowed all day and all night, and when George and I rose to leave on the next part of our trip the following morning everything was blanketed in white. When the sun topped the mountains the glare from the snow was so great that we had to put on our coloured spectacles brought for this purpose. Four pack mules, two riding horses and two muleteers formed our small caravan, and we were only minute black specks in an undulating wilderness of white as we picked our way through the heavy snow to the summit of the pass overlooking the valley. Towards evening we arrived at a small village, called Nga-Shu, built on the side of the mountain and commanding a wide sweep of valley where hundreds of yaks grazed around the sprawling black goats'-hair tents of the nomads.

A few days later we passed through Gada, or Tailing, with its gleaming-roofed monastery set like a jewel in the centre of a smooth green plain. Leaving Gada, and crossing the billiard-table-like plain, the trail wound upwards steeply into the clouds covering the mountains ahead. The muleteers suggested another and easier route, and we turned off the narrow, rutted trail on to the springy grass of the mountain on our right. Gradually the gradient increased until we were lying along our horses' necks as they struggled upwards, at times climbing steep shelves of earth like mountain goats instead of horses. After several hours it appeared that the muleteers had lost their way and had no idea of where we had got to, and I had to take a reading from the compass. The arrow indicated a mountain stream and for some time we followed the course of this, up a narrow cut in the mountain so sheer that our legs and loads scraped the sides as we passed; then straight up the mountain again to cross the shoulder at its lowest point, and at last we reached the ridge and could see the right trail several hundred feet below. While the horses rested George asked the muleteers why they had chosen to come that way. 'Oh,' said one of them, whose name was Gombo, carelessly, 'the other way is very steep.'

Several days later we arrived at Tao-fu, our intended destination for this trip. It was evening when we rode wearily around the mountain and into the town, and by the time we had had a wash and a meal we were too tired to go out and have a look round. We had to eject a calf, a dog, some hens, several armfuls of wood, straw and dirt, before we could find sufficient space in a room of one of the houses to spread out our camp-beds and gratefully drop off into a dreamless sleep.

Although Tao-fu was 10,000 feet above sea-level, as soon as the sun came up we had to strip off furs and woollens and wear only shirts and riding-breeches. Word had already gone ahead of the skill of the 'foreign doctor' and a queue had formed before we finished breakfast. Much as I might have liked to think so, my fame had not reached here from Kangting; the explanation was much more simple and much less flattering. Two or three days previously we had caught up with a caravan travelling to Lhasa. We had travelled along with them, and then stopped at midday to share a meal together. During the meal one of the traders asked if I could do anything for his horse which had suddenly become ill. We walked over to where the animal was lying on the ground, retching and twitching in pain. It looked like a case of poisoning of some kind, either fodder or grazing, so I ordered the Tibetans to hold the horse still and, taking some homœopathic pilules, I dropped them into the horse's mouth, closing the mouth and nostrils with my hand so that it would have to swallow. Half an hour later the horse struggled to its feet, and a few hours later along the trail the trader saddled it up again and rode it, with admiring congratulations to the miracle-working foreign doctor who had saved his valuable animal from death. It was this story, probably embellished, that had got around and brought the crowd of patients so early. When I took my box of medicines outside and set them on a table outside the door of our roof-top room, the crush of patients—each one thrusting out his arm to have his pulse taken as that was a well-known custom of the lamas whether they knew what to look for or not—was so great that George had to use his great weight and strength to hold them back and give me sufficient space in which to work.

Each day between seventy and a hundred patients came along to be attended to in the morning clinic, some having made several days' journey over the mountains when they heard of the treatment to be had in Tao-fu; and in the afternoons George and I visited the houses in the small town treating patients who were too ill to come to us, and preaching at every opportunity.

The first major conflict with the lamas happened while we were in Tao-fu. Tao-fu had one of the largest monasteries in the area, with a roster of two or three thousand monks, and it dominated the town and surrounding valleys. We had been called to treat two Chinese soldiers who had managed in some mysterious way to contract relapsing fever. Both were lying on filthy beds in a squalid shack in a congested part of the town, and I ordered them to be washed and shaved all over, and the huts to be cleaned in some way; then I would bring medicine to de-louse the men and huts, relapsing fever being a lice-borne disease and dangerous in such a close-packed community. When I returned with the D.D.T. I found an embarrassed crowd gathered, who informed me hesitantly that the lamas had ordered them not to allow the foreigners to sprinkle them with D.D.T. as the medicine would kill the lice, and to kill anything, even a louse, was a great sin. No amount of argument or persuasion would move them and the matter had just to be left there. We were furious at the priests, who never put in an appearance to argue their own point of view but left it to the credulous and frightened villagers, and we decided to approach them about it.

The meeting with the lamas was precipitated because of another incident of that same afternoon. We had just returned to our room when there was a commotion outside and several burly Tibetans arrived, carrying a young girl whose face was covered with a dirty rag, and followed by an anxious, murmuring crowd. When they laid the girl on the floor of the room and I removed the blood-stained rag I saw that she was only a youngster of about nine years and her face was a bloody mess. At first I thought she had been shot, or kicked by a mule, common enough accidents in Tibet, but there were too many loose shreds of skin for that, and then out of the din of clamouring voices I made out that she had been mauled by a mad dog. I had no further time for talk then, as I went to work on her face, but after I had patched it up as best I could and given her a sedative to put her to sleep for some time, I discussed the matter further with those who had brought her, and it transpired that the dog which had mauled her had not just recently gone mad but had been so for some time and had savaged several people. When I asked in amazement why someone had not shot the brute, for every Khamba prided himself on his marksmanship and it should have been an easy matter for them to get rid of it first shot, I was told that the lamas said that it was wrong to kill and no one dared disobey.

The next day we visited the lamasery to tackle the lamas on their own ground. The lamasery itself was like a small town, with narrow lanes between the various buildings, some of them temples, some living quarters. As we passed through the living quarters of the lamas, stopping here and there to talk with some of them and give them gospels, or booklets on Christianity, we were greeted most of the time with mocking questions and sallies. Even the idols in the dark alcoves of the dirty temples smiled sardonic-ally.

A lama held aside a curtain and we passed into a large, light, airy room, the floor of which was clean and polished, and the walls hung with intricately embroidered tapestries in a variety of colours. Four lamas in cleaner, better robes than the others we had seen, were seated in a row on a luxurious carpet on the far side

Gigantic richly-embroidered tapestry of Chenrezi, chief deity of
Tibet, exposed for public worship outside Tibetan monastery.

of the room; in front of them, on low, ornamented gilt tables each had a manuscript open, and a bowl of tea in a silver- and gold-embossed holder. They did not rise but smilingly motioned us to take a seat on the carpet beside them, and then ordered the priest at the door to bring tea. When the butter tea had been poured and we had taken the usual sip, replacing the ornamented cover on the top of the bowl to keep the tea warm, the polite questioning began. Which country did we come from? Were there many horses and mules in our country? How did we travel? How long did it take to come from our country to Tibet? How did we travel across water? Before we had come anywhere near the point where the 'doctrine' would be discussed a curtain separating us from an inner room swung aside and an old man appeared. The four lamas immediately leapt to their feet and bowed low in obeisance, tongues out and breath-sucking noisily. He motioned the others to be seated, and smiled as he introduced himself to us. He was the *Kembo*, or Abbot, of the monastery. There was a raised dais on the other side of the room, almost like a throne, richly carpeted and tapestried, with bowls and religious symbols in gold and silver on the table in front, and he took his seat there and began the questions all over again. He was better informed than the others and showed no surprise at the mention of ships, automobiles, even aeroplanes. However, the reason was soon made clear. He had only recently returned from a journey to Nanking where he had been a Tibetan representative from Kham to the Chinese Government, and where he had also acted as a delegate at a 'Conference for Association of Religions'. He was full of enthusiasm for this idea and asked our opinion, obviously expecting that such magnanimity on his part as a Buddhist would call forth equal enthusiasm on our part as mere Christians. When George went on to point out the significance of the difference between union and unity, and the unequivocal words of Christ: 'No man cometh unto the Father but by Me,' 'There shall be *one* fold and *one* shepherd,' 'I am the Way, the Truth and the Life,' 'There is none other name under heaven given among men whereby we must be saved'—his enthusiasm evaporated, and his nods became merely a courteous recognition of the doctrine and not agreement with it. It was only a step from this to the matter of killing, as an example of our differences, and the battle was on. The lamas were at an immediate disadvantage when George brought forward the very pointed argument that even at that very moment in the kitchen beneath us huge sides of meat were being cooked for the lamas' meals, meat which the lamas had ordered from butchers who were employed by them to kill. A great amount of voluble casuistry was used to get out of that one, involving the low position of the butchers in the Wheel of Life and the merit they obtained by slaying the animals to provide for the lamas, and the equal merit the lamas obtained by bestowing dispensations on such unworthy objects. We followed up this advantage by introducing the lamas' orders to the people not to allow the lice to be killed, and also the case of the mad dog. There was a distinct hesitation on the part of each one to answer this and they gazed uncertainly at one another, until the old Abbot mildly reiterated the old argument that each louse had a soul and was also on its way to enlightenment.

'In that event each worm has a soul,' I burst out, unable to contain myself any longer, 'and has an equal right to be allowed to work its way to enlightenment through the bowels of the priests. From now on I am going to tell every priest who comes to me for medicine for worms, in front of all the people, that of the two pills I am giving him one will kill the worms and the other will clear them out of his system, and if they really believe what they teach they will keep their worms.'

As nearly every Tibetan had worms, from eating raw meat amongst other things, and suffered great discomfort in consequence, this was an ultimatum with a vengeance. They looked at each other in dismay and it was left to the wily old Abbot to suggest that as there were different orders of importance among souls perhaps it would not be so wrong to kill the worms to save the lamas' lives or give them greater freedom for meditation? George was quick to reply that in like manner perhaps it would not be so wrong to shoot the mad dog to save little girls' lives and kill lice to save men? The point was willingly conceded and after

Butter images in front of unexposed embroidered tapestry of Chenrezi. Religious symbols on ceremonial occasions are made from intricately moulded and highly coloured designs in butter.

The Task

several more bowls of tea the Abbot asked if we would like to see the inner shrine of the monastery, the *sanctum sanctorum*.

We passed through the curtain into a long narrow room with two other curtained doors leading off to the sides. On either side of the room, which was brightly, almost gaudily, painted in brilliant colours portraying historical and mythical events of Buddhism, generously interspersed with the earlier beliefs and practices of Bönism, the primitive demon-worship of Tibet, there were closely set rows of idols and images of saints and divinities in various postures, with bowls of water and burning butter-lamps placed at odd intervals in front of them. Passing through another curtained door we entered the inner shrine. It was even more beautifully painted and ornamented, at least what could be seen of it, for most of the place was in darkness except for the lights from the butter-lamps and the butter-candles in their egg-cup-shaped candlesticks of gold. Life-sized golden images of Buddha and his disciples smiled enigmatically out of slanted, elongated eyes from all around the room, and the spaces between them were filled with glass-faced cupboards holding the hundred and eight wood-carved sacred Scriptures of Buddhism. The smell of incense hung heavily and sickeningly in the room, and the far-off beat of a drum and sonorous clang of a gong stirred the already quickened pulses into something like fear. There was too much of something concentrated here that upset the educated human equilibrium and clamoured with silent menace for recognition and ultimate submission. The externals were beautiful, but they hid something that fantastically dilated the eyes, flickered the nostrils and caught the breath in fear.

Outside thunder growled, the late afternoon sun slanted up the valley tracing a lovely pattern of light and shade on the surrounding forested mountains, and the air was heavy with the promise of rain. But it was a natural heaviness, and would cleanse, and afterwards the sun would shine again and everything would live.

There was no more opposition from the lamas and they came round for their medicine for worms with the others, and stayed to watch wonderingly as I stitched up wounds, removed teeth painlessly—comparatively!—and cured long-standing complaints that their prayers and incantations had failed to touch. More and more people were coming from a distance and it appeared as if we should have to remain there for months to deal adequately with them all. We finally set a date in advance so that all in Tao-fu would know when we were leaving and be able to receive treatment if needed; the others from the surrounding mountains and valleys would just have to be disappointed. Cases so advanced that it was impossible for me to do anything were constantly being brought in, and it was no use trying to tell beseeching relatives that nothing could be done, for their faith was so great after some of the things they had seen and heard that any refusal would have been taken as unwillingness to help rather than inability.

And all the while the lamas watched and waited in the background for someone to die on my hands. Their reputation and power was being undermined by these foreigners who came with their wonder-working medicine and the new doctrine which told of forgiveness and salvation being free like the medicines they gave. It was too attractive and acceptable to be permitted, for once such a doctrine began to spread the superstitions and parasitical practices of Lamaism were finished. For it was Lamaism that was practised in Tibet, not Buddhism.

As early as the fifth century A.D. the Chinese described the Tibetans as 'ferocious barbarian shepherds', and they were then a nation of very warlike people under their own kings and chiefs, who were chosen for their great personal strength and success in war. This was long before they knew anything of Buddhism, or owed any kind of allegiance to China, when they were even without a written language. They were divided into clans, or tribes, and each clan made war on another to increase its own strength and wealth. They claimed that they were descended from a monkey that came over the Himalayas and married a she-devil of the mountains; the young progeny ate some magical grain given to them by the Compassionate Spirit of the Mountains (who afterwards became the Dalai Lama) and wonderful things began to happen—their tails and hair grew shorter, and finally disappeared, they began to speak, and they were men.

About the seventh century the Tibetans overran Upper Burma and Western China and forced the Chinese Emperor to a humiliating peace. It was a part of its terms that the Chinese Emperor should give his daughter in marriage to the twenty-three-year-old Srong-tsan Gam-bo, King of Tibet at that time. This Chinese princess was an ardent Buddhist, as was the other wife of the king, a Nepalese, and between the two of them they prevailed upon the king to introduce Buddhism into Tibet. He sent for Buddhist priests from India and reduced the Tibetan language to writing according to the Indian alphabet, and into this new written language he caused many of the more important books of Buddhism, both from India and China, to be translated.

The new religion proved rather a mixed blessing to the country, for ultimately, after passing through various stages, it became a disastrous, parasitic disease which fastened on to the vitals of the land. The form of Buddhism which was introduced became mixed up with the black practices of shamanistic Bönism and gradually became a cloak for the worst forms of oppressive demon-worship, by which the poor Tibetan was placed in constant fear of his life from the attacks of thousands of malignant devils both in this life and in the world to come, and forced to make never-ending payments to the lamas of large sums to avert these calamities. The priests—'lamas' in Tibetan—multiplied rapidly and soon usurped authority in matters of state, and finally gained full control, overthrowing the kings and assuming the kingship from among themselves. The 'priest-king' structure in Tibet, as in other lands, proved a very retrograde movement. The lamas ruled the country entirely in their own interests, and unlike the early ecclesiastics of Britain or other countries they never even attempted to preach or to educate the laity, but kept the latter in ignorance and abject servitude, with the result that the former virile Tibetans became the most priest-ridden people in the world and, sapped of their vigour and independence, gradually deteriorated as a nation.

The Task

It was this power that the lamas had to safeguard in their own interests, and that kept foreigners out of Tibet. The people must never get to know that there was a better way of life outside what the lamas gave to them. They had been successful in this concealment for centuries because of the natural barriers formed by the gigantic mountain ranges surrounding their country, so difficult to negotiate that even Genghiz Khan passed round them on his march to conquer the world. Then latterly the idea of a 'buffer state' in international politics helped them, for it kept out by mutual agreement those from surrounding countries who in the ordinary course of events would have overrun Tibet and so brought knowledge of one kind or another that would have eventually undermined the power of Lamaism. The fact that two-thirds of the people had to suffer appallingly to support a priestly third, who contributed absolutely nothing to the country, neither troubled the lamas themselves nor the nations who exploited the situation to serve their own political ends. The soul or body of the individual meant nothing to them, either in the remorseless Wheel of Life or the equally remorseless wheels within wheels of international politics.

Almost the last patient to be attended was a nomad woman, lying in a tent outside Tao-fu. Her lower abdomen, rectum, inside of legs, vulva and vagina, was one mass of running suppurating sores. She had just given birth to a child. The child, with a three-inch length of umbilical cord still tied with a dirty piece of rag, was covered from head to foot with the same suppurating sores. It was syphilis, of course, and both the husbands, one aged 47 and one aged 27—neither of whom knew who was the father of the child—were also suffering from an advanced stage of the same disease. As I sought to clean up the mess I retched time and again, and finally I had to go outside and vomit. The woman was in agony and lay on her lice-ridden, blood-and-pus-soaked sheep-skin gown, groaning in pain, her head threshing from side to side, but murmuring in hope and gratitude through it all: 'Ka-tru, Ka-tru. Ka-drin-chay.' ('Great favour' or polite 'Thank you'.)

She managed to sleep that night for the first time since giving birth to the baby, and was comparatively comfortable the next day, although still asking plaintively and fearfully: 'Will I die?' Four days later her husbands had to return to their nomad encampment and she would have to ride over the mountains with them. There were so many who were so ill and so little could be done to help.

George was complaining of a sore throat and headache when we left Tao-fu, and by the time we stopped at a nomad camp in the late afternoon he had a high fever. He was afraid that he was in for an attack of pneumonia and pleurisy as twice before he had had similar onsets and symptoms, and had gone down with those illnesses. Being caught with any illness at that altitude of 14,000 feet was dangerous but the dangers resulting from complications of pneumonia were even greater. I gave George as many M. and B. tablets as I dared and packed him off to bed quickly, dosing him repeatedly throughout the night. In the morning he was still a bit groggy, although the fever was reduced, and insisted on travelling homewards as soon as possible instead of hanging around.

We made Gada in one day's riding, with George reeling in the saddle as we arrived. Leaving early next morning we passed the day's stage by eleven o'clock and camped towards evening with some nomads in a high valley. George felt much better and by the next day, apart from slight weakness, was almost normal again.

It was just as well, for as we descended out of the cotton-wool clouds wreathing a pass, and crossed an open plain wide of the trail, George's horse suddenly floundered and with a wild shout he hurled himself sideways and backwards from the saddle on to the solid ground. But even in that short space of time the horse was already up to its belly in soft oozing mud, and sinking rapidly. Being relieved of George's 210 pounds gave it a better chance, but if the muleteers had not grabbed the reins and its tail, and helped to pull it to safety, it would have disappeared in the mud in its panic-stricken struggles. Fortunately, George had only touched the edge of the morass or it would have been 'finis' for both. Farther on, one of the mules inadvertently strayed into another marsh, and the muleteers had to tear off their boots frantically and work their way from hummock to hummock towards the animal and strip off its load, throw ropes round its neck—a difficult job as the mud was already over its shoulders—and nearly strangle the mule as they heaved it out of the clinging morass.

A few days later we rode into Kangting, bearded, tired and dirty. Geoff and Gordon had been working hard on the house during my absence and had transformed the place by inserting an extra window in each room, with glass panes instead of the usual rice paper, so that apart from occasional gaps in the walls of the house where the wooden boards had warped and allowed the wind to whistle through, we were really comfortable. During the war an enterprising foreigner in the Army had managed to install electricity in the town and a good light was obtainable, much better than in many of the large cities down country in China. John Ting had been a great help in arranging things, but had since left to go to Shanghai and Nanking, so that he could see his family and collect his wife on his return before the country collapsed. The economic situation was farcical, and in one day the rate of exchange for the pound jumped from one and a half million dollars to four and a half million dollars. Geoff calculated that he had spent between five and six hundred million dollars in just over a month, including all expenses in getting the house ready.

Yet in the midst of it all God continued to supply our every requirement. From China itself there was encouraging news of God moving in blessing amidst human chaos, and Samuel Tsang wrote to us telling of two thousand people accepting Christ in Shanghai, and twelve hundred in Nanking, in special meetings being held there. There was a great spiritual awakening throughout the country and from all over the eastern provinces came reports of Chinese giving their wealth—and even the poor giving their little out of their poverty—to help others, as the words of Christ gripped them. Samuel Tsang had just been on a visit to the eastern provinces and wrote of the decision of about three hundred Chinese evangelists to put into effect immediately a comprehensive programme to preach the news of Jesus Christ over the whole of China, in every major town and city, by 1952. In his letter he suggested that we should seek to know the Lord's will as to whether we should travel down to Fukien and meet Watchman Nee and the other leading evangelists and teachers and then afterwards go round the assemblies in China, preaching, and laying before the newly converted Chinese believers their responsibility towards the people in West China and Tibet.

The prospect and potentialities of such an opportunity throughout China, before Satan swept in with the forces of materialism in the Communist régime, were so tremendous and overwhelming that it required the explicit command of God to remain where we were and study the language, to keep us in Kangting. All the need in the world, all the opportunities in the world, were not sufficient warrant to move one step in the service of God. Other parts of the field had nothing to do with the labourer; it was for the Lord of the Harvest to direct His own affairs and thrust out His own labourers where and when He chose.

'If thou passest on with me thou wilt be a burden to me,' said David to his friend and companion, Hushai, who wished to accompany him into exile in the mountains, 'but if thou return to the city . . . then mayest thou for me defeat the counsel of Ahithophel.' And Hushai, who reluctantly turned away from David, was the means used to bring David back to the throne. So many friends and companions of Christ, too, had become a burden to Him in their mistaken zeal, and the mission field, so-called, was cluttered up by many who, although sincere and godly people, ought to have been at home serving their Lord there. They had allowed 'need' or 'opportunity' or a passing emotional conviction to determine their sphere of service, instead of the command of God. China was tumbling on to the lap of the greatest anti-God régime the world had ever seen, innocent believers were already being raped and ripped open, their entrails dragged out of their living, tortured bodies by slowly moving vehicles while they were tied to posts, their tongues and eyes torn out, and a thousand other fiendish tortures inflicted, because they were faithful to God instead of the State. Surely now was the time to establish them, pour the living Word of God into them, to help them face the tribulation that was pouring down upon them from the north.

But the command of God to us remained inflexible: 'Study the language and keep your faces towards Tibet.' It was a more difficult decision to take than it had been to decide to remain amidst the collapse of government, of currency, of administration, for the possibilities in China were imminent and real while the possibilities in Tibet were distant and ideal. The final tragedy was that there were so many better equipped in knowledge of the language and Scriptures who ought to have been able to help these believers by their own professed principles and yet it appeared that no one but Geoff and I, novices in language and Scripture, were prepared to consider it; in fact, even in their last days before fleeing from China, many of those same missionaries were still denouncing those who would have to remain and die for what the missionaries supposedly believed in themselves. The missionaries could go to other non-Communist countries and begin once again to build up their self-conceived structure but always they could run away and leave the native believers to pay the price of *their* ignorance and folly, and to die as they blindly sought after a simple obedience to the Scriptures that ought to have been taught by the missionaries in the first place.

Chapter Nine

THE OPENING

I stepped up my language study with my teacher, Gezang Wangdu, to three hours per day, spending the rest of the time studying by myself, or with George Kraft in the caravanserais, or around the camp-fires with the Tibetans. Geoff and Gordon shared a teacher they had found, called Beh-ma, an unkempt, wild nomad, clad in a dirty yakskin gown, who was amazingly well-taught in Tibetan. Through these two we gradually built up the necessities for outfitting a caravan, from the wooden boxes to hold sixty pounds of equipment or goods per side of animal to the animals and saddles for carrying them.

We had also become very friendly with our next-door neighbour, a man called Chia, and his wife and family. He was part Chinese and part Tibetan, and held an influential position under General Liu Wen Huie, Governor of Sikang Province, and his wife was a Tibetan from Lhasa. Part of his work was to act as a liaison between the Tibetans who came into Kangting and the Chinese Government, and it was through him and one of his contacts, the Secretary of the Governor of Chamdo, in East Tibet, that we received our first offer of help in getting into Tibet. In order to be ready to leave at a moment's notice, should permission come through quickly, we decided to speed up our preparations and take a short trip by ourselves into Kham, to test our language and our handling of a caravan.

We headed south-west towards Minya Konka with five horses and four yaks in our caravan, one cook, one teacher, and two muleteers—both women, wives of Beh-ma! After travelling for three days we stopped in a nomad encampment near to Beh-ma's home country while he went off on a visit to deal with some family affairs. When he returned three days later we left the encampment and took a steep trail leading over the face of a nearby mountain. A magnificent sight greeted us on the other side, where the mountains sweeping down to the dark valleys were carpeted with flowers of every colour—blue gentians, white edelweiss, pink primulas, light-green shrubs, dark-green pines, firs, birches, rhododendrons—and then up and up on the other side, past the tree-line to the snows, until clouds drew a jealous curtain over the peaks.

Another few days' travel, and then we camped above the tree-line below the mighty Minya Konka. The Minya Konka lamasery was only a small huddle of buildings cowering in the shadow of that magnificent range.

Early next morning we got up to watch the clouds lift slowly from the valleys. As we sat at breakfast, drinking bowl after bowl of scalding tea, the curtain rose on ridge upon ridge of virginal beauty in front of us until the 25,000 feet massif stood fully revealed, blushing rose-pink in the morning sun, reluctant patches of evaporating clouds lying like filmy vestments about her feet.

We stayed a few more days exploring the lamasery and the surrounding mountainside, and then began a leisurely return by a different route. While crossing the river at the foot of Minya Konka we almost lost Gordon. He was never very happy on a horse, preferring to walk, and in order to ford the river we had to proceed upstream over a precarious narrow shelf, with the horses up to their knees in the rushing water. The sides of the mountains on both banks were so steep that we continued along the river for some time, picking our way with the greatest of care, and then finally decided to attempt to get out at a point that was still difficult to negotiate, but possible. Beh-ma took it first, moving easily in his saddle from long habit as the horse scrambled upwards. Gordon was next, and after a long, dubious look at Beh-ma's disappearing figure above, he urged his horse forward out of the water and on to the bank. The horse lunged upwards powerfully, lifting itself out of the water with a bound, and

Mt. Minya Konka, one of the world's highest peaks, towering 25,000 feet on the China-Tibet border. Several days' pony journey from Kangting and conquered in 1936 by two daring young Americans.
(See 'Men Against the Clouds.')

The Opening

Gordon began to slide out of the saddle as he tilted backwards, only saving himself by grabbing wildly at the horse's neck. The horse kept going, scrambling and leaping forwards to avoid going over backwards, and would have made it safely but for Gordon, who either forgot or was unable to adapt himself in the saddle to help the animal, and at the next steep point horse and rider teetered slowly over backwards into the river. Fortunately, Gordon was able to get his feet out of the stirrups before they fell and both landed in the river at different places so there was no serious damage done, although a soaking in an icy-cold river, while clad in woollens and furs, at 12,000 feet was bad enough. Gordon walked for the remainder of the trip.

On our return we found the situation even more chaotic. Mail delivery was more irregular as the larger cities fell to the Communists, and more and more people, peasants, soldiers and police, were taking to banditry to find money and food. However, letters had come through to us containing cheques to the value of £400, and with this we immediately bought two hundred bales of tea for one thousand million dollars. Tea, rice, silver and gold were the only stable mediums of currency. It was forbidden to hoard rice, and silver and gold could not be used for small everyday transactions, so bales of tea were being used all over the area by Tibetan traders and Chinese merchants as the only means of carrying on business.

An unexpected difficulty cropped up suddenly when Gordon announced that he would not be travelling with us into Tibet. After some hesitation he confessed that he had fallen in love with one of the workers of a new group of missionaries, Mildred Hostad of the World Mission Prayer League, and he had already applied to join her mission. This was a blow, for Gordon had been a chemist, and had a good knowledge of medicine, and would have been an excellent colleague, but there was nothing that could be done about it. He was moving down to the W.M.P.L. headquarters in Kangting and expected to get married as soon as it could be arranged.

The spiritual opposition against us increased steadily and it became daily more difficult to pray and study the Scriptures. What would normally have been an ordinary early morning devotional reading and prayer became a matter of two or three hours' concentration, demanding all one's physical energies. When prayer for any specific matter was required, demanding more exercise than usual to get into the presence of God and the calmness of communion, it became a battle, and the effort left one soaked with perspiration and physically exhausted. About this time, too, Geoff began to have distressing symptoms that could not be placed in any category of illness, and between the attacks he showed no symptoms of illness at all. At first Geoff would appear in my room dazed, or even asleep, knowing nothing until I had awakened him, except for an impression of overwhelming evil from which he had tried to get away. It was not a nightmare, for there was no form attached to the experience, no images in the mind, only the sense of a presence of evil that sought to destroy. The attacks became more violent, when Geoff was unable to come through to my room at all, and simply collapsed on the floor beside the bed, with the bedclothes and his pyjamas stripped from him, lying in all his misery, and still with no remembrance of anything except this sense of overwhelming evil. Finally, I was awakened one night by the sound of crashing glass, and I rushed through to Geoff's room on the top floor to find him standing by the window about to jump out to get away from the evil. He was still dazed and bewildered when I got him back into bed, and he did not comprehend what he had done and was about to do until some time later.

It was now too serious to ignore, and we decided to make it a matter of prayer. Ed Beatty of the C.I.M. had told us of two young Tibetans who had been converted, and then immediately afterwards had become seriously ill. He had brought them into the C.I.M. compound thinking that perhaps their food was being poisoned because of their new profession of faith, but the attacks continued and increased in violence until they died—and the symptoms were the same as Geoff was showing now. It could not be food-poisoning, for we were both eating the same food, and in any case on the morning after the attacks Geoff was all right, with no diarrhoea or nausea. A part of the practice of black magic by the lamas was to cut signs on the doors or walls of houses, and then lay a curse on the inmates, or to obtain pieces of a person's clothing, or hair, or nail-parings, and then mould them with some clay into a small image, and finally stick a sliver of wood into the entrails of the image, soliciting the help of the spirits to afflict the object of the curse; we therefore removed every piece of paper bearing symbols which we could find, and cut out every symbol from the doors and walls. Then we made the attacks a matter of prayer, taking it to God and asking Him to frustrate and defeat those attacks of Satan that we might go on to complete His purposes. After that there was no recurrence of the attacks.

The words of Archbishop Trench which I read somewhere at that time left a deep impression on me as I pondered over the significance of the supernatural in the lives of men:

> *If we with earnest effort could succeed*
> *To make our life one long connected Prayer,*
> *As lives of some, perhaps, have been and are!—*
> *If—never leaving Thee—we had no need*
> *Our wandering spirits back again to lead*
> *Into Thy presence, but continued there,*
> *Like angels standing on the highest stair*
> *Of the sapphire throne—this were to pray indeed!*
> *But if distractions manifold prevail,*
> *And if in this we must confess we fail,*
> *Grant us to keep at least a prompt desire*
> *Continual readiness for Prayer and Praise—*
> *An altar heaped and waiting to take fire*
> *With the least spark, and leap into a blaze.*

It was Edward Payson who wrote in one of his famous letters to a friend: 'Religion consists very much in giving to God the place in our views and feelings which he actually fills in the Universe. We know that in the Universe He is all in all. The best advice I can give to you is to look to Him. This I doubt not you

do; but you cannot do it too much, If we would do much for
God, we must ask much of God; we must be men of prayer; we
must almost literally pray without ceasing.' Like Daniel, Prime
Minister in one of the greatest empires the world has ever known,
who opened his window toward heaven and prayed three times a
day. Like Luther who said, on being asked what his plans were
for the following day: 'Work, work, from early until late. In fact,
I have so much work to do that I shall spend the first three hours
in prayer. If you are too busy to pray, you are too busy.' Like
Cromwell who, looking one day at statues of famous men, turned
to his friend and said: 'Make mine kneeling, for thus I came to
glory.'

The unrest increased in Kangting, and rioting broke out in
different parts of the town. Chia, our friendly neighbour, sent for
me one day and asked for medicine as he had a cold, and then informed me that he was leaving immediately for the mountains
where fighting had broken out among the Tibetans and he had
been appointed to act as mediator. It appeared that a well-known
trader had been shot by a lama's servant in a quarrel between the
trader and the lama, and the lama's servant in turn was immediately shot by the trader's servant. Friends of both took up the
feud right away and a tribal war started. A detachment of soldiers
had been sent out to put down the disturbance, but nothing further had been heard of them, whether they had been liquidated in
the struggle or were simply pretending to have difficulty in getting into contact with the combatants. The Chinese had no desire
for mountain warfare with the wild Khambas unless with greatly
superior numbers on their side. Out of their long experience of
fighting with the Chinese the Tibetans had coined a saying, 'Beat
a Chinaman enough and he will speak Tibetan,' and the unfed,
unpaid soldiers of General Liu Wen Huie at any rate had no wish
to hear the war-song of the Tibetans:

> *The scabbard of my blue steel*
> *Is the liver of my enemy. . . .*
> *No thought of death finds any cover in my mind!*

The Opening

I carry the red life on my finger tip!
I have taken the vow of a hero!

The situation had grown so serious that finally Chia had been despatched to clear it up. It was not just the tribal war that was disturbing, but conditions locally were such that it might flare up into widespread rebellion and rioting. No money at all was available in Kangting, and the Chinese merchants held up supplies of tea to boost the prices and make huge profits. The Tibetans immediately retaliated by refusing to come into the town to trade, and camped outside where their simple food needs were easily supplied in *tsamba*—the barley-flour, staple diet of the Tibetans—and dried meat; in this way they could hold out indefinitely. It was the poor townspeople and peasants who suffered in the boycott, for with no currency, no tea, no bread, no vegetables available, they were unable to find food. A one-pint cup of rice cost four million dollars, and a small packet of tea twenty-five million dollars.

The stack of tea that we had laid in on our return to Kangting rapidly disappeared in such circumstances, and soon our problem would be the same as everyone's, even although we still had several cheques worth £300 or £400. It was then that I remembered a friend of mine, John Mackie, a Scotsman, who had gone to India to take over the running of the Central Asian Trading Agency, a business formed to carry the message of Christ into the countries of Central Asia through trade. Before leaving Britain I had discussed the possibilities of the Trading Agency with Mackie, but had agreed to leave the matter open until we saw how the land lay. It now seemed a good idea to get into touch with him to see if he could send supplies from India, through Tibet, to us. We explored the possibilities of meeting somewhere in North Tibet, or even Sinkiang, Mackie leaving from Peshawar and ourselves from Kangting, but the chances of meeting in such vastness were too remote; so we arranged that Mackie should fly to China instead and we would travel to Chungking to meet him and see if anything could be done to fix a line of supply for the time, not so far distant now, when China would fall to the Communists.

In the midst of all the local confusion word arrived from my teacher's family to say that his mother was dangerously ill and would he come quickly bringing the foreign doctor with him. It was a simple matter to arrange a caravan quickly, as we now had our own animals and equipment, and within a few days Geoff and I, the two teachers, two muleteers, one of Beh-ma's wives, eleven yaks, four horses and three pigs were on the trail out of Kangting once more.

Autumn had worked lovely changes in the scenery and snow lay well down the slopes of the mountainside, even in the heat of the sun. The change each day in temperature varied as much as ninety degrees, from fifteen below zero in the early morning to eighty degrees above by midday. Soon we were above the snow-line and camping in a high valley between 15,000 and 16,000 feet, where the wind swept the snow into our faces in a million pricking needle-points and the cold numbed us into silence. The effect of the light from the moon in that world of white was hauntingly beautiful, though, and the stars were so bright and seemed so near that they were like tiny chandeliers suspended in the air.

The mornings were the worst. It required considerable effort to get out of the double-layer sleeping-bags and face the early-morning frost. The only streams that were not frozen were those that tumbled steeply from a height, and even those had their banks packed with solid ice and only allowed a narrow, jagged channel for the icy flow. In our attempts to wash the water froze on our fingers as we scooped it out of the stream, and the breath froze on our moustaches and beards making it difficult to speak. Our way lay across a snow-field on which no trail showed and we had to plough knee-deep through the snow to the summit of the pass. Here the virgin snow stretched away until it swept upwards again to the mighty peaks of the Minya Konka range where it remained frozen in serrated majesty against the deep cloudless blue of the sky.

Beh-ma left us a few days later to go to his own part of the country, where we should meet him again after we had visited the old teacher's, Gezang Wangdu's, mother. We turned south down another valley. Woodland glades with the sun slanting through branches and lying in a yellow tracery of intoxicating beauty on the carpets of multicoloured flowers. The river a still mirror of sky-reflecting blue, except where it was whipped into a creamy foam in the occasional rapids. The only snow to be seen now lay on the summits of the distant mountains.

A turn in the valley, a thinning of trees, a few whitewashed houses gleaming in the late afternoon sun against the dark background of trees and mountains, and we had arrived. A room had been prepared for us and in a matter of minutes we were sitting at tea, waiting for our supper of solid flour-and-water scones, fried yak-meat and eggs. When we had finished supper we descended the stairs to the main living-room to have a look at the teacher's mother.

The living-room was much the same as in all Tibetan houses, but here, instead of the plain mud walls, wooden panels had been built in half-way to the ceiling, giving the room a more finished appearance. There was no stove but the more usual open fireplace extending well into the room from one wall, with two large cross-pieces of iron supporting two iron cauldrons. Along the whole of one wall, and reflecting the light from the blazing logs on the fire, were several rows of brass plates, jugs, pails and ladles. The firelight flickered redly also on the faces of the family as they squatted round the raised wooden shelf of the fireplace, a ledge about six inches from the floor which served as a table, and on which were laid out bowls of tea, *tsamba*, cheese and dried raw meat. Large sides of black, smoked meat hung from the roof-beams, with huge rounds of cheese, and other oddments.

However, except for a hasty glance round, I had no time to take much in for everyone rose to their feet when we entered, and the teacher led the way by the light of a spluttering pine torch to a bundle in the darkness of the far corner, which turned out to be the mother. She was lying on a pile of sheepskins, with a sheepskin covering her, and her laboured breathing filled the room with an ominous sound. I knelt down by her side, almost overcome by the stench, and saw that she was tremendously bloated from the feet upwards, obviously from advanced dropsy. I was puzzled by the smell, and asked for the light to be brought closer, and then sat back on my heels at the sight. In the swollen barrel of the woman's abdomen there was a gaping wound, with a pool of pus lying inside. I asked the teacher what had happened, for there seemed to be no connection between the wound and the dropsical condition, and the teacher replied that the lamas had cut a hole in her abdomen to let the accumulating water run away. True enough, on closer inspection I found the round burn marks which the lamas usually made with lighted incense sticks as part of their treatment, around the edge of the wound.

The mother was old, seventy-one, the teacher said, and very far gone. It would be dangerous to do anything with a case so obviously near death, and all that would be involved in such an event. Yet the lamas themselves had failed, and if we were able to help such a seemingly hopeless case after their failure it would be a wonderful testimony to the power of our God. I gave Geoff a brief outline of the position and suggested that we pray to find out the will of God, and if we received assurance that God would heal the woman then we could go ahead. Geoff agreed, and I told the assembled family what we intended doing, and kneeling there as we were we asked the help of God. I arose, assured that all would be well, and set about the task of cleaning up the wound first of all, and then gave the highest dose of aminophylline that was permissible. The effect was startling, for in a few minutes her breathing eased, and shortly afterwards she fell into a deep sleep. We sat around the fire for a little to keep our eye on her, but soon the droning '*Om Mani Padme Hum*' of the blind old uncle and aunt in the half-darkness of the other corner of the room crooned us into a doze, and we excused ourselves and retired to bed.

For several days I was kept busy attending to the usual influx of patients, and then the old teacher asked me if I would visit a brother of his who was ill in a nearby monastery. Like almost all monasteries in Tibet this one was situated on a high promontory commanding a wonderful view of the valley and the mountains beyond. The whitewashed wall with the beautifully coloured frescoes and paintings, and multicoloured glass windows, blended well with the surrounding greenery of the forests. The various houses of the lamas' living quarters were grouped about the large temples of the monastery in a semicircle on the concave platform of the mountainside and facing north so that the sun poured its light upon them all day.

We passed through the crowds of curious lamas and made our way to a building high up on the mountainside and separate from the others, and climbed the stairs to the top floor. Here several young acolytes were gathered and on a few words from the old teacher one of them went through a curtain into an inner room to announce our arrival. The old teacher had not seen his brother for eighteen years, as he was a recluse who had taken certain vows and shut himself away from all men except those who came to consult him on spiritual matters. He had not been well for some time, and he had discovered, by natural or supernatural means, that a foreign doctor had arrived in the valley and had sent to his brother to bring him along to see him.

He arose from the usual carpeted dais as we entered, an emaciated elderly man of medium height, and courteously motioned us to be seated on the lower carpeted dais opposite him. He gave a sharp command to the acolytes and they began hurrying about fetching tea and *tsamba*, meat and delicacies, laying them on the low tables in front of us, while the hermit entered into a deep conversation with the teacher. In the meantime we looked round the room.

It was only about twelve feet square, dark, lit by one small window and the usual butter-lamps, and sickly with the smell of incense. Behind us, and immediately opposite the hermit-oracle, in a cavity in the wall, was a golden idol with silk scarves, prayer-flags, flowers, *tsamba*, wheat and water offerings in front of it on a shelf. On all the walls were hung silk-framed *trankas*, or religious scrolls, while from the ceiling rows of prayer-flags with mystic words stamped on them hung from the rafters. Beside the lama were scores of objects used in the pursuit of his religion, the most prominent being the thunder-bolt and bell and prayer-wheel, which were the most commonly used. But it was on the wall behind the hermit that the most striking objects were to be seen. There were four long scrolls hanging from roof to floor on which were depicted in white on a black background pictures of the various stages in intercourse with the spirits of the nether world. The most sinister and frightening of all was the last one where the priest was seen with a hollow reed protruding from the top of his shaven head.

I had heard of these oracle-priests who went into a trance and who in the process of projecting their spirit on some errand had the reed inserted by an acolyte to keep the way back into themselves clear for the spirit's return, so that it should not find another body and leave them without a spirit and consequently damned for ever. Although I knew of many of the fantastic practices of those who dabbled in the black arts of forbidden knowledge, I had thought this one rather too far-fetched to be believed, but here was the evidence before our eyes.

The initial contact with the spirit world seemed to be the same as that practised in the western world by so-called spiritualists, the shamans of Asia and witch doctors of Africa, the simple act of submitting oneself to the control of the demon. There was a considerable difference between 'obsession' and 'possession', the former being only a condition of ultra-sensitive psychic awareness of the supernatural, while the latter was a submission to the control and 'possession' of one's will and body by one or more of those supernatural beings. The more willing the submission to the widening sphere of obedience demanded by the rising demonic hierarchy, the greater the forbidden knowledge and power communicated by them through their willing medium. Against such a hierarchy of evil, Milton's *Paradise Lost* might be enlightening and Goethe's *Faust* might be real, but only the Word of God could provide the defence and the means of attack. Strangely enough—although not so strange when one thought of the limitations of Satan's power which was imitative and not creative—

the secret of victory over the whole demonic hierarchy, including Satan, lay also in submission, in the measure in which a person was prepared to submit himself to the Spirit of God so that the power of God, working through him, to that extent could overcome the forces of darkness. The more abandoned the submission, the greater the power.

The fundamental difference between the two submissions was inimical and vital; the submission to Satan meant a repudiation of moral and social responsibility on the part of the individual in that the person possessed by a demonic spirit was not capable of ratiocination at any point during the trance and became an open channel for any form of communicative evil; the end result being mental, physical and finally spiritual destruction. On the other hand, the person who submitted himself to the direction of the Spirit of God through Christ was at all times profoundly aware of external circumstances and individual responsibility, could weigh all things in the light of sacred or profane knowledge and take a decision for which he was then and for ever personally accountable to God and man; the end result being increased mental vigour, physical well-being and spiritual peace. That both were diametrically opposed and incompatible could be proved by the simple experiment of bringing both protagonists together when, as in the days when Christ was on earth, the one in whom the Holy Spirit had control could, by exercising His authority, still command and overpower the evil spirit in control of the other, so that he was unable to enter into the usual trance of possession or manifest the usual phenomena.

It was the inevitable torment of immanent destruction that was troubling this hermit-oracle now. He was a bundle of twitching nerves, he could not eat, and if he did then he suffered excruciating pain. He could not sleep, nor could he concentrate to read or study, and his spiritual life suffered in consequence, so that he worried about his place in the next life. Could the foreign doctor help him?

How could the doctor help him by medicine when it was his spirit that required treatment? And how could the foreigner communicate his thoughts in a language that he had been studying for only about a year? However, I did my stammering best, leaving some medicines as well as some Gospels and booklets, and finally left the hermit-oracle to face his lonely death and judgement.

The old teacher's mother was steadily improving, and after several days I decided that we could safely depart, leaving with her some medicine and instructions as to how and when it should be taken. We were loaded down with presents from the family and from grateful patients, most of the presents consisting of *tsamba*, meat and butter. Butter was the most usual form of present and already we had collected over twenty pounds of it, with more constantly coming in. With butter the price it was in Kangting, if we chose to sell it on our return our trip was already showing a considerable profit, and we had still to pay a visit to Beh-ma's part of the country where there would probably be more gifts.

We had to follow a different trail to get to Beh-ma's place, and after leaving the old teacher's valley we turned up another and began climbing almost immediately. Hour after hour we plodded upwards until we were above the tree-line and out on to the barren slopes of the towering mountains. All around the mountains dropped steeply into the dark valleys and then rose sharply again on the far side, until they disappeared for a time on a coronet of cloud. One bank of cloud moved slowly over and down the peaks of one mountain mass like some gigantic waterfall. Peak after peak, covered with snow, filled the whole horizon in a series of stupendous serrations, terminating in the greatest of all, Minya Konka itself, reaching into the blue infinity in unparalleled grandeur and beauty. Snow lay thick on the pass, and it was well on into the afternoon before we could stop among some shrubs and make a fire to cook a meal.

A few days later, while we were riding slowly through a peaceful sunlit valley with a few houses scattered here and there, the morning air was shattered by a loud whoop and a horseman swept into view, stretched in a flat gallop, followed by another, and another, and another. They pulled their horses to a slithering halt in front of one of the houses, and we decided to go over and see what was happening. Inside the house there must have been about a hundred shouting, drinking men and women, decked out in all their finery, and we were told that they were celebrating some Tibetan holiday.

After we had partaken of some of the lavish hospitality thrust upon us by the slightly tipsy revellers there was a rush to the door for the horse-racing. Somehow or other one of our muleteers, Jay-tru, had got hold of a spirited bay, which he said belonged to a relative who lived near by, and he sent it weaving in and out among the writhing mass of riders in short bursts of speed as we made our way to the place where the races were to be held, a flat part of the valley floor about five hundred yards in length. Here Jay-tru and another rider, a young lad no more than twelve years of age, riding a small, black pony, rode to the far end, while the others dismounted and formed a semicircle at the finishing line. There was no starter, both riders facing up the course, pacing slowly forwards and then whirling round suddenly when they reached the end of the field to head for the crowd. The long-legged bay leaped away in a flashing gallop leaving the young fellow looking even smaller as he rode bare-back two or three lengths behind. However, the small black horse came on at terrific speed, legs flashing in a blur of action, and with the small rider lying along its neck, arms flailing in reckless encouragement, it flashed past the crowd the winner by a neck.

There were several other races which appeared to be personal challenges, then Jay-tru asked us if we should like to join in a big race where several horses were taking part. Geoff declined, but I thought I would see what I could do against these expert horsemen. I was riding a small grey, a good enough animal but not up to the standard of some of the horses there, all of which had been specially fed to ginger them up for the races, whereas the grey had been ridden from dawn to dusk for several days. About ten riders moved across the field, the horses cavorting and pulling at the bit as they felt the excitement of the riders, until we reached the far side. Here several false starts were made as the horses reared out of position, and then suddenly we were away. The horses bunched together, riders crowding knee to knee, and the crazy Tibetans just rode their horses forward and out of the mêlée by jostling their neighbours out of the way. It was mad riding at a reckless gallop, and a flashing whip would cut across the flanks of a horse unexpectedly as a rider drove to get up front. I rode neck and neck with a Tibetan who lay along his horse's neck and urged it along faster by yells and a wide sweep of his arm, his hand almost touching the ground as he tried for more speed. We were still together as we crossed the finishing line, and I had the satisfaction of knowing that I was in the first four.

We had to hurry away to catch up with our caravan which had plodded ahead with the other muleteers, and a few hours later we arrived in Beh-ma's valley. The same celebrations were going on here and as we rode forward several horses thundered past in another race the one in the lead ridden by a striking young Tibetan. His teeth flashed white in a reckless smile as he released a piercing 'yee-hee' in his horse's ear, and his body rose with the bound of the horse as if he were part of it, as he swept by to win by several lengths. That, Jay-tru told us, was his brother.

Beh-ma came hurrying over, followed by a few women and villagers, and led our horses to some nearby tents, confiding to us that although that was his house just across the stream he preferred to live in a tent, being a nomad, and we could pitch our tents next to his. The racing finished, the drinking and dancing went on far into the night, and finally we had to excuse ourselves as we were almost falling asleep on the floor.

We lived royally for the next few days since Beh-ma had large herds of yak and insisted on providing us with fresh meat. A yak's heart or liver, or a side of meat, would be ready for us at every meal, with bowls of thick, creamy yak's milk. As it was a remote, sparsely inhabited valley there were not so many patients, but gradually they began to come in from the surrounding mountains. Two women who had travelled for several days came to see if I could do anything for the younger of the two who was suffering from toothache. She was in a very low condition for the tooth was so bad that her face was swollen until she could no longer open her mouth to eat, but fed only on tea and soup. It was impossible to get her mouth open to have a look at her tooth, and there was no hope of getting forceps in, and I had to tell them reluctantly that I could do nothing for her; she would have to travel to the hospital in Kangting to get proper treatment. They pleaded with me to do something as it was impossible for them to go to Kangting, and if she had to suffer any longer she would die. Finally, I agreed to try. I gave her a tablet of Kerocaine to hold in her mouth, my one syringe being broken, and waited for some time to see if it would help deaden the pain by absorption. Then with Geoff and her companion holding the woman's hands in her lap I slowly eased her jaws apart. The lips split at the corners in the process, and I was able to get my finger into her mouth to feel the tooth. It was a lower molar and it was rotten right down to the socket, with the gum swollen and suppurating. Even with special forceps to keep it from breaking it would have been difficult to extract, but with only the usual forceps it became a nightmare. I had to forget the suffering woman in front of me and brutally force aside the infected gums to get right at the root of the tooth, and then slowly and carefully begin easing it out of its socket. Although rotten it was still bedded down firmly, and sweat broke out on my forehead and began trickling down my face. My arm grew numb and cramped with the pressure I was exerting, and I signed to Geoff to put his hand on my wrist and assist me in levering the tooth. It came away at last, and the woman slumped forward on the three-legged stool on which she had been sitting, tears streaming down her face. She had not uttered a murmur throughout the whole operation. Two hours later, after a mouth-wash and a couple of aspirins, she and her companion swung into the saddle and began the long journey homewards.

As the reader will remember, the reckless horseman of the races held a few days previously was Jay-tru's brother; and when he knew that we required a servant he offered himself for the job.

The Opening

His name was Lobsang Sherab, or Loshay for short, and he was something of a character. He had already walked to Lhasa, five months' journey away, and had only just returned; he was still only twenty-one and, disliking the monotony of the nomad's life, herding cattle every day, he now wanted to leave the valley again. His mother was dead, but his father and brothers and sisters were alive and Beh-ma was his friend and guardian, in Tibetan fashion. It was left to Beh-ma to see the family and act as guarantor for him regarding his future behaviour, and we had to agree to look after him in every way, according to Tibetan custom, providing no wages, but food, clothing and an occasional gift if he deserved it.

It was the end of November before we returned to Kangting, leaving Beh-ma behind to attend to some local affairs. He was involved in an election of some kind among the people of that area and the proceedings were expected to go on for a few days longer. We had seemed so far removed from the world while at Beh-ma's that it came as a shock to find that the situation had deteriorated so much that the American Ambassador had advised all American citizens to leave China as soon as possible, and British subjects were waiting from day to day to hear the same from the British Ambassador. Some of the missionaries were already preparing to leave Kangting, and to raise sufficient money to clear expenses had put a stall on the streets with clothing and other articles for sale. The banks had closed and no money was being brought into Kangting from down country. Merchants refused to cash cheques, for money was depreciating at such a rate that the cheque was valueless by the time it could be presented in Chengtu eight days later. It took ten days for the missionaries to receive cheques from their headquarters in Shanghai, and by the time they arrived in Kangting the cheques for three months' living expenses could buy food for only one day.

Geoff and I now had six bank books and several hundred pounds in cheques. It looked as if we should still have to leave the Tibetan border, and China, without God being able to accomplish His purpose through us. It was an impossible decision for us to take. The economic ruin around us was only an incidental event in God's purpose in and through the nations and should never militate against His purpose in and through us. Where the Spirit of the Lord was there could be no confusion, and it was our duty to leave the arranging of supplies to God while we went ahead as if external circumstances were normal. It was the old story of God and Elijah repeated. If a thousand missionaries left China because it was only common sense in the circumstances then it was still nothing to Geoff and me. The others could probably explain away their retreat and still preach the omnipotence of God, but we were bound to the mill-wheel of God's purpose and must go on until all His enemies were ground to powder. The only alternative was to acknowledge the inability of God to arrest circumstances or overcome an ideology that was openly and blasphemously antagonistic to Himself.

In any case the situation was not so hopeless as at first it seemed. We received a letter from Samuel Tsang, our Chinese Christian business friend in Chengtu, to say that he had twenty-five thousand million dollars belonging to us from previous cheques deposited with him and that if we wished he would take our English cheques and supply us with the equivalent value in goods and medicines. That meant finding a way to get the goods across the bandit-infested mountains between Chengtu and Kangting.

In the meantime, another young fellow had arrived in Kangting with a letter of introduction to us, a Chinese-Tibetan called Wang Ming De. Younger than John Ting he had been trained in the same Bible School, but where John was a dynamic preacher of the gospel, Wang Ming De was a lucid teacher of doctrine. Since coming to Kangting Wang had gathered together those who had been converted under John Ting's ministry, and who had since drifted away for one reason or another, or had lost their first ardour for want of further inspiration, and he had been teaching them fundamental principles. John Ting was on his way back to Kangting from his visit to Shanghai and when he arrived and joined forces with young Wang Ming De we could look forward to an even greater awakening than there had been previously, with greater possibilities of establishing the work of God according to the Scriptures. Wang's mother was a Tibetan and he could speak the language fluently. He was convinced, too, that God would have him work with Geoff and me, so here was a promise of things to come in these eastern parts of Tibet at least. If Satan was working in his way, God was also working in His.

Peking fell to the Communists, and Nanking and Shanghai were threatened in the new drive southwards and westwards. Preparations were being made in Chungking and Chengtu for a 'last stand' by the Nationalist Government, and the Governor of Sikang Province, General Liu Wen Huie, ordered the provincial government and troops from Kangting to Ya-an to be close to Chengtu. The Tibetans were fighting with the Chinese soldiers outside Kangting, and there were rumours of their carrying the war into Kangting itself. In Kangting looting and rioting flared up from time to time as the people and soldiers tried to take what they could not buy. In the midst of it all one of Beh-ma's wives arrived, grief-stricken, to say that they had been attacked on their way into Kangting and that Beh-ma had been shot. The murderous attack had taken place only one day's journey outside Kangting, on the other side of Jedo.

Following hard on the news of Beh-ma's death there came a message one night about eleven o'clock for me to go across to Chia's house, and on entering the living-room I found him lying on the floor in a pool of blood, with a deep gash in his head from his forehead down past his temple. The room was full of gesticulating, excited people, all trying to recount what had happened. Chia, it appeared, had stood on a table to move a picture on the wall and had fallen with the picture on his hand, his head striking the jagged-edged glass frame when he hit the floor. Mrs. Chia was white-faced and frightened. The relatives, who had been hastily sent for, were distraught and voluble, and three lamas watched for anything that might be to their advantage. They had gone as far as they could go when they had put a handful of dry *tsamba* on the wound to absorb the blood and to stop the flow, and now they waited to recover what advantage they could as we took over. The situation was fraught with difficulties, for Chia was an important figure and if he died while being treated by a foreigner it would place us in a very dangerous position indeed. However, there was always God to outweigh any human considerations and a quick plea to Him for help gave the assurance to go ahead.

I ordered two wooden forms to be placed together, and stretched Chia out on that as an operating table. Geoff scrubbed up as assistant to pass instruments and help when required, and then I shot in a local anaesthetic beside the temple and proceeded to repair the gash. There was complete silence all the time I was working, except for the rattle of forceps being dropped into the basins, and when one of the children began to cry Mrs. Chia picked him up and opening her blouse breast-fed him to quieten him, while she continued to sit beside her husband and watch him anxiously. I finished the suturing of the ragged edges, cleaned up the matted hair, and then gave Chia a strong sedative to put him to sleep quickly. There were murmurs of amazement now from the relaxing watchers, and some of them came forward with Mrs. Chia to thank us profusely. I assured them that Chia would be all right in a few days and that there was nothing to worry about, and then we went home, tired after the strain.

Chia improved rapidly after the stitches were removed, and, heaping us with gifts in his gratitude, he asked what else he could do to help us. His gratitude was even greater than it would normally have been for he had been told by one of their oracles that this was to be his unlucky year, and he was convinced that but for our help he would certainly have died. I told him that we would keep his offer in mind but that there was nothing that we required at present unless he knew a means of getting some goods which we had bought in Chengtu into Kangting. I only mentioned this in passing, not expecting any suggestion from Chia, but he reacted immediately.

'Oh, I can fix that for you all right,' he said, surprisingly. 'If you can get the goods delivered to a friend of mine in Chengtu I will see to it that they are brought safely into Kangting.'

'But how can you manage that?' I asked in amazement. 'I thought the road was so plagued by bandits that nothing was being brought in except under heavily armed escort?'

'True,' replied Chia, 'but then, you see, part of my job is to arrange trading matters for the Governor and I can have your goods brought in with his caravan, where they will be perfectly safe from bandits.'

He even suggested what type of goods we should buy in Chengtu to bring the best value in Kangting and, when we finally left, in Tibet, including opium if we wanted it. We declined, explaining why with our beliefs we could not trade in opium, but accepted his other suggestions with alacrity.

We had now almost another £1,000, received from one source and another in answer to prayer, including the proceeds from the sale of furniture and other things in the house. A young couple from the World Mission Prayer League, Clarence and Helen Hjelmervik, had been looking for a house in Kangting and we suggested that they take over our house in 18, Kwang Ming Lu, and allow us to live with them as boarders until we left for the interior. They were only too pleased to do this and moved in quickly, Helen rapidly transforming house and meals from bachelor confusion to almost unbelievable orderliness.

It was taking a tremendous risk to send so much money to Samuel Tsang by letter when there were so many robberies on the trail, and we talked over the possibility of travelling down country ourselves to buy the supplies. It would also give us a final opportunity to meet the believers in Chengtu and Chungking once more. While we were discussing the possibility a letter arrived from Samuel Tsang in which he suggested again that we try to come down country and talk over the work in China, particularly in the west, with himself and Watchman Nee, his brother-in-law, keeping the possibility of a quick visit round all the assemblies in China before us in prayer.

We decided that we would go to Chungking anyway, and then

see what God would have us do from there. The possibility of meeting leading Chinese Christians and addressing scores of thousands throughout the country at such a critical time appealed very strongly to us and it would have to be carefully considered before we finally decided one way or the other. The work in Tibet was as great, if not greater, in importance in the sight of God than the work in China, even if less spectacular.

Instead of walking to Ya-an, as was customary, we took three of our horses and Loshay with us to cut down on the length of time required on the road. It was already dark when we rode into the outskirts of Luting, and the bridge over the river dividing the town was scarcely visible in the darkness. It was a suspension bridge on four iron chains, over which had been laid loose wooden planks, with two iron chains on either side as hand-holds, strung about sixty feet above the roaring river and about a hundred yards in length. I looked at what I could see of it and asked Loshay dubiously: '*Dro a nyen?*' (Is it all right to go on?). '*Dro nyen ba*' (probably all right to go), he replied laconically. It required some effort to get the horse started on its way across the bridge but once on the swinging structure it picked its way slowly and steadily forward behind me. Geoff followed with his horse, and the bridge rocked wildly at the new strain and almost threw me over. Loshay had just started on his way when Geoff's horse stumbled and with a frightening crashing of boards went right through, only kept from pitching into the river by one of the chains passing under its belly. The horse had the sense to stop struggling or it would certainly have dropped into the river far beneath, taking us with it, but how to get it up on its feet without the same thing happening again was the problem. I dared not go back to help Geoff, for if I left my horse by itself it would begin to move and the added rocking of the bridge would throw us all into the river. It was left to the imperturbable Loshay to ease his way forward and with prodigious strength lift first the animal's fore-legs and then its hind-legs on to the planks held by Geoff. After that we moved across one at a time, treading delicately and praying most of the way, while the others stood still.

The Opening

It was the horses that got us into trouble again just over the pass into Kan Hai Tze. We crossed the pass in deep snow and mist, and picked our way with increasing difficulty down the trail on the other side. Slipping and slithering on the icy steps that had formed we fell into snowdrifts on each side of the trail, and finally, after about five hundred yards, the leading horse slipped and was unable to rise. We had to cut notches in the ice about our feet in order to get a grip while we attempted to lift the horse, but it only floundered around and made the surface of the ice more mirror-like than ever. It was already getting dark and the mist was steadily thickening, shutting out everything around us, when we finally gave up the attempt and looked at each other silently. We were hours from the nearest village, could proceed no further on this trail, and could not possibly get back to the last village. Our only hope lay in getting the horses back up the trail to the top of the pass and then finding our way round by another route until we came to a house on the mountainside where we could stay for the night. And we still had to find a way to get that horse on to its feet before we could even begin the journey back up the trail. It was a moment requiring consultation with God and we got our reply immediately. Take off the loads, take the saddle-blankets and saddle-rugs and spread them around on top of the ice to give the horse a footing, and then, while moving back up the trail, put the blankets and rugs down at each step for the horses to walk on. It was slow, tedious, back-breaking work, and even when we had reached the top of the pass we had to return ourselves and carry the loads on our backs. We stumbled on through drifts in the gathering darkness as we zigzagged down the mountain until we finally came on a small filthy woodman's hut where they reluctantly agreed to put us up for the night. The other bridges and landslides and dangers of bandits were simple to face after such an experience.

When we arrived in Chengtu we found that Samuel Tsang had left for Shanghai on urgent business but would meet us in Chung-king, so when we had bought all the trading goods that we required and made arrangements for them to be delivered to Chia's agent in Chengtu, we left for Chungking. We still had some things to buy that were not obtainable in Chengtu, but when all our purchases were complete there was still no sign of Samuel Tsang. Chungking was in one of her sulky moods and lay under thick clouds so that no plane could touch down. In the meantime we were almost put under arrest by a supercilious official, supposedly a distant relative of Chiang Kai Shek's, who claimed that we must be spies as my passport was from the United Kingdom and I was from Scotland which was not in the United Kingdom, while Geoff, who was formerly a banker, had become a missionary for suspicious reasons! However, after a lot of arguing, and a nominal fine for not registering when we left Kangting, we were dismissed.

While we waited for Samuel Tsang to arrive we looked up the assembly of believers in Chungking and found them a sound, healthy, dynamic group of about eighty people. The Saturday night meeting was turned into a 'fellowship' meeting where Geoff and I could address the believers, one to speak on the recent historical development of New Testament principles and practices in Britain, and the other to give an exposition of Scripture—both by interpretation, of course, as our language was not up to such a demanding standard. I led off on the historical development of New Testament truth and as I used name after name connected with those early events I turned to look questioningly at the interpreter to see if he understood. However, he seemed to have no difficulty and fluently coped with the difficult address while the audience sat in deep concentration. Geoff followed with an exposition of the Scriptures on the sufficiency of God to support that which was of Himself, and the meeting closed. In the general discussion that followed, I commented on the ease with which the interpreter had dealt with all the strange names, many of them names that were not familiar to the bulk of Brethren believers in Britain, and was told to my surprise that the interpreter's name was Newton Wang, after the Benjamin Newton of those early days, and that he had made a study of the history of that time, as had many of the others.

One of the most difficult questions to answer was the one put by a brother who asked why there was no great movement of the Spirit of God in Britain in many conversions as there was in China, when the reason for the great blessing in China was simple obedience to the Word of God, and yet that same obedience was being practised in Britain without the same results. It was difficult and embarrassing to explain to these Chinese believers that the early and simple obedience taught and practised by the men mentioned had resulted in a great wave of conversions and deepening of spiritual life in Britain, but that gradually that simple obedience had degenerated into an empty traditionalism, a ritualistic practice of early methods which had sapped the movement of its vitality and power and left the testimony vitiated and stagnant.

It was a wonderful experience to be approached by three of the elder brethren afterwards, and after a few minutes' conversation to be asked courteously by them if we would come along on the Sunday and remember the Lord—'breaking bread'—with them as an assembly. Here were men who, apart from foreign missionary tutelage, had been taught of the Spirit to handle the things of God in simplicity and wisdom, without any nationalistic feelings or opinions of men to intervene, and who could meet with their foreign brothers on the ground of that same Word. When we finally left Chungking for Kangting, as we felt we could no longer wait for Samuel Tsang who was still waiting for a plane to fly to Chungking, those same believers handed us a gift of money, 'as from the Lord', to 'bring us on our way' to Tibet, even as the early churches did with the early apostles. The theory that foreign money was necessary to support the poor native believers, or church, who were too poor without the help of the missionary or the missionary's money, was exploded by those believers and others throughout China as well. In Shanghai, for instance, where the hall in which they met was too small to contain the growing numbers, a sum of two thousand ounces of gold, amounting to roughly £40,000 at that time, had been given by the Shanghai believers alone to build a place to hold 5,000 people, and that in a time of unparalleled economic depression; while in other places, believers were selling their houses, lands and possessions and giving their money to the furtherance of God's work while they devoted themselves to travelling with the message of the Gospel of Jesus Christ.

When we arrived in Kangting, John Ting had returned with his wife and 70-year-old mother-in-law. The stories of his visit down country to China were already circulating widely and being repeated with amazement. While on his way between Kangting and Chengtu, the group of people with whom he had been travelling had come to a river that had no bridge and had to be forded. On this occasion the rains had begun and just before their arrival a dam had broken farther up in the mountains and the river was already rising rapidly with a sullen roar even as they watched. On one side of the trail the mountains rose sheer and impassable, while on the other, the river emptied itself into another larger river which was impossible to cross. They could not wait indefinitely until the river dropped, out in the open with no shelter and with constant threat of attack from bandits, nor could they return to the previous village almost a day's journey away now. The situation seemed hopeless when John said quietly that he was a Christian and his God was a mighty God who could open a way through rivers if necessary, had done it in the past, and could do it again. It was necessary now, for He had sent him, a simple believer, on His work, so he would now pray to Him and ask Him to hold up the water in the river in front of them and let them through. He prayed, and then taking a small child from his mother he stepped into the boiling waters of the mountain river where they swirled about his knees, and motioned the others to cross while he stood with bowed head and prayed. They hesitated, but then in amazement saw that the water, while it still rushed downwards, was no longer visibly rising as it had been, but steadily dropping until it was only up to John's ankles, and they crossed over one by one in single file to the other side. When the last one passed over, John followed, carrying the child, and as soon as he put his foot on the bank of the far side, the waters broke from above with a thunderous boom and poured down to make the river impassable.

Before they had time to talk about the miraculous event they had just experienced, there was a loud outcry from the coolies with the caravan, who pointed ahead and informed them that their predicament was now worse than ever, for there was only a wide stretch of marshland ahead and they were the only ones who knew the path through it. Now, in the heavy rains, that path had been covered in a sheet of water and it was certain death to attempt to find a way through, for a false step to left or right would mean a horrible end in the soft mud. They were still so overcome by this new menace that they forgot the quiet Christian in their midst until he again spoke and told them that the same God who had led them through the river could take them through the marsh safely, and walking forward he called them to follow him. He had only been over that trail once before and knew nothing of the path, but with quiet confidence in God he led them through step by step until they reached their destination for the night. It was no wonder that every one of these people in that caravan, listening to John tell of his God and His Son, Jesus Christ, and how they here might get to know Him, became Christians on the spot, for they had met Him for themselves in his servant.

When John returned to Kangting with Wang Ming De, he again preached to crowds during the Chinese New Year with the same results as before, and many of those who had been converted on a previous occasion but had drifted away because of the empty formalism of traditional practice, returned again and were filled with a new vision and fire. Amongst them were several, like Wang Ming De, who were part Chinese and part Tibetan, with a knowledge of both languages, and they too caught the vision of travelling westwards into Tibet with the message they had just heard and believed.

At the same time Kangting and the whole of Sikang Province seethed with revolt. More than two thousand bandits, deserters from police and army, who had taken their rifles and revolvers

with them, were marauding continuously between Chengtu and
Kangting, and swooping on the outlying villages to carry away
rice and food. This left Kangting without supplies, and the
students in the government schools, the police, the army and the
poorer people who could not pay black-market prices, looted and
robbed the shops looking for food. It was only a matter of time
before the Communist 'Fifth Column' took over, or a mass riot
took place, or the Tibetans moved in and took over from the
Chinese. The racial antipathy that had existed for centuries between the Tibetans and Chinese had been exacerbated over the
past years in Kangting, particularly when the Chinese soldiers
quartered there treated the high-spirited Tibetans, who came into
the town, ruthlessly and with contempt whenever they could find
occasion. With their forces defeated and support gone, the Chinese
were in fear of the powerful Tibetans who were now in the
majority in the town. It only needed a spark to set the whole place
alight.

I thought the spark had been struck one night when, after a
burst of gunfire, there was a rush of footsteps outside and a heavy
battering on the door of the house. Two Tibetans whom I knew
were there, and they urged me to come with them quickly as one of
their friends had been seriously hurt. I threw a few things together
into a bag and hurried after them into a nearby caravanserai
where I climbed the stairs and entered a narrow room, packed
with Tibetans, who drew aside to let me pass to the bed. I found
a powerfully built Khamba lying on his back on a wooden pallet,
with a dirty, blood-soaked cloth over his face. When I had carefully pulled it aside I found a scarcely recognizable blotch underneath. I replaced the rag quickly and asked what had happened.
Several voices took up the story and finally I understood that the
man had been cleaning his gun, to be ready for any emergency in
the town, and had accidentally pulled the trigger; it was an auto-
matic and he had put three bullets in his skull. Taking away the
rag, I looked at the mess again and saw that the bullets had blown
away the nose, gone through the right eye and passed out
through the top of the head where there was a gaping hole under

the matted hair. I was still not sure if one of the bullets might not
be inside the skull, but as I questioned the spectators they
pointed to the roof, where a large hole let in the fading daylight,
and said that they had all gone out there. It was impossible to do
more than clean up the powder-blackened mess in those surroundings, and I ordered some of the man's friends to improvise a
stretcher to take him to hospital. The man was still concious,
groaning: 'Will I die? Will I die?' as I gave him a shot of morphia
to keep him quiet and deaden the pain, while his friends lifted
him and carried him to the Catholic Hospital on the other side of
the river.

The French Catholic Hospital was desperately under-staffed
and the doctor there was a young nun who had only recently
come out from France, on the completion of her training, and
with only a short experience of surgery. The Mother Superior
had to act as nursing sister and, if she assisted, someone else had
to give the anaesthetic, or if she gave the anaesthetic, someone
else had to do the scrubbing up as assistant. I had helped on occasions, although I was devoting most of my time to language
study, and I had to assist on this case now. With one of the man's
friends standing by, and Geoff in the background, we fixed up a
morphia anaesthetic by continuous drip method into a vein, as
the man's face was so mutilated and requiring such extensive
treatment that it was impossible to put a mask on his face. It was
an amazing exhibition of the tremendous vitality of the Tibetan,
for the man was conscious nearly all the time of the operation,
and yet only groaned on a few occasions. The nose was only a
few shreds of skin on either side of a blackened hole and we had
to improvise in building up a new nose for him by putting in two
pieces of rubber, from an old stethoscope, as nostrils, and stitch-
ing the shreds of what remained of his nose over this. It required
thirty-eight stitches before we had finished putting it together.
Then there was his eye. Nothing could be done about saving this
as everything had been blown away, leaving only a powder-
smudged gap. We cleaned it up, after probing inside up the path
of the bullets through the skull to see if any remained, and

brought the loose folds of skin around the eye together to close
the gap. There remained only the hole in his head. It was an ugly
ragged wound just above the hair-line, which we could only
clean up as best we could, sprinkling the wound and the gauze
dressing liberally with sulpha powder, and hoping it would come
together of itself if the man survived at all. The operation had
taken about five hours, and we were weary as we left the hospital
about nine o'clock at night, but we still had another call to make.

Some days before, a well-dressed Tibetan had called at our
house to ask for medicine because he had not been keeping well
and had heard from many people of the skill of the foreign doctor.
There were several other Tibetans with him but they kept in the
background and by their conduct indicated that they were either
servants or bodyguards. For this was Pangdatshang, the famous
leader of the Khambas. After diagnosing heart trouble I had put
him on a course of digitalis and then called in to see him some
time each day. He lived in a large house in the centre of the town
that had formerly been a caravanserai but had been altered to suit
the present owner. He lived on the second floor, attended by
scores of servants and surrounded at all times, every day, by a
constant stream of traders, officials and merchants. There were
many stories told concerning him, some almost legendary, but
the bare outline of his history was that when the thirteenth Dalai
Lama fled to India, the elder Pangdatshang, father of this present
one, had fled with him, taking his family. Because of his loyalty
and help he had been rewarded on the Dalai Lama's return to
Lhasa, and from then on began to build up a large trading connection with India. This he had expanded by sending his eldest
son, Yangpel, to Peking to establish an office, and Rapga and
Topgyay, the younger sons, to Kham in East Tibet to handle
affairs there, and gradually established the family concern as the
greatest trading house in Tibet, with links from Peking to Calcutta. When the father was murdered in one of the inter-family
feuds in Lhasa, the eldest son, Yangpel, came from Peking to take
over the family business in Lhasa.

By this time the Pangdatshang family had established them-

selves as powerful figures in Kham, with thousands of armed subjects under their control. In the jockeying for power in Tibet,
following on the death of the thirteenth Dalai Lama, Rapga and
Topgyay rebelled against the Tibetan Government and with their
armed Khambas marched on Chamdo to try and seize power.
They were defeated through counter-intrigue by the lamas and,
fighting a retreating battle, crossed over the River Yangtze into
Chinese-occupied Tibet. Here the Chinese were alarmed at so
large a force of armed Tibetans appearing, even in retreat, and
the Governor of the province, General Liu Wen Huie, ordered
his troops to engage them immediately. After a protracted
struggle through the mountains and valleys of Kham, sometimes
fighting Chinese Nationalists and sometimes the retreating forces
of the Chinese Communists on the 'Long March' from Kiangsi
to Yenan in North China, they were ultimately defeated and the
remnants of their army scattered. Rapga and Topgyay fled, the
former making his way to Kalimpong in North India, near the
western Tibetan border, while Topgyay disguised himself and
disappeared down country in China.

After some years Topgyay gradually made his way back to
Kangting and there slowly built up the trading business of the
family again. By the time the Second World War broke out he
had gained all that he had already lost, and added more. He was
wealthy and influential, and among the Khambas, who loved a
fighter, he was a hero who had fought in two wars, with many
fabulous stories about his fighting, his markmanship, his riding
and generalship circulating round the camp-fires of Tibet. His
position was reinforced when he was made a colonel by Chiang
Kai Shek and held responsible for the Khambas of East Tibet
should they be required to repel the Japanese invaders during the
Second World War. Now he was officially recognized as leader of
the Khambas, and while he held a position that was inferior to
General Liu Wen Huie's, yet the Governor of the province was
apprehensive of his growing power, for Topgyay had far more
and far better men at his command than had the Chinese Governor. However, Topgyay showed no signs of using the great

possibilities that were at his hand, although there were many rumours of intended uprising against the Chinese, and they remained ostensibly friendly.

Then had come the collapse of the Nationalist Government and the rapid advance of the Chinese Communists. General Liu Wen Huie, ever an opportunist, was caught between two opposing forces. He was a notorious war-lord, fabulously wealthy through exploiting and oppressing the people, a dealer in opium and a perfect mark for the advancing Communists coming from the east. On the west there was Topgyay, the man he had attacked when in retreat from Tibet, with his thousands of loyal, fighting Khambas who hated the Chinese for their supercilious attitude and high-handed methods whenever they came into contact. When the Governor and Government officials, with the main body of troops, withdrew from Kangting to Ya-an because of the scarcity of food and the Communist threat from down country, the way was left open for Topgyay to take over control whenever he wished. Over the past few months rumours that he was just about to do so had risen and died at intervals, but they had never materialized.

This was the man with the bad heart who had called on me to ask for medicine, and on whom we had to call after the operation on the wounded Tibetan. When we entered the room in which he was sitting we found him surrounded by several other Tibetans, all discussing the case of the man who had shot himself. We were immediately bombarded with questions as to his condition and they were amazed to learn that he still had a good chance of living. Topgyay ordered a meal to be brought for us, and while we ate he calmly suggested that we should come with him into Tibet. At first we thought that we had misunderstood his meaning but gradually it dawned on us that he was serious in his offer. He expected to leave for Tibet shortly and would like us to accompany him as our medical knowledge would be useful to him and to his people.

In the days that followed on this startling offer of Topgyay's his family fell ill, one after another, of an epidemic of measles which was sweeping the town. When this happened every so often hundreds of children died, either from the measles or from the complications following, and Topgyay was very anxious lest his own children should die. He called me in to treat them, and it meant almost living in the house, and during those days Geoff and I became very friendly with him. When his brother Rapga arrived from Nanking, also unwell, Topgyay suggested that I should come and live in the house with them.

This growing friendship with the most controversial figure on the Sino-Tibetan border caused increasing disapproval among some of the other foreign missionaries, who had never approved of our ideas or methods very much anyway. It had been the belief and practice of missionaries, on the border particularly, that they must never do anything that might bring them under suspicion by the authorities of anything savouring of 'political' interest. Missionaries everywhere bowed and scraped to the petty whims of any ragged local functionary in their anxiety to preserve their own and their Mission's position from becoming involved in the possible stigma of indulging or interfering in politics. This fear arose out of an unconscious guilt complex through owning, in a country that was not their own, property and land held often on dubious deeds founded on even more dubious treaties permitting them to be there in the first place. Rarely mixing with or showing interest in the people except for personal and professional reasons, they wore an air of superiority that more often than not became a denunciation of everything Eastern and a dictatorial insistence that the Western way of life was the only one possible for the Christian, in religion, in culture and very often in governmental structure and administration. All this left them open to suspicion and accusation of more 'interest' than their profession warranted, and so they reacted by avoiding contact with those in a higher stratum of society whom they suspected of having more open political views and attachments, lest they should be thought of as taking sides in politics. This suspicion on the part of officials increased the nearer one got to the borders, particularly the Tibetan border which was so controversial anyway, and the missionaries' reluctance to do more than hold occasional 'gospel meetings', or 'open airs', or give out gospels and leaflets, increased accordingly. There was very little attempt to get among the people and live with them at any level. Thus the Christianity of the missionaries had come to mean something remote from everyday life, something restricted to a Sunday, a building and a token baptism. The thunderous cliché, 'A missionary's job is to preach', became an easy dictum whereby the missionary could justify his professional existence by holding a few traditional services each week and thus exonerate himself from the *prime* injunction of his divine calling, which was to obey the will of God. This function did not necessarily involve preaching but it certainly necessitated a constant exercise of the spirit to apprehend the mind of God in every circumstance, whether to preach, or to work with one's hands or to keep silent amongst seemingly great opportunity—even as the greatest missionary of all showed and taught.

Now we believed that God had brought Topgyay to us in the working out of His purposes. We therefore ignored the disapproval of fellow missionaries and the mounting suspicion of petty officials and cemented our growing friendship with him. Another factor which brought us together was the illness of Topgyay's wife who, with diabetes, required an injection of insulin every day.

It was during those daily visits that I came to know the real plans for the rumoured uprising in Kham and Tibet. I had come to be such an accepted member of the family that Topgyay discussed everything quite openly in front of me, and although many of his visitors cast many uneasy glances towards the listening foreigner Topgyay serenely told them to go ahead with whatever they had to say. The news usually consisted of listing the number of able-bodied man and guns available in each district or monastery to be placed at Topgyay's disposal when he required them. Only six men were aware of all that was involved in the proposed revolution, though, and they were sworn to secrecy by oath before the gods. Topgyay even showed me the document that had been signed by them as part of my daily language lesson. His sense of humour saw something funny in the situation that a foreigner, and a missionary at that, should be learning the Tibetan language on the plans of a revolution.

The plans were simple and daring. Topgyay and his five friends with their army would take over Kham, or Sikang Province as the Chinese called it, including the capital Kangting, and two other Tibetans with their friends from the northern Tibetan province of Amdo, or Tsinghai, Lobsang Tsewang, more commonly known as General Huang, and Geshi Sherab Gyaltso, would take over control of Amdo. These two provinces had formerly been part of Greater Tibet before they had been arbitrarily annexed by the Chinese and were still, except for a few armed garrisons, inhabited completely by Tibetans. The two provinces and groups of leaders, declared rebels and viewed with suspicion by the Tibetan Government in Lhasa, would then approach the Lhasa Government with the suggestion that they officially recognize the two provinces as part of Greater Tibet, and then they would fight against the Chinese to hold it and contend for the disputed independence of Tibet. If the Lhasa Government turned down their suggestion and offer they would then march on Lhasa, calling on Khambas and Amdowas in the Lhasa Government Army and monasteries to desert and fight with their own leaders, and so take over the government of the country by force. The military strategy was to be left to Topgyay and the plans for political administration to Rapga. Rapga had been a keen student of politics ever since he had left Tibet, and had been expelled from India because of his intention to form a 'Progressive Party' in Tibet to overthrow the old, crippling, reactionary régime. He was a clever scholar and had translated the 'Three Principles of the People' by Dr. Sun Yat Sen, as well as pamphlets on International Law, and extracts from Karl Marx, into Tibetan. These had earned him the reputation of being 'Communist', and even 'terrorist', although he disagreed on many points with Marxism. He was a fervent nationalist and advocate for Tibet's independence, and he was in Kangting at that time because he had finally broken completely with Chiang

Kai Shek over the latter's policy of ultimate absorption of Tibet into China.

In the midst of plans and rumours and riots Topgyay calmly held a party at some hot springs just outside Kangting, at a place known as Erh Dao Chao. It was to be a week-end affair and he had taken over the springs and all buildings to house his guests. Geoff and I were invited with all the top Tibetan officials and traders and Chinese merchants, and saddling up our horses in their best saddle-rugs we joined the gaily dressed company. We had only just been served with tea and sweetmeats when a rifle-shooting competition was announced and officials, traders, servants, muleteers and soldiers streamed out to where a target had been rigged up across the river, about four hundred yards from the narrow ledge from which the shooting was to take place.

Topgyay led off with his three bullets, the amount to be allotted to each person, and when the echoes died away the servants appointed to score came out from behind the stone barricade, checked the target, and signalled 41 out of a possible 60. The next person to shoot, a Chinese official, came forward, shot his three bullets and scored a zero. Whether it was the angle that was difficult, or the wind coming up the valley and off the river that was hard to gauge, no one seemed to know, but Tibetan after Tibetan, many of them with reputations as crack marksmen, registered a zero. Jigme, Topgyay's son, had defeated the best that the Chinese, Canadians and Americans stationed in that area during the war had produced, and that when he was only thirteen years old, yet he scored a paltry 4. Rapga, who in his younger days amused himself by shooting eggs held in the hand of a servant, scored nothing at all. Kora Lama, a fighting, trigger-happy friend of Topgyay's, scored 30, showing that it could be done. Then Topgyay turned and offered Geoff and me the choice of guns to shoot next. Geoff followed the others with a zero, and the Tibetans watched interestedly to see how the other foreigner would fare. I had a growing reputation among them as a horse-man, and they waited to see if my shooting was on a par with my riding. I chose a Remington rifle, tested it for weight and balance, and then, sighting carefully, fired my three bullets. The signallers came out, took down the target, examined it and then waved three red flags and four white—34. I was second to their leader, the famous Pangdatshang. The shooting went on, with the nearest after that only 27.

When we got back to the hot springs a gargantuan meal had been prepared, for which two yaks and four pigs had been slain. By the time the main dishes and then a multitude of subsidiary dishes had been got through, very few were able to give of their best in the Tibetan singing and dancing which followed. Everyone, whether they had a melodious voice or not, had to sing a song from his or her own country or part of the country, and Geoff and I were not excused singing something from England and Scotland. Afterwards some of the Tibetans waited up to play mah-jongg and gamble, but most were glad to retire for the night.

Shortly after this conditions in Kangting became so bad that the Chinese merchants came to Topgyay and pleaded with him to take over control of the town. The wily Tibetan leader, who was not yet ready to declare himself, finally agreed to do so for a month on condition that the Chinese merchants clubbed together, donating several ounces of gold each, to pay for rice for the Chinese soldiers and police. He pointed out that the soldiers and police could not be blamed for not keeping order when they were not being paid by the officials to do so, and if they were to be kept from rioting then the cause of their complaint would have to be removed. This gave him control of the town without leaving himself open to the charge of rebellion against the Government.

It was through Topgyay that God miraculously cleared up the problem of supply while we were in Tibet. When he suggested to us the possibility that there might be a war, and that we might have to take to the mountains with only a pack-mule and a horse at any time, we agreed to face whatever the future held in carrying out God's will for us, and then on this commitment he offered to let us have whatever we required in the way of animals, equipment and food. Naturally, he said, he could not provide us with tins of foreign food, but if we could live like Tibetans he could give us *tsamba*, raw and dried meat, butter, cheese, milk and sometimes other things as they were available. He urged these things on us as a gift, maintaining that he had plenty of everything and was not interested in acquiring wealth, and also he wished to provide something as we were providing so much in helping his people. But we insisted on keeping an account with him of all that we got so that we could pay some time, for we felt that the great name of our God could not be compromised by having it said in the future that His servants were dependent on the charity and provision of a believer in strange gods. Topgyay give what he could, but let us preserve our independence from men and honour any debt incurred to leave the glory of our God unimpaired. We would go forward in faith, taking all that we required for God's work at our hand, believing that when the time came in the future to pay the debt, either in India or Britain or America, wherever Topgyay had accounts, God would have the money ready for us to pay for His own work through His own channels. Topgyay also agreed to supply the other missionaries with what he could should any of them wish to take advantage of his offer, but only the Hjelmerviks, of all the missionaries in Kangting, were able and willing to accept; the others were either disinclined to take the risks involved, or were tied by Mission principles and practices. Clarence and Helen Hjelmervik had a small daughter about eighteen months old, but they were prepared to face the unknown future with God should He lead in this way.

We intensified our preparations for leaving, and it came as a welcome relief when Topgyay suggested a hunting trip into the mountains. Geoff, Vik (as Clarence Hjelmervik was known) and myself, with Topgyay, seven servants, animals and guns, made up the party, and we would just carry on as long as we felt like it. We travelled over a part of the country that we had not visited until now and bagged several deer and mountain goats, increasing as well our knowledge of the language and life among the Tibetans.

Kangting was in a ferment when we returned. One of Topgyay's servants had got into trouble with some of the Chinese soldiers and had been put in prison. A few of his Tibetan friends had broken into prison and freed him, and now the whole town was seething with the excitement and expectation of fighting between the two factions. The Governor had become more than suspicious and was sending in a constant stream of small detachments of troops to Kangting, ostensibly to control the outbreak of riots but actually to outnumber and outwit Topgyay. Already there were more Chinese troops than Topgyay had Tibetans, but he shrugged that off with a casual: 'Oh, one Tibetan is better than ten Chinese.' When he got to his room, after his arrival in Kangting from the hunting trip, he had a few minutes' conversation with Kora Lama and then sent him to the north part of the town with some men to take up positions there and await a signal; others were sent to the west gate and ordered to walk back up the main street, carrying guns but doing nothing. On no account was a Tibetan to fire first, but as soon as a Chinese fired they were to give them everything they had.

On the streets shopkeepers who were still open to trade hastily threw up wooden shutters, and street hawkers melted away. From the west gate of the town, down the empty street, came one of Topgyay's chief lieutenants with several others behind him, hands on the butts of shouldered guns. A Chinese soldier flattened himself against a doorway and was not aware that a Tibetan was in the next doorway to him waiting for him to make one move towards his gun when he would jump out and finish him. An ominous silence hung over the whole town. Topgyay's men walked to the bridge, met other Tibetans there, moved onwards, and there was a considerable slackening of tension. The Chinese had lost the psychological advantage, and from now on the Tibetans would call the tune. People began to appear on the streets, and here and there the voices of hawkers could be heard once more calling their wares.

A few days later while I was sitting talking to Topgyay Kora Lama came in to say that another two foreigners had arrived in town, one of them a woman. Topgyay immediately sent one of his servants to find out all he could about the new arrivals. It appeared that one of the nuns in the convent was seriously ill and a surgeon had been sent for from Chungking, and this was the surgeon with a friend. Topgyay could find out no more and he was increasingly intrigued by the stories that were brought to him about the new woman. She was French, she was good-looking, she was young, she had yellow hair, she wore trousers tucked into Tibetan boots. With each report Topgyay looked more knowing and pleased with himself, until he finally unburdened himself of his great idea that the time had come for me to get married! It had always amazed and grieved him to think that two such healthy specimens as Geoff and me, permitted, unlike the lamas, to marry, were not married and apparently were not interested. He had offered to find Tibetan wives for us who could easily be got rid of when we wanted to leave Tibet for our own country. Now here was an unexpected provision of an excellent wife for one of us. From the reports that he had he did not think she was suitable for Geoff, but she was just the match for me.

I decided that I would put one over on Topgyay, the practical joker, and held a dinner party at our house to which we invited the new arrivals, and then, without mentioning this, we invited several Tibetan friends, including Topgyay and his family. Topgyay's face was a study when he was brought face to face with the French girl, who at my suggestion was in borrowed Tibetan dress for the occasion, but he quickly recovered and was soon in conversation with her through his nephew, who could speak fluent English.

The following morning Topgyay sent for me, and when I arrived he announced that he had made his decision—I must marry the French girl. He had found out the night before that she was unmarried, that she was twenty-one and that the surgeon was her brother-in-law; she was on holiday, had been visiting her sister in Chungking and had taken this opportunity of travelling with her brother to see Tibet. He, Topgyay, had then craftily suggested to her that to see the 'real' Tibet she would have to cross the mountains, but that if she wished to do this he could provide her with as many animals and soldiers for escort as she required. He had even volunteered to go with her, taking his wife, and his bearded foreign friend (myself!) as interpreter, to show her the country. It was here the cunning of his plan came out. When we arrived in the mountains he would say that his wife was not feeling well and must return to Kangting, but the two foreigners, the French girl and myself, were just to go on with the animals and have a good time. Even if I did not do anything to the French girl, he finished triumphantly, I would have to marry her to save her reputation, for that was one of the crazy things foreigners believed!

He had it all cut and dried except for one thing—the heroine was missing; and with relish I told Topgyay and Kora Lama what had happened. Late the night before a cable had arrived from the French Consul urging them to return to Chungking immediately as the situation there was critical. They had left that morning early, and precipitately, and were already well on their way. Topgyay's reaction was sudden and characteristic. He called for one of his captains and shot out a string of commands. 'Take all the men available—seventeen?—all right!—ride over the short cut in the mountains to intercept the foreigners' party. Attack this, robbing it to give an appearance of banditry, but taking only the young yellow-haired woman, letting the others go. Then proceed to a certain part of Kham with the woman and hold her there until the bearded foreigner comes to claim her.'

He smiled triumphantly as he finished the orders and the captain left the room, and then he explained his new plan. His men would take the French girl to a hide-out in the mountains, until I came to collect her. Even if I did not want to go the French Consul would send an S O S to Kangting for a search party to be sent out to look for her. Either I, or George Kraft, would have to go, or both, as we were the only ones capable of such a task, and even if George Kraft went alone, it would be no use as the men would only hand over the girl to the bearded foreigner as commanded. I would then have to go and fetch her, and, as a further attraction, he added complacently, the girl would look on me as a hero, thinking I had rescued her from the bandits, and could not possibly refuse to marry me under these circumstances. The soldiers had their horses saddled and ready to leave before I finally convinced Topgyay that he could not arrange a marriage between westerners as a joke and at last he reluctantly called his men off.

Chapter Ten

THE ARRIVAL

The American Ambassador sent a final warning to American subjects that America was about to withdraw diplomatic recognition from China and advised all American subjects to leave China as soon as possible. Every day Geoff and I expected word from the British Ambassador with advice to the same effect, when it would be very difficult for us to ignore it and proceed as planned. Some missionaries of the World-Wide Evangelization Crusade arrived from a place called Kantze, several days' journey to the north of Kangting, with the news that young Wang Ming De had had great times preaching there, and that there were now nine baptized believers all meeting together, with five others waiting for baptism, when they left. The Word of God was spreading, and being firmly established where He had never been named before, according to His promise. Wang Ming De would leave Kantze shortly to join us and the believers would be left without any 'outside' help, but because they had been grounded solidly on the Scriptures they would require no help but could grow and expand under the work of the Spirit as God had purposed in His wisdom from before the foundation of the world.

With preparations well ahead for leaving at any moment, Helen Hjelmervik suddenly took ill and her condition rapidly worsened. The Catholic doctor tried everything, and then advised an operation that could only be performed in Chengtu, seven days away over the mountains. It would mean that Helen would have to be carried all the way there on the shoulders of coolies, and also that Vik would have to go with her. There was little possibility that

196

they would get back in time to travel with us into Tibet. However, we agreed to meet somewhere on the Indo-Tibetan border, or even in Tibet itself, some time in the future, and then we parted.

Events were now rushing to a climax. Peking had fallen, so had Nanking and Shanghai. Chungking and Canton were threatened and Chiang Kai Shek arrived in Chengtu to make a last stand in West China. He sent word to Topgyay ordering him to put the war-time airfields of Kangting, Ying-Kwan-Tsai and Litang into good order to receive the expected air traffic, and to hold himself ready to fight the Communists if called upon to do so. The Communists turned towards him and the west. It was time for Topgyay to decide what he must do.

I was sitting with Topgyay, Kora Lama and a few other friends discussing our final plans, when a messenger from Lhasa with important news was announced. The messenger, still dusty and smelling of horse-sweat from his ride, came in, bowing low, and in a few words gave the news that the Tibetan Government had ordered all Chinese to leave Lhasa immediately. The news was an unexpected bombshell in that gathering, for no one knew exactly what the implications were. Had the Tibetan Government decided to declare their centuries-old independence, and make a stand against China? Or was some major power such as India, Britain or America supporting the Tibetan Government and strengthening its hand in expelling the Chinese in order to anticipate and frustrate any conquests by Communist China? It was an important point to Topgyay and his factions, for in the first case their revolution against China would have the approval of the Tibetan Government; but in the second case the revolution was finished before it had begun, for while the Khambas and Amdowas could overthrow the Tibetan Government in an internal rising, if the Tibetan Government in Lhasa was being supported by a foreign power or powers, then they would help the Government to put down the revolutionaries from East Tibet. After a long discussion, it was finally decided that the Tibetan Government would never have taken such a drastic step on its own initiative, and therefore it must have had a major power behind it to support it in its decision, in which case the revolution would have to be postponed until the air cleared a bit. It was a four-months' journey to Lhasa, and rapid news could not be expected or rapid decisions effected. They would have to disband for the present, take to the mountains and watch events to the east and west from there. Even if the Communists succeeded in overcoming Chiang Kai Shek quickly, they would have to regroup and consolidate before turning their attention to Tibet, and in that time the Khambas could decide what they would do.

In Kangting everything had come to a standstill waiting for the end. Whatever happened it could only result in good for the people. If the Communists took over they would have law and order and food; if Pangdatshang took over they would have law and order and food. No one believed that Chiang Kai Shek had a chance, and no one wanted him to have one! They had had enough of the Nationalist régime. It was known that General Liu Wen Huie, true to his foxy reputation, was already negotiating with the Communists to hand over Sikang Province, which would leave Chiang Kai Shek without a rearguard or way of escape. China, or five thousand years of civilization that was China, had come to an end.

The caravans of yaks for our goods had come and gone. Forty loads had been taken, including seventeen boxes of medical supplies, each one weighing seventy pounds; ten thousand copies of Scriptures, with loads of silk and brocade and other goods for trading; only personal belongings, with food and medicine required on the trail, were left. Topgyay wanted to wait until the very last minute possible, watching events in China, and then leave at a moment's notice for the mountains.

It was a dangerous game to play at that stage for the Governor's soldiers were again returning to the town in even greater numbers to prepare for the hand-over to the Communists, and already one plan for the murder of Topgyay had been discovered. But Topgyay only smiled when this was pointed out to him, and patted the bulge in his gown where he kept his revolver. He had only seventy men and there were hundreds of Chinese soldiers now in town, but he was serenely confident that he could beat off any attack in Kangting with his hand-picked seventy.

The decision to move came suddenly, as was expected. News was brought to Topgyay that Colonel Fu, the man who had led the Chinese Army against him almost twenty years before, was on his way to Kangting with orders from the General to stop Topgyay leaving Kangting, and if necessary to kill him, and that he would arrive that night. Even at that, Topgyay could not resist a gesture, and he invited Colonel Fu to a meal with him on the night of his arrival, at which he blandly informed Colonel Fu that he was leaving next morning. It was a masterpiece of strategy for Fu had not time to get his forces together and he dared not challenge his wily and powerful Tibetan enemy without a completely prepared plan of campaign.

Kangting was tense with expectation from dawn the next morning, as all over the town people debated whether Fu would risk giving battle after all. He had several hundred troops to Topgyay's seventy, but he also had the memory of a thousand of his troops being defeated by ninety-eight of Topgyay's. By eleven o'clock crowds of people were making their way to the south side of the city where Topgyay lived, to watch the preparations for his departure.

In Kwang Ming Lu Geoff and I, wearing the heavy Tibetan gowns which we had found to be more comfortable than western clothes on the trail, packed the last of the cooking utensils into one of the boxes and gave the order to Loshay to load the animals and proceed to Pangdatshang's compound to join the others. We had been invited down to a final meal with the Krafts before leaving and from there we took our farewell of the other missionaries who had gathered to see us off. We were never likely to forget the kindness of George and Pearl Kraft, nor the inspiration of their spiritual lives. George had taught us much of the language, but he had taught us more of God.

Pangdatshang's compound was a milling mass of people and animals when we arrived, and the streets outside were so packed with people that we could only force our way through the crowds with difficulty. If any fighting was to be attempted it would have to be done outside the city for no one could move to advantage in this crush. For once no one paid any attention to the foreigners as we came downstairs and swung into the saddles of our horses. Every eye was fixed on the doorway for Topgyay, the one in whom the Khambas had placed their hopes of liberation. Servants were there with each member of the family—Jigme, the eldest son, and Abu-Chungwa the youngest at seven, and Amo Chewa and Amo Chungwa, the girls of six and three. Amo Chungwa, although only three, would be riding her own horse all the way, a month's journey, and a special wooden guard had been fixed on the saddle to hold her in position. Each member of the family, as they appeared, was draped round the neck with a ceremonial white scarf, the customary greeting of the Tibetan, and as Rapga appeared he was almost carried away in the rush of people presenting him with scarves. Finally, Topgyay appeared and there was a loud murmur from the crowd, the nearest the East gets to a cheer, and Topgyay disappeared from sight as traders, officials, muleteers and merchants, Tibetans and Chinese, heaped him with scarves until he was only a moving white bundle struggling through the crowds to where a servant held his famous pacing mule.

With a wave of his arm Topgyay signalled the riders to move and the armed escort sent their horses into the crowd. It was a miracle that no one was trampled on for the narrow street was jammed from side to side down its whole length and beyond with a solid mass of people, and the mules and horses of the riders were high-spirited and excited, rearing and straining at the bit to get ahead. All the servants and muleteers were armed, as well as the soldiers, and red, green and yellow coloured prayer flags fluttered from the barrels of the rifles slung across their shoulders, giving a brilliant flash of colour to the riders as they weaved through the drably dressed crowds. Stirrups and silver god-boxes glinted, claret-coloured brocades and orange silks, heavy yak-skins on powerful shoulders topped by uncombed, matted hair, loomed up and passed, and still the caravan of riders moved through the crowd. There were over a hundred and fifty riders, like bobbing coloured corks in a dark sea of people, as we left the town. We were well up in front just behind Topgyay, and were in constant danger of being unseated as Topgyay swung his arm scattering Chinese silver dollars among the beggars, who dived beneath the horses' bellies in their mad scramble for the money. All along the way Topgyay received white scarves—silk ones from the officials, muslin ones from the poorer people—and occasionally he leaned forward and draped them back over the people who had given them to him. The two Catholic nuns smiled and waved, their white habits startlingly white against the dark maroon of the Tibetans' dress and blue gowns of the Chinese.

Then, near the gate leading out of the city, a figure emerged from among a large detachment of soldiers—it was Colonel Fu! A ripple of excitement ran through the crowd, stifling into an electric tension as the two met, Fu on foot and Topgyay riding. Fu smiled and said something, and called to an officer to come forward. The man had a scarf in his hand and Topgyay swung from the saddle easily as he dismounted to receive it. There was a rising murmur of conversation among the crowd when they saw that the crisis was passed, and Fu and Topgyay walked together to the airfield just outside the town. Here, after a great deal of bowing and smiling, everyone swung into their saddles again, following Topgyay, and Kangting was behind.

The winding trail to Jedo was a thread on which were strung the black beads of yaks and the coloured beads of riders, about three hundred animals in all. Only about sixty riders would be going the whole way, the others were friends accompanying Topgyay on the first half of his journey, according to Tibetan custom, and they would return from Jedo.

Every house in Jedo was packed with the sudden influx of travellers, and some of the Tibetans hastily pitched tents for the night. We learned that we should have to stay in Jedo for the next day as well, as some of the loads had to be sorted out from the mix-up of hurried departure, and also Topgyay's wife and her servant were not feeling too well. Geoff and I managed to find a little room, with two others, where we were all jammed on top of each other, and wept copiously from the smoke of a fire set in a hole of the floor between us.

We left Jedo on a brittle, ice-hard morning. The muleteers had been up before dawn getting the cumbersome yaks loaded and on their way before the riders were up and about, but even so there was great confusion as saddles were sorted out and slapped on frisky animals in the early morning cold. At long last, however, we got away, and Gesang Ay-Shi, Chia and a few more of Top-gyay's friends said their final good-byes and dropped behind on their return journey to Kangting, and the caravan strung out and settled down to the normal pace it would now keep all the way to Pangdatshang's hide-out in the mountains.

It took us two days to reach Nawashi, where George Kraft and I had ridden in one day on a previous occasion, because of the size of the caravan and also out of consideration for the women and little children in the party. We pitched our camp almost opposite the same house in which we had found that remarkable 'prayer-meeting' going on during our earlier visit.

When everyone had eaten, and lay sprawled easily about the various camp-fires, there was a stir of interest as a peculiar figure was seen stumbling towards us. It was an old man, dressed in a filthy lama's gown caught carelessly at the waist with a piece of rope, and he gazed at us unseeingly, mumbling all the while. The Tibetans stared at him in awe for this was a famous lama, a former oracle, and they still held him in reverence and fear although he was obviously mad—or perhaps it was partly because of that. He sat down beside a fire while everyone stood up in respect, and Topgyay ordered food to be given to him. He looked at the dishes blankly and then, muttering all the while, picked up a handful of rice and held it out watching it dribble through his fingers. Some of the men said, 'See, he is feeding the gods we cannot see,' while others thought he was offering them the food and stretched out their hands to receive it. The old man smiled stupidly and picked up more rice and *tsamba*, thinking it a game, and passed it round

Breaking camp at dawn in Tibet. Thick-walled, stone and mud houses of a Tibetan village in centre and left background of picture.

the various people now crowding around him to receive the 'sacred' food, which had been blessed through his touching it. Suddenly, still muttering and dribbling at the mouth, and scattering imaginary handfuls of food as he went, he turned away and stumbled down the trail in the direction of his cave in the mountain, where he was said to sit naked every day in the freezing cold. The spirits he had served so faithfully were now taking the price of their forbidden knowledge and power in robbing him of his mind and body, and would shortly claim his soul. The folly and tragedy of *Faust* was still being enacted in the twentieth century.

Several days later we approached the first of thirteen passes over 15,000 feet in height between Kangting and Batang, a busy little town on the upper reaches of the River of Golden Sand. The riders on the best horses always surged to the front on such an occasion as it was an opportunity to test the stamina of their horses and enhance their reputation by being first at the top. Our caravan had been increased by several young fellows from Batang, who had been working in Lhasa and had been expelled by the recent edict of the Lhasa Government—some whispered, because of Communist sympathies and activities—and they increased the exuberance of the caravan with their enthusiasm in riding and singing and dancing. When the caravan reached the top of a pass Topgyay would dismount and hang a prayer flag or scarf on the stack of prayer flags already there, while others would add a stone to the huge cairn always found in such places; at the same time they would offer a prayer to the gods who dwelt on the tops of the mountains.

Nyachuka, or Yakiang as the Chinese called it, was the first town to be passed through since leaving Kangting and we looked forward to it with interest. The trail dropped suddenly, became increasingly rough through a series of deep gorges, and then emerged from the depths of the valley on to the banks of a large, deep and swiftly flowing river, beside which were perched the squalid Chinese-style wooden houses of the village of Nyachuka. There we were entertained to tea by the headman while the villagers got ready the boat that was to be used to ferry us over to the far side.

The river at this point was extremely rough and rapid, due to the rush of a nearby mountain torrent pouring itself into the main stream. The horses and mules, with the loads, were ferried over first, and they were only driven on to the large, unwieldy, flat-bottomed boat with the help of sticks, stones and curses—the last most of all. It took hours to get them across the fifty yards of river but at last it was accomplished and the boat was ready to take the human freight. The passage, seen from the shore, was a nerve-racking process, but experienced in the boat itself it became torturous. We eased our way up the river by poling along in the shallows of the bank until we approached the confluence of the two rivers where the boat began to rock wildly in the cross current. Here it was thrust out into the roaring main current of midstream with a great chorus of shouts and rifle shots—to scare away the destroying demons who haunted that spot in midstream—and after being carried swiftly and helplessly downstream for some time we were deposited in the shallows of the far side, where we again poled ourselves to the landing-point. We camped for the night a little way up the mountain on the far side overlooking the river, while fifty-five yak-loads of ammunition were ferried over to be added to Topgyay's caravan.

Each day we travelled slowly, strung out in a long line across mountains and plateaux, leaving some time for rest or hunting. The scenery changed from icy, windswept snowy passes through undulating flower-carpeted grassland, to thickly forested valleys and sparkling rivers. Every day scouts went ahead to patrol the high points, searching for roving bands of Chinese deserters or even the more dangerous groups of bandits who, although Tibetans and subjects of Pangdatshang, swooped down so fast on a caravan that they shot first and asked questions afterwards. Topgyay had once before been attacked by one of these groups in this country and he had no wish to have the experience repeated.

On the sixteenth day out from Kangting we made preparations to enter Litang, one of the highest towns in the world, at an altitude of 14,500 feet. It was bitterly cold when we crawled out of our sleeping bags to take the bowls of butter tea which Loshay had ready for us. Fires blazed all around the camping-place and the servants and muleteers would saddle or load an animal and then return quickly to the blaze to thaw out fingers numbed by the frozen leather of girths and thongs. More than one looked longingly at the towering peaks where first the rose-colour, then yellow of the sun crept slowly and tantalizingly downwards, with its promise of heat for cruelly cold bodies. We had passed through one gloomy valley and were well up a second before the sun finally touched and caressed the whites, reds and greens of clothing, the dull blue of rifles, and silver and gold of god-boxes, or glinted on the movements of gaily saddled horses and pacing mules as they passed and re-passed each other on the way to the summit. Away ahead the flat plateau that was Litang, the 'Nickel Plain', shimmered in a golden heat-haze.

As we rounded a bend in the trail there was a thunder of hooves, a cloud of dust, and several galloping riders swirled up in a confused mass, their horses rearing to a slithering halt. The leader, a giant of a man in a huge yak-skin gown, stepped forward and had a few words with Nyima Tsering, one of Topgyay's officers, then moved towards a point on the trail where Topgyay and the others were already approaching on their horses. He produced the ceremonial scarf and garlanded Topgyay, who returned it and then passed up the lines of bowing, respectful riders on either side of the trail. These were all from Topgyay's own part of the country, soldiers in his past fighting, led by the famous captain, Gyabon Bundi, the giant in the yak-skin. More and more riders were arriving constantly from Litang and, as we left the mountain trail for the flat table-land of the plain, the single file of daily riding disappeared in a changing pattern of bunched riders as friends sought out friends to talk animatedly. The horses caught the excitement from the fresher horses from Litang and pulled restlessly at the bit, and the speed of the party increased imperceptibly. Some of the more high-spirited horses had to be brought round in a wide circle and back to join the group, so restive were they to get away and gallop over the football-field-like plain stretching away into the distance. The riders were not averse to this restlessness on the part of their animals and used it to exhibit their skill as horsemen with a nonchalant and apparently unconscious control. A grey horse, small even for a Tibetan horse, persistently moved out of the group in a head-tossing, fast-moving circle, the rider, a lama, having great difficulty in controlling the lovely animal and bringing it back again. On at least two occasions he had to get off and quieten it before remounting and rejoining the others. Finally, the lama turned its head towards a long shoulder of mountain running into the plain, and to take the fire out of it sent it forward at a gallop. After several tremendous leaps it settled down to a flashing gallop that stopped the conversation of every rider in the caravan, and as it took the side of the mountain in its stride at the same speed and disappeared eventually over the top, they broke out in cries of admiration. A good horse was as highly prized as a good gun in Tibet and they had just seen one of the finest of its kind. The Litang contingent, in reply to the excited questions of the others, shook their heads gloomily and spoke of a 'demon' being in the grey, for it had already killed a man, and they were daily expecting it to kill its present owner who was becoming more and more afraid of its uncontrollable strength.

Groups of riders varying from six to thirty were now coming across the plain to meet the caravan, lengthening the triangle of riders spear-pointed to Topgyay and the headman of Litang, until there were over two hundred riders strung out in a weaving pattern of interchanging colour as we changed places at a fast gallop, a canter or a trot.

People were now walking out to meet us, and a group of Tibetan women had gathered on a small knoll. As Topgyay swept forward they ran towards him to offer bowls of curds, milk, tea, wine and other foodstuffs as token gifts. Topgyay smiled and leaned sideways in the saddle, dipped his fingers in the bowls as he went by, and shouted that his wife was coming up behind. We thundered round a slight rise in the plain and a group of Chinese officials stepped forward to be introduced to Topgyay. After a quick handshake and acknowledgement all round he was back in the saddle and sweeping forward again.

A collection of filthy, square-built mud houses, looking like a sprawling archaeological site in their collapsed, broken-down condition, was next, and this was pointed out to us as being part of the old town of Litang which had been devastated in an earthquake the year before, claiming over a thousand lives.

We finally reined to a halt on the outskirts of Litang proper, beside a large, solidly built house of the usual Tibetan design. Servants were running all over the place leading in horses or driving back curious onlookers. The Pangdatshang family were to have the upstairs as their quarters while Geoff and I had the ground floor. The downstairs of this house was different from others we had visited, for, instead of being used as a stable for animals, it was stacked with bales of tea, all hided ready for despatch. Nor did it appear to have been used as a stable in the past for the walls from floor to ceiling were covered with the highly coloured religious paintings usually seen on the walls of monasteries, wall paintings which were still in reasonably good condition although here and there some of the colours had flaked off with the plaster.

When we went upstairs to join Topgyay and the others for tea and sweetmeats the same high standard of artistic decoration was everywhere in evidence, with more than the usual multiplicity of household idols, all of gold and silver. We drew Topgyay's attention to this and asked if this were the house of some very wealthy Tibetan of whom we had not heard, and he told us that it was the house in which the sixth Dalai Lama had been 'incarnated'. He pointed out five lumps of wood, two large and three small, hanging above the outside door; these, he said, indicated that five other incarnations had been born in that house, two great and three lesser in rank and importance.

It was strange in the sunlit quietness of that afternoon to hear the quiet voice of Rapga say that the last time he had been in that house was in 1934 when he had passed through from Markham, after their defeat, on his flight down country. Topgyay had fled by Yunnan, but he, Rapga, had come through Batang and Litang. General Liu Wen Huie had sent for him to come to Ya-an, where he was at that time, and 'courteously' provided an escort of ten men to take him there and look after him on the way. Rapga suspected Liu of conspiring to use him to further some plans of his own, but could not do anything about it, and agreed to go and meet him. In Kangting he took to smoking great quantities of opium until the Chinese officials there reported that he was taking to opium in despair over the failure of his plans for an uprising in Tibet and that he could be written off as harmless. Consequently, while travelling from Kangting to Ya-an, the escort was reduced to only four men, for it was not considered worth while to send more on such a short trip with Rapga as he was so much under the effects of opium. One day out from Ya-an Rapga changed his expensive Tibetan gown, giving it to one of his servants, and putting on an old Chinese gown he slipped away in the darkness, leaving the servant to impersonate him, and his other servants to help carry out the bluff by waiting on him hand and foot until they reported in Ya-an. The ruse was successful and Rapga managed to find his way to Nanking in Central China, and then from there to India.

And now here he was again, on the eve of another revolution, returning along familiar trails. At each step on the way and often between the day's stages, delegations appeared and the burly, quiet-spoken leaders of these delegations had pledged their loyalty in any future fighting under the Pangdatshangs, giving an account of the men and guns they could produce if called upon. The three weeks had unfolded an impressive array of men and munitions with the possibilities inherent in their being united for the first time in centuries under an able leader, instead of warring among themselves. Topgyay decided to wait in Litang for a few days, within reach of news from down country, and then begin the last stage of the journey to Bo, marked Poteu on the map, the mountain retreat of the Pangdatshangs.

We had been invited to attend a feast shortly after our arrival, and after a wash-up and change of clothing we started for the town, followed by servants, bodyguards and a crowd of townspeople. The path from the house into town lay across a wide open space on which an incredible sight met our astonished eyes—incredible for Tibet, and even more incredible for Litang, one of the largest monastery-towns of Tibet. At intervals of every fifty yards or so there was a small camp of nomads with a series of rough wooden frames pitched around their tents. On these were hung the steaming carcasses of freshly slaughtered yaks. Thousands of crows were perched on the cross pieces, picking at the carcasses, while overhead huge vultures circled on a slow wingbeat. Everywhere scavenging dogs tried to snatch at entrails, while one or two more audacious than the others tried to drag away the huge yaks' heads that were lying scattered on the ground. Nomads, stripped to the waist, were covered in blood, steaming in the cool of the afternoon, and crowds of porters, men and women, were lined up with baskets to carry the meat away into the monastery. For it was the monastery that had ordered the slaying of the animals to supply the priests with meat for food and also to stock against future profitable trade. Three hundred yaks were being slaughtered every day and the butchering had already gone on for several days. Rapga and Topgyay said nothing but shook their heads disapprovingly as they looked at the carnage, until one sight was too much and Rapga whipped out his camera to photograph a maroon-robed lama carrying a yak's head in one hand and a lump of meat in the other. The lama looked up and saw Rapga pointing the camera at him and, dropping the yak's head and the meat, ran quickly behind a nearby tent and hid himself.

About two or three hundred yards beyond the nomads' tents the path turned to the right below a slight overhang of rock, on which were a pile of stones and prayer flags, and then rose sharply to enter the main street of the town. The street was wide, about forty feet from side to side, running north and south, the northern end terminating in the Chinese magistrate's *yamen*, or offices and quarters. The houses on either side of the street were all one-storied and flat-roofed and they were built in a continuous block from the top of the street to the bottom. The doorways led straight off the road and nearly all of them had two or three steps down into the rooms. Through a gateway to the left of the Government Offices the road led into the market part of the town. Here the 'road' was only about ten feet wide with small, busy shops lining each side for over a hundred yards or so. Like the houses on the main street they had steps leading down into the entrances and from what we could gather this custom was to help keep out as much of the dust as possible from the dust-storms which swept the Litang plain from time to time. There was a surprising variety of goods for such a remote place, coloured silks, carpets, saddlery, religious paraphernalia, exquisitely worked silver goods from the famous workshops of Dege, flour, sugar, matches and household utensils—and, of course, butchers' shops with freshly slaughtered meat. At the end of the street there was another gate leading into the monastery, larger than the town itself.

As we passed through this gate we came upon one of the most ironical incidents in the religious history of Tibet. Just a few yards across the threshold of the gateway leading into the monastery an emaciated horse—its ribs showing, its bloated belly heaving in agony, its eyes opaque with approaching death—almost blocked the entrance. No one would kill the horse to put it out of its pain, for the lamas said it was a sin to kill, but five hundred yards away three thousand yaks had been killed by the orders of the lamas and the meat was being carried into the monastery through an alleyway not five yards away from the dying horse.

There were probably only about two thousand people in Litang, if that many, but there were over three thousand lamas in the monastery and about another thousand on the roster, although these were away either on pilgrimage or for some other reason. The buildings of the monastery were larger and in better condition than any of the houses in the town, and were built about the monastery in irregular groups, making the lanes between them narrow and crooked. Towards the rear of the monastery on higher ground facing south and overlooking the town, newer buildings had been built and some more were in process of construction. Many of the older buildings had been destroyed in the previous year's earthquake. The main worship-hall of the monastery, in contrast to most of the places we had seen so far, was spotlessly clean. The floor was well laid in lengths of smooth wood, not yet polished. The roof, about sixty feet above us, was supported by red-painted pillars intricately carved and inlaid with a variety of colours and lavishly overlaid in parts with gold leaf. The whole building was designed so that the eye automatically was led to the north side where two huge wrought-iron gates, about twenty feet high and twenty feet wide, guarded a dark enclosure beyond. It was so dark beyond the gates that at first nothing could be seen except a few butter lamps burning at some distance above our heads. Gradually, as we strained to look upwards beyond the butter lamps, at a height of about forty feet, the outlines of a gigantic gilt face could be seen gazing blankly and serenely into the distance. The dark outline of the whole image was just visible, after gazing for some time, but it was the effect of that enigmatic face suspended in darkness that remained vivid in the memory when everything else had faded.

The host was an interesting character, a Chinese and not a Tibetan. Rapga informed us that his name was Liu, that he had been a major-general in the Nationalist Army but had left everything to become a lama. He must have had influence with General Liu Wen Huie, or even high up in the Nationalist Government, for he had not only been appointed head of Litang monastery but also of all the monasteries in Kham, or as the Chinese insisted on calling it, Sikang Province. This use of influence to gain high position detracted considerably from the sincerity of the renunciation and the Tibetans suspected him of being a spy. He was tall and thin, with a narrow inscrutable face, and typically Chinese in speech, manner and gesticulation although dressed in full lama regalia. The other guests were the magistrates of Batang, Litang and Nya Chuka, so provincial officialdom was well represented. There were over twenty dishes in the feast and, with an appetite

born of the wide open spaces and sharpened by the monotony of
trail diet, we contributed little to the usual conversation until we
sat back replete at the end.

The days that followed were filled with a round of feasts and
discussions as rider after rider came in with news. Jekundo in
Amdo Province—or Yushu in Tsinghai Province, according to
the Chinese—an important town on the northern trail into Tibet,
had fallen to the Communists; and the Tibetans in Kham were
cut off from the Tibetans in Amdo. It came as a surprise, for
everyone had expected the Chinese Moslem generals in north-
west China to make a stand against the Communists; but they too,
steeped in corruption, were swept away by the moral judgement
of Communism and the Communist Forces poured through to the
Tibetan border unopposed. The Amdo Tibetans had been caught
unprepared by the unexpected collapse of the Chinese Moslems
and with no set plan were easy prey for the well-organized Communists. Jekundo was only fifteen days' journey away over the
mountains, and news was already filtering through that the Communist commanders were calling on all the leaders in Sikang to
surrender to them, and ordering all towns to prepare to welcome
them as 'liberators'.

Topgyay weighed the situation coolly and carefully and decided to wait on for a few more days in Litang. He could always
leave for the mountains beyond at a moment's notice and even if
there were Communist spies among the officials there were not
sufficient soldiers to stop him. He was very suspicious of Liu, the
head of the monastery, but that did not prevent him from spending a lot of time in his company. It was a battle of wits to see who
could get more out of the other without giving too much away.

It was during one of our visits to the monastery that we got
mixed up in two invitations to feasts. While we sat around one of
the sunlit, warm rooms of the head lama's part of the monastery,
servants brought in huge platters with sides of meat, pork, mut-
ton, stews, soups, vegetables, steamed breads, and sweetmeats.
An invitation had come to attend a feast that day and everyone,
on seeing Topgyay willing to remain, assumed that this was it. The

meal lasted for about two hours and afterwards the Abbot asked if we would like to see the inner shrine of the monastery. On the way there we had to pass through a room in which was the tomb of the 'incarnation' of the previous Abbot. It was a tall, cone-shaped edifice reaching to the roof of the room and covered from top to bottom in gold. Our host informed us that 113 ounces of gold had gone into the gilding of the tomb. Around the various ledges and in the various alcoves of the structure there were solid gold offering bowls and religious symbols, while turquoises and rubies gleamed in the insets.

The inner shrine was the dwelling place of the guardian-god of the monastery, the 'unholy of unholies', never shown to an outsider. Here the chief 'deity' to whom all their prayers were directed dwelt in awesome power. The Tibetans might 'propitiate' the beneficent deities, keeping them quiet and satisfied by giving them their due respect in token offerings, but they 'solicited' the approval of the demonic hierarchy whose powers they feared above all others, and their offerings and worship were proportionately increased by the powers displayed by these so-called 'guardian-gods'. The serene and smiling Buddha might be given the public place of importance in the main worship-hall but the real centre of worship and power lay in this small, dark room, dimly lit by spluttering butter lamps and smoking incense-sticks, which housed several grotesque and obscene idols, and whose focal point was in the dead-white leering skull suspended from a beam at the rear of the room. The force of evil was almost physical in its impact. In such a setting and atmosphere the dread 'Ro-lang' ceremony became a reality. Spoken of with bated breath by the Tibetans I had had it corroborated in my studies of some manuscripts obtained for me by my teacher. *Ro* was the Tibetan word for 'corpse', and *lang* the Tibetan word for 'to rise up', and together they described the dread rite of laying out a newly dead corpse, or corpses, in the temple or some lonely spot, and then by incantations and black practices calling a spirit back into the dead body, and at last challenging the writhing, thrashing corpse to a contest in which only one could conquer. The bodies of lamas in grotesque attitudes and with hideous agonies twisting their dead faces had been found on lonely plateaux as a witness to the penalties meted out to those who invoked the powers of another world.

We came out into the afternoon sunshine to find a Chinese soldier waiting for us with a red card in his hand. It was the official invitation to the feast we had agreed to attend that morning! Topgyay had not paid sufficient attention and had thought that the invitation to the monastery was also the invitation to the feast we had agreed to attend that morning, whereas he had agreed to attend another and that only two hours after the baronial repast provided at the monastery! He looked at us in despair and then speaking in Tibetan, so that the soldier would not understand, he suggested that we waste as much time as we could both on the way and when we arrived, so as to postpone eating until the last possible moment. It was only a temporary expedient, though, and the meal had to be faced. Chinese custom dictated that after the host had called on the honoured guest to partake of each new dish as it arrived then each guest could call on a fellow guest to take part and the guest called on was obliged to do so. It pleased Topgyay's sense of humour to call on Geoff and me time after time to eat more, and then try and avoid eating himself by dipping his chopsticks into the dish and then engaging his host's attention so that he would not see that he had merely extracted gravy and not meat. Topgyay excused himself at the eighteenth dish, and a few minutes afterwards I joined him in the stables to bring up most of that excellent meal. We had to return and continue eating, of course, for it would have been a great insult to the host had he known we were away being sick.

Like the ancient Romans after indulgence, it was decided the following day that we should attend the hot sulphur springs in the vicinity of Litang. We were about an hour's horse-back ride away and a small party was to be formed. Geoff and I had not been too interested at first, as our horses were grazing up on the mountains somewhere, until Rapga's son, Sonam Dorji, said that the much-admired grey horse we had seen on the day of our arrival was outside, having been sent by the owner as a courtesy gesture for someone to ride. The only person capable of riding the horse was Topgyay, and he declined the honour since he had been out of practice for many years and had no inclination to break himself in on a reputed killer. He finally agreed after much persuasion to let me ride the grey, although he insisted on a promise that I would not gallop.

When we went outside to where the horses were tethered in the large compound, a large crowd of townspeople had gathered to watch the colourful cavalcade move off. Everyone stood back as I approached the grey terror, which drew back farther as it watched me come nearer, eyes rolling and ears laid back. With the halter stretched taut, and unable to retreat farther, it suddenly turned and flashed out with its hooves and I had to slide aside nimbly to avoid them. The movement brought me close to the horse's neck and I remained there, without moving, speaking quietly and soothingly, oblivious of the crowd. The horse's ears gradually flickered upwards and then, as I lifted my hand towards its neck, flattened again. With my fingertips I slowly began to stroke the arching neck, travelling farther with each stroke until I was moving near the head to where the reins lay on its neck. Picking them up gently I continued stroking with the other hand, talking quietly the while, and at the same time eased my left foot off the ground towards the stirrup. The silence could almost have been cut as I fitted my foot into the stirrup and began to throw the weight of my body on to that leg slowly so as not to upset the horse. Then with a sudden movement I swung myself up and across and I was in the saddle, settling myself for the battle. The grey began pitching immediately, throwing its head high in the air and then plunging downwards as it tried to hurl me from the saddle. It was like a bolt of chained lightning as it curvetted about the compound, its legs like steel springs hurling it upwards each time it touched the ground.

After a short time testing the horse's mouth and my seat in the saddle I took it through the gateway on to the plain. There it became almost frantic in its attempts to break away, go wild, and gallop. Already the crowd had lost their initial fear and were shouting and whooping in encouragement, but I had given my promise to Topgyay and to Geoff and I held it to a jolting trot. The others were now mounted and came out on to the plain at a fast canter, pulling at the bit for a gallop, and the grey went away on a bucking spree in the excitement, leaping and rolling like a ship gone mad, its nose almost sweeping the ground in its attempts to get free. The jolting drove the hat from my head and I automatically made a grab for it with my left hand. It was my undoing. The grey rocketed away in a thundering gallop over the undulating plain, weaving crazy wild patterns as it sought to throw me off. The wind sang in my ears as I exerted all my strength and skill to bring it under control but it had a mouth of iron and I began to feel my legs go numb and knew it was only a matter of minutes now before I was thrown, and probably dragged and kicked to death. With the thought came the determination to have one last attempt at breaking the brute. I had gone round in a wide circle and was now almost back amongst the other riders again, who had pulled their horses to a stop as they watched the exhibition of riding; both man and animal were under judgement by the ruthless standards of Tibet. As I swept past them in a cloud of dust and stones I went almost as savage as the horse. When the horse threw its head down I broke the movement with a jerk and wrenched it up again. When the head came up with the flailing forefeet I beat it down by bringing my riding whip down between its ears. When it sprung to the left I wrenched the reins and bridle to the right until its body curved in a semicircle and it had to move crabwise, and when it swung to the right I did the same to the left. We were like a couple of mad things and I was covered from head to foot in the bloody froth blowing backwards from the horse's mouth. Then, miraculously I was moving along with the others, the horse still quivering and breaking into an occasional flashing gallop, but always coming round in a wide circle to join the others for a little while. We were almost at the hot springs, situated in some low foot-hills, and I decided to give the horse its head and test its stamina by putting it at one of the steep sides of one shoulder of the mountain. It responded like a flash of lightning and was away before the others could draw breath. I let loose a Tibetan 'yee-hee' in its ear and lay along its neck as the staccato beat of its gallop blurred into a roll. I was almost intoxicated with the speed and power of the animal under me and it was still straining in a gallop when we topped the ridge and dropped down on the far side, and I had to fight like mad to bring it to a standstill.

In the hot springs as we lay and soaked, the performance of the horse was the sole topic of conversation. I lay back with my eyes shut, aching in every bone and muscle, my body quivering with the strain and reaction, my fingers raw flesh where the reins had burned and skinned them, while Topgyay tried to persuade me to buy the horse. He knew the lama owner, he said; he knew he couldn't ride the horse and that he was afraid of it, he knew that he could get it at a bargain price, why didn't I buy it? I would never get a chance like this again for a Tibetan never sold his horse if it was a good one. The lama would sell this one because he could not ride it, and was afraid, too, that it might kill someone one day and he would be held responsible.

I wanted that horse but I was sore and exhausted and knew that it would take weeks of such riding before it could be brought under proper control, and the thought in my present battered condition was almost too much for me. I finally agreed that if I could ride it back to Litang again without being unseated I would buy it at whatever price Topgyay fixed. It was agony on the return journey. The horse knew it was on its way home and refused to stay with the other riders, and I had to fight it all the way, but I stayed on. I had to be helped from the saddle by Loshay when we arrived, but my reward came when Loshay whispered that I *must* buy the horse, that there was none like it and I was the master. Loshay had been one of the most insistent against trying to ride it before we left for the springs and he himself was reckoned one of the finest riders in Kham.

Before we left Litang we almost had a murder on our hands. Loshay came to us one afternoon to say that one of the silver-embossed tea bowls had been stolen, and would we give him permission to see if he could find it? It was an awkward situation for we were guests of Pangdatshang and his servants were the only ones in the house with our own. It followed, then, that if our servants had not taken the bowl one of his servants must have done so. The feudal customs of the Tibetan demanded that the servants of one lord provide hospitality for the servants of the other: so many of Pangdatshang's men had been given tea by Loshay and any one of them might have taken the bowl. However, he said that he had suspicions about one of them and that he would be careful in his investigations.

Three hours later there were sounds of shouting and quarrelling outside and on going out to investigate we found Loshay being hustled into the house by some of his friends while he shouted imprecations over his shoulder. We gradually got him quietened and discovered that he had gone into the town with a friend looking for the man he suspected. Meeting him on the main street, he had gone over to talk to him and while speaking he put his arm round his shoulders and then dropped it until he could feel in the bulge of the waist of the man's gown where the Tibetans carried all their odds and ends, including their tea bowls. It was a dangerous move for it might have been the man's own tea bowl that was there, but he had too guilty a conscience to bluff it out for he went for his sword instead. Loshay drove his fist into the man's face and as he fell over backwards he leapt on to the hand holding the sword, kicking it out of the way, and then pounded the man's head against the ground. The man picked up a large stone and battered Loshay in the face with it, driving him over on his back; and then, clawing at each other, they fell into the river. Even there the fighting went on, each one trying to drown the other in the shallow bed while the interested spectators crowded the bank without attempting to interfere.

Still struggling, they savagely fought their way out and as they battered each other on the bank Loshay slipped in the mud and the thief leapt to a low wall and, picking up a large coping stone with two hands, brought it down on Loshay's head. Only Loshay's thick hair saved him from instant death. As it was he reeled backwards and collapsed in a heap. The thief took one quick look at him and then turned to stagger away, the crowds watching him silently. Loshay struggled to get up on his knees, blinded with water and blood and sweat, and seeing the thief getting away, picked up what was nearest to hand to throw at him. It happened to be a huge curving yak's horn, left over from the slaughter, and he hurled it with the deadly accuracy of the nomad, trained to hurling and slinging stones from childhood. The thief either sensed danger or took one last look to see if he had killed Loshay; whatever it was he turned round just as Loshay hurled the horn after him and the point took him in the middle of the forehead, splitting his skull like an egg-shell. It was then that Loshay's friends had grabbed him and hustled him into the house.

The man was a muleteer of Topgyay's so we decided that we had better go and report the incident to him before he heard of it from other sources. He heard us through in silence and then shrugged his shoulders, saying that it was all right. Loshay had been within his rights according to Tibetan custom, and as he had found the man with proof of his thieving on him, he was at liberty to kill him if he so decided. If the thief had got away with stealing the bowl then Loshay might have been suspected of the theft and his name for honesty destroyed; it was up to him, therefore, to decide on the punishment for the man who had thus endangered his reputation. After some persuasion Topgyay finally agreed to send two soldiers to bring in the muleteer for medical treatment, but when they went to get him they found that he had disappeared without trace.

The sun was shining brilliantly when we left Litang on the last stage of our journey. There was the usual procession of local dignitaries with farewell gifts and the usual pandemonium of departure, and then we were outside the compound and on our way. Stretched away out across the plain in groups of various sizes, was the caravan of over two hundred animals—yaks, horses and mules. At irregular intervals groups of the townspeople had gathered to wish Topgyay a safe journey in Tibetan fashion. As he rode, each group came forward with gifts of curds, milk, wine and sweet-meats on trays, to present to him; some he touched with his fingers in acknowledgement, to others he just smiled, bowed, spoke a word of thanks. The older people offered the gifts to him as a courtesy gesture, while he in turn gave money, silver Chinese coins, to their children.

The flat plain stretched away into the distance in a shimmering haze, early morning though it was, until it was caught up in the circle of bluish mountains. The ground underfoot was so frost-bound that the horses had great difficulty in keeping on their feet. From Litang the plain had looked like a large, flat billiard table, about ten miles by eight in diameter, but in actual fact the plain was in three distinct levels, with as much as fifty feet or so abruptly separating them in sharp drops. Much of the plain was tufted grass but there were large stretches of hundreds of yards where it was smooth and level. The one shallow river cut the plain in two, here and there widening out into a wide gash on the surface, but most of the time remaining narrow and almost hid-den. It took us about two hours to reach the river, which we forded by riding obliquely downstream and then upstream again at the same angle. The mountains reared away from us, dark green slashed by large yellow stretches of sulphur deposit. All around clouds of steam rose from hidden thermal streams.

With a stiff climb ahead I had my saddle transferred to the grey to test it on the mountains and begin the process of breaking it in. There were several hectic minutes while I mounted and settled myself in the saddle, and then I turned its energies towards the mountains. It ate up the first climb easily ahead of the others, then topping the rise on to a flat stretch put its head down again and went into its celebrated bucking exhibition. However, it did not last so long this time and I managed to turn it towards the mountain trail again. It was almost normal while travelling alone, only straining powerfully at the bit, but as soon as I brought it alongside the other riders it surged forward to get ahead and refused to stay in line. When we arrived at the open space beside a river that was to be our camping spot for the night, Topgyay suggested that I race the grey with one of his own, his top horseman riding it instead of himself. I agreed, and we paced our horses to the end of the valley, turning round suddenly at a shout and sending them hurtling up the course. The grey rocketed past Ju-gar on Topgyay's horse and passed the finishing line about twenty yards ahead of it, an easy winner, and not fully extended, for I was still a bit afraid to let him right out.

Darkness stole down on one of those nights that are never forgotten. In the flat clearing above the river, with not a tree in all the vast amphitheatre of mountains, several fires blazed with wood carried from the lower pine forests, where different groups were preparing the inevitable butter tea. Line upon line of yaks and horses were tethered to one side, and in a wide semicircle on the other the loads of boxes, tea and ammunition were stacked to form a wind-break. The haunting notes of a Tibetan song hung in the air. A dog barked occasionally. And the moon with divine artistry sketched the scene in silver and black.

We were up before dawn next morning as we had a hard day ahead, with what the Tibetans reckoned the highest pass in Kham to cross. This was known as the Gara La, or 'Blacksmith Pass', and if higher than the previous Ra-nga La, must have been in the region of 19,000 feet. All around the scenery was bleak, barren and uninteresting except for the hypnotic charm of vastness—no trees, no bushes, no vegetation of any kind—just stretch after stretch of stones and shale and sandy soil with the savage rocky peaks for ever towering above. As we drew near the top of the pass there was the usual drawing away of the younger element as they jockeyed for good positions in their dash for the summit. On previous occasions Geoff and I had not bothered to enter the race for the top as the others had by far the better horses, but now I was tempted to see what the grey could do in the test of stamina as well as speed. I eased it forward imperceptibly until I was lying fourth from the front, the leader about twenty yards ahead, and the summit about three hundred yards away, and then I kicked it into action again. It was a narrow trail and I was spattered by a stinging hail of dust and small stones from the hooves of the horses ahead, until I swept past them and reined in at the stone cairn on the summit.

Two giant pyramid-shaped peaks stood sentinel on the pass and formed a frame for one of the most magnificent panoramas to be seen anywhere in the world. Visibility was perfect and range upon range of snow mountains stretched away into the deepening blue distance, crowned by a magnificent towering virgin peak, startlingly like the Matterhorn, which blindingly reflected the rays of the sun. Below, fold after fold of valleys cradled the dark green and black of forests and away to the left a blue lake lay quietly sleeping.

Down in the valley, up on to the high grasslands again—tossed by the horse and only by a miracle rolling clear of its flailing, murderous hooves—ramming the giant captain in one bucking spree and lifting him clean out of the saddle to fall with an earth-shaking thud and kept from serious injury only by the huge sheep-skin absorbing the shock—and then on again to the next pass.

Here a large company of riders were drawn up beside the cairn and stack of prayer-flags, a long trail of white smoke rising in the still air from a pile of cedar branches offered to the gods of the mountains for bringing the caravan through thus far safely. The leader was a small, powerfully built Tibetan with a crippled leg, and he limped forward to greet Topgyay warmly. He was a very influential nomad chieftain who had been of great help to Top-gyay in the past, and he and Topgyay sat by the side of the cairn talking animatedly, while the nomad chief's riders provided bowls of fresh curds. The scene was unbelievably beautiful. Over a hundred heavily armed, colourfully dressed riders sprawled around on the rich green of the grass, while the groomed horses with their gleaming saddlery and blazing rugs filled the background as they nibbled the grass, reins trailing. All around mountains fell away sharply into dark abysses or soared upwards intoxicatingly to rend the unclouded blue of the sky with their jagged outlines. And above them all, nearer now than on a previous occasion, the 23,000 feet Matterhorn-like peak towered in flawless majesty, each

Caravan of horsemen, with rifles slung on shoulder, travelling just beneath the snow-line (about 17,000 feet in Eastern Tibet).

detail of its outline etched sharply against the deep blue of the sky in the clarity of that altitude.

When the curds were finished the riders mounted again and rode down the far side and across a wide valley to where there was a large cluster of black tents, and dismounted before the largest of them all. The inside of the tent covered an area of about thirty-six feet by eighteen feet and showed considerable evidence of the owner's wealth. All around the sides, built up like a wall, were skin-covered boxes containing the possessions of the nomad chief, as well as bags of grain, *tsamba*, skins of butter, saddles, and rugs. The floor was thickly covered with carpets in a variety of designs and colours, and down the length of each side of the tent were two rows of small tables. On the tables were intricately designed china bowls in silver and gold holders, for the tea, and then bowls of nuts, sweetmeats, *tsamba*, dried meat and dried fruits. In the centre of the tent a clay stove had been built, standing about three feet high and about five feet long, on the three open holes of which huge metal cauldrons were bubbling with tea. The tent was the centre of attraction for the whole nomad community and every opening was jammed with oily, dirty faces gazing wonderingly at the Tibetan leaders they had heard of by name only and the foreigners they had never heard of at all.

We stayed the night with the nomad chieftain, leaving early next morning. The deeper we penetrated into the mountains the more wild and glorious the scenery became. Undulating grasslands carpeted with flowers, barren plateaux with not a shrub for miles, forested valleys with flashing silver streams pouring into deep turbulent rivers, all slid past the seemingly tireless horses. With scarcely a house to be seen in all the remoteness, it always came as a shock to turn a bend in the trail and find a group of horsemen approaching to greet us or to join us. Lamas from near or distant monasteries on fat sleek mules, gold god-boxes gleaming dully against the deep maroon of their robes; wild nomads on shaggy ponies, massive in their huge yak-skin gowns; well-dressed, silent, dangerous-looking men on restless horses: all appeared at intervals along the trail, to come forward, present scarves and presents, talk in low tones to Topgyay for a few hours and then disappear again in the maze of valleys.

Topgyay murmured to me regarding one group as they approached that they were the killers of a medical missionary who had come up into Kham some years before. There were about thirty of them, well mounted on good horses and armed with rifles, swords and revolvers. When they had finished the usual talk Topgyay sent for me and informed me that these men had heard of my prowess as a rider and wanted to know if I would give an exhibition. My grey had been sent up the mountain but they offered to produce a wild horse from amongst their string that only their leader could ride, and I agreed to ride that. It was only when I walked forward to where four men were holding the large white brute that I remembered the difference between the high Tibetan saddle and the flat English one I always used. I was about to ask for it to be changed but it had taken so long to saddle the struggling horse that I decided to leave it as it was.

I had one passing qualm again as I shuffled down into the saddle and found myself uneasily perched on top of a saddle blanket, a saddle rug and eighteen inches of wood topped by two other smaller saddle rugs, and then everything was forgotten as the men jumped aside and the huge white horse exploded under me. It had several different tricks from the grey, but lacked the speed and sudden dynamite of the smaller terror, depending on its brute strength to unseat the rider. I fought it for some minutes, and then turned it down the valley, drumming my heels against its flanks, to try it at speed in the open. The animal went away in a series of powerful leaps, trying the grey's tricks of arching its back in the air and throwing its head down between its forelegs. It was an easy move to counter and I usually leaned forward until the grey's head had almost reached the bottom of its swing and then swung it suddenly upwards again. But I forgot about my unexpected height in the Tibetan saddle on this occasion and as the white horse leapt into the air, throwing its head downward, I leaned forward as usual but, because I was so high and the distance to the end of the swing greater, I was jerked right out of the saddle and catapulted through the air in a wide somersaulting arc. I tucked my head well down between my shoulders as I landed and rolled over and over before coming to rest beside a huge boulder. The horse was well on its way down the valley and the Tibetans were rolling on the ground in their amusement. It must have looked funny to them, although I might have cracked my skull open in landing from that descending parabola. By the time the horse was caught the riders were ready to leave and no further exhibition was possible—much to my relief. I had enough to contend with every day in my own horse.

The groups of riders increased and the caravan now consisted of over two hundred riders, moving swiftly ahead of the slowly plodding yaks. Only one more day and we should arrive in Bo-mi, or Bo-ko, or just Bo, as it was variously called, our objective in the hinterland of Kham. This was not the family estate of Pang-datshang, which was still several days distant at a place called Bumda, in Markham, or South Kham. 'Bumda' was the correct romanization of the first part of Pangdatshang's name and not 'Pangda' as it had been rendered.

We were up early on the day of our expected arrival, muleteers, servants, soldiers and escorts grooming their horses and cleaning rifles to spruce up their appearance for the great event. We had scarcely pulled out of the valley when more groups of riders began to appear and form up on either side of the trail. Topgyay dismounted each time now, receiving scarves, presents and greetings with a warm smile, for these were his close friends and followers, the remnants of his earlier defeated army. Up again and into the saddle and forward at a fast trot, the excited riders passing and re-passing each other in sharp bursts of speed, restraining their powerful horses before they could pass Topgyay in the lead. A bend in the trail and more scores of riders massed on the skyline above us.

We were like a small army as we crossed over the ridge and on to a high bare plateau, moving swiftly forward to where a large crowd of people were gathered round a large white tent. There was a rush as we swung to a halt and then we were surrounded by laughing, shouting people who inundated us with scarves and greetings. We walked forward to the tent where tea and steamed bread, *mo-mos*, and cold cooked meat had been prepared for our arrival. Several men came forward to talk with Topgyay as we ate, probably headmen and leaders of the various groups represented, until we were at last ready to move on.

The summit of the last pass before our arrival lay ahead and, as soon as Topgyay waved his arm as a signal to mount and move, some of the riders sent their horses ahead to get the advantage of good places on the trail in the race to the summit. It was an unparalleled opportunity to establish a reputation for rider and horse as there were representatives from all over Kham, and whoever excelled in that race would be spoken of at every camp-fire throughout Tibet for months to come. At the same time the great number of riders made the race to the summit infinitely more difficult for there were now almost three hundred horses to pass and re-pass on a narrow trail, often winding above steep drops of thousands of feet to the valleys below. The skill of horsemanship lay in gauging the strength of one's horse up sheer faces in short gallops or sudden spurts to pass a rider on a widening part of the trail, or in trials of nerve by passing on ledges above dizzy precipices.

We were late in getting away in the crush of men and animals; I on my grey, Geoff on his bay and Topgyay on a powerful black pacing mule were about two-thirds of the way towards the tail of the caravan. Topgyay got no special privileges in a race of this kind and had to move ahead by skilful manœuvring like everyone else. About half-way up the mountainside a line of yaks and muleteers partly filled the trail, and as we weaved in and out amongst them at a fast trot, Geoff and I just behind Topgyay, we caught up on Loshay our servant, driving our pack animals with the others. Loshay drew aside to the edge of the trail and then, pointing to the grey and the summit ahead, yelled: 'Ride!'

I had been holding the grey in up till then, content to let Topgyay set the pace, knowing that he as a veteran would be skilled enough to gauge the distance to a fraction—when to ride fast, when to conserve the horse's strength. However, with Loshay's shouted advice in my ears and the feel of the powerful muscles of the grey moving smoothly and impatiently beneath me, I sent the grey ahead. The ground banked steeply at the side of the trail at this point, with about twenty riders strung along the centre of the trail, watching for any attempt on the part of the others to overhaul. With a sudden kick and lunge I threw the grey up the banking on a quick gallop, and before the others could move aside to block me I slithered past in a cloud of stones and dust. It acted like a signal to gallop and every rider settled down low in the saddle to meet the challenge.

I had timed my burst well, for there was an open stretch ahead, dotted here and there with low scrub; and with the grey stretched in a weaving gallop I passed rider after rider, while they hesitated whether to accept the challenge now at this pace or dismiss it as reckless show-horsemanship. Three times I brought the grey to a walk to give it a chance to recover its breath for a spell, and then on the occasional widening spaces in the trail I used its lightning speed to swerve round the riders jealously guarding their places in the line. Soon I could see no riders ahead at all, and I wondered whether I could have passed everyone already, but on meeting me some of Topgyay's soldiers shouted that there were still others ahead. The horse responded to the touch of the heel and leapt forward again, the spurts of stone from its flashing heels starting small landslides down the mountainside. It was crazy riding, slithering on loose sand and rocketing round bends at full speed, but the excitement and intoxication from these mad horsemen from the roof of the world was infectious, and no odds were calculated.

The trail opened out into a large hollow in the mountain, just below the summit, and here about twenty riders had dismounted from heaving, steaming horses beside a group of nomad tents. They greeted me boisterously as I came up and told me to dismount and take a bowl of tea as that was the custom when it was offered. While drinking they would see if any others caught up for the last dash to the summit. A few more came in, swelling the group of horsemen to about thirty or forty, and then there was a shout and movement towards the horses. The horses, instead of being exhausted, seemed more restive than ever, and I had some difficulty in getting up on the rearing grey. When I did, the other riders were already thundering down the valley towards the narrow trail leading on to the shoulder and final stretch to the summit. Only one horse at a time could cross that shoulder and whoever came out there first had the race in his pocket. It was about five hundred yards to the start of the narrow ledge leading upwards, and already the leading riders were almost half-way, with the others bunched close behind and riding like men possessed. There was only one way to get ahead and that was to take the risk I had already taken farther down the trail, by sending the grey on to the steep banking at a hammering gallop, like a motor-cyclist on the 'Wall of Death', and hope that its speed would help it to keep its balance. It was too fast and exciting to feel danger of any kind, and a yell tipped itself out of my throat as the grey slithered down the incline just in front of the nose of the leading horse where the trail narrowed. No one could possibly pass me now, and I came out on top of the shoulder as I had foreseen, with a clear run to the summit. I reined in at the cairn and prayer-flags with a piercing 'Yee-hee' cry of victory, twenty yards ahead of the nearest rider. As man after man slid off his steaming horse he took up his position before the grey, nibbling quietly at the bare grass now, and paid homage to a great animal—even their voices subdued in awe at such a performance.

As each rider or group of riders arrived, they dismounted, joined the main body of riders who had arrived first, and heard again the details of the finish, until Topgyay himself appeared. When he had heard the result and had a short rest, he gave the order to start moving again, down into the valley. Two thousand feet of pine forest lay between us and the valley floor where a cluster of houses, dominated by a large white building, indicated the village of Bo. On the other side of the valley, sheer rock buttresses towered thousands of feet above the forests, snow on the summits. The path wound down steeply, and the riders, walking now and leading the horses, picked their way with difficulty through heavy, loose earth and dead, rotting wood. The silence and gloom were oppressive, broken only by the rattle of gunfire, as here and there an exuberant rider let loose a round of ammunition to indicate our approach, and by an occasional brilliant shaft of sunlight streaming through an opening in the heavy foliage above.

After descending for about two hours, at long last the trees thinned and we came out once again into the open and sunshine. The riders all mounted again and moved at a fast trot along the narrow path, but keeping their places now and not trying to pass each other. Children scampered excitedly across the fields towards the houses, where the spaces between the houses were black with crowds of people. Two old men drew to the side of the trail as the horses approached, one of them peering shortsightedly at the riders. Topgyay had passed when the almost blind old man let out a cry and stumbled after him, tears streaming down his face at his failure to recognize his old leader. Topgyay leaned forward and patted his shoulder and then handed him his reins to give him the honour of leading his horse home.

Over the narrow wooden bridge spanning a brawling stream, and we were among the crowds, a narrow lane through them being chalked on the ground all the way to the big white house in Tibetan 'lucky' signs. As we entered the large compound of the white house the crowd rushed forward and caught the bridles of the horses, the riders dismounted, the escort and soldiers wheeled and disappeared into the village, and we had arrived.

The house was built like a fort, square, thick-walled, broad at the base and tapering towards the roof where multicoloured prayer-flags fluttered in the afternoon breeze. The door into the house was a massive, two-leaved affair facing into the compound. The ground floor was a storehouse of sorts, the whole of the first floor a huge kitchen and servants' quarters, and the second floor the living quarters of the family. There was the usual main living-cum-reception-cum-dining-room, but in addition there were several other rooms leading off the main room which Topgyay told us were bedrooms. Along the whole of the south wall of the main room were set removable latticed windows, with thin white cloth instead of glass, which could be lifted out to let the sun in and the family out on to a sheltered veranda. Here the wall of the house had been continued straight up to the roof to keep out the fierce winds, and a window of thick glass had been set into the wall so that the inmates could still look out on the superb view southwards down the valley. Inside there were the usual long low daises, thickly and richly carpeted, and the small ornamental tables set at intervals before them. On the walls heavily embroidered tapestries and religious *trankas* hung side by side with Chinese scroll paintings. The floors were of polished wood and the ceilings supported by massive ornamental pillars. After Topgyay and the family, most of whom had never seen this 'home', had explored every room, familiarizing themselves with each place, we returned to the main room and tea, when Topgyay apologized for the crudeness of the building, which he had designed himself and which he had only expected to live in for a little while in those early tempestuous years.

When we had eaten we all went outside for a look round the village. The valley had been uninhabited when Topgyay first arrived there on his fighting retreat from Tibet about fifteen years before. It was an excellent place for his headquarters and so he had cleared away large areas of forest, built houses for his men and scoured the surrounding countryside for women to be wives to them. He had not been able to find enough to give them one each, but as polyandry was widely practised in Tibet anyway, the ratio of one woman to three men, which was the best he could manage before his flight, was not too bad compared with some areas. Over the years the soldiers-turned-farmers cultivated the valley and now large areas were ploughed although productivity was very low, the altitude being toward 13,000 feet. Water was obtained from a narrow river flowing through the valley from north to south.

The white house was packed with family and servants, and until we could have a place of our own built, Geoff and I were allotted a 'log cabin' about twenty feet by twelve feet, on the flat roof of one of the Tibetan houses near by, approached by a notched log from the outside. It was a stark but solid enough protection against wind and snow. The 'fireplace' was an oblong block of clay about three feet by two, in the middle of the floor, with no chimney or escape for smoke except a small hole in the roof. On either side of the fire there were two wooden pallets, on which Loshay had already stretched out the sleeping-rolls, for beds. When our boxes were stacked up inside, there was barely room for two people to move about at one time. However, Topgyay had invited us to have our meals with them in the white house until our own house was ready, so it was only a matter of adapting ourselves until then.

Chapter Eleven

THE ULTIMATUM

I t was impossible to carry on any extensive medical work in such cramped quarters, but it was equally impossible to turn away the many who began to come for medicine soon after our arrival. Word soon travelled throughout the area that the 'foreign doctor' friend of Pangdatshang had arrived and people began to trickle in from the mountains, pleading for medicine. As a temporary expedient we pitched our tent on the roof of the Tibetan house as well, beside the log cabin, and this had to serve as a consulting-room and dispensary in the meantime.

Time disappeared from our lives in the narrow confines of that valley, and the primitive evening and morning were the only divisions of our existence. Each day the sun rose above one range of mountains, pursued its serene untroubled course across the blue vault and disappeared behind the other range on the west. Each night the fire flickered on oiled, slant-eyed faces—still and intent as they listened to the music-box of the foreigner, with the strange sounds, or to the foreigner himself as he told of a strange new doctrine—and died away in the star-hung immensity overhead. Beyond the mountains nations might reel to their ruin but here there was peace.

Yet the surface impression was false. There were conflicts in that valley that reflected the same conflicts as the world outside—conflicts in the souls of individuals as they were torn by fear and pride, avarice and hatred; conflicts between families as they squabbled for land and wealth and revenge; conflicts between tribes as they fought to increase influence and power. As in every other country and people in the world, the problem in the final

232

analysis was the basic one of the individual soul. Here were the seeds of all conflicts and here were the possibilities of peace. A soul at rest with itself had to be first of all at rest with God. The soul that had become knit with God in the great peace of reconciliation was a soul empowered by the Spirit of God to live above all conflicts. That was why the artist in the exhibition of paintings depicting 'Peace' won the first prize with his painting of a bird in its nest in the crook of a bending branch over a raging torrent, while the others with their paintings of white doves, quiet landscapes and cows grazing, missed the significance and prize.

Hardly a day passed without someone riding into the valley for medicine, or with news from some part of Kham of the Communist advance, or for talks on measures to be taken in the event of having to fight the Communists. A large delegation of officials, about thirty strong, came from Batang about two days' journey away, to return guns and goods stolen from the fleeing Pangdatshangs in the fighting years before. The officials of Batang, known throughout Kham for their treachery and distrusted because of their mixed blood, being of Tibetan and Chinese parentage, had weighed up the situation, seen that the retreating Pangdatshangs had little hope of success and attacked their depleted forces to gain favour with the Chinese Army. Now, almost sixteen years later, Pangdatshang had returned in power and they were quick to make amends by returning the looted guns and goods taken at that time. There were long speeches of apology and explanations for the past and then long discussions on what was to be done in the future.

Rapga sat silent and inscrutable, but confided in me later that they did not trust the Batang officials, many of whom he suspected of being secret Communists who only wanted to betray them to their leaders. A feast was given, mah-jongg was played, a shooting competition was held and a horse-race run, and once again the valley was quiet for a little while—until another group came along from the Konka Lama, from the country adjoining Pangdatshang's, who had also traitorously fought him, and now sent to make restitution.

Topgyay's riders, travelling constantly throughout Kham, brought him word that they were now encircled. From Jyekundo in the north right round by Chengtu and Chungking, and now Kunming and Likiang since Canton had fallen, the Communists were consolidating their position in China. It was only a matter of time before they advanced into Kangting, and then Kham, to subdue the rebels there. Topgyay prepared to fight. Without any knowledge of Communism himself, he listened to Rapga, instructed in the revolutionary theories of Sun Yat Sen and Karl Marx and others, and learned from him that the approaching struggle would be no 'clean' war of strength and skill with the victor taking the spoils, but an end to their race and religion and culture and freedom, and an absorption into a ruthless, godless, materialistic machine.

Topgyay offered Geoff and me an opportunity to escape before it was too late, but we refused to accept it. God had brought us thus far and it was impossible for a follower of Jesus Christ, the Son of God, to flee from Karl Marx, His creation. Topgyay was impressed and grateful, for in the fighting ahead many would be wounded and require medical treatment which no one could give if we did not remain. However, this possibility raised problems, as we had not enough left of the common medicines which would be required in such great quantities and there was no way of getting supplies of them from China, where the Communists were now in full control.

Talking over the problem with Topgyay we finally decided that Geoff should make an attempt to get to India through Tibet and there contact John Mackie. If Mackie could buy the medicines in India and send them to Kalimpong on the Tibetan border, Pangdatshang had a manager there who would send them across Tibet to Kham. He could also send in supplies of tinned foodstuffs by this way, for we had been living almost continuously on the *tsamba* and dried meat of the Tibetans, with occasional meals of rice and vegetables, for some time now. Geoff was the obvious choice to make the trip for not only had he been handling all the financial side of the venture so far, being a banker by profession, but also he had no knowledge of medicine to carry on in Kham himself, and there was every possibility that fighting would break out before anyone could arrive back from India, with crowds of wounded to be attended to every day.

Topgyay had assumed a breathing space of from six months to a year before the Communists would launch an attack on Tibet, probably a year with all the commitments that they still had in China. But within a few days he received a rude shock when a rider from Batang rode furiously up to the white house with letters which turned out to be important communications from the Communists.

There was the usual long Communist preamble on 'democracy' and 'liberation', and all the new freedoms the people would enjoy under the new régime, and then came the important contents. They had learned of Pangdatshang's plans for a revolution against the reactionary feudal government in Lhasa and they approved of his plans and desire to further the interests of the people. He was to go ahead with these plans and they would supply him with arms, ammunition and necessary financial assistance; the only difference was that it would not be a factional uprising as planned before but a 'people's' revolution against the Tibetan Government. He was not to consider fighting against the Communist army or resisting their orders in any way, for they were not viewing him simply as an intransigent war-lord to be punished in a foray after which they would withdraw their forces as had happened in years gone by; nor would they be put off in their intentions if he linked up with the Tibetan Government against them, for they intended to liberate the whole of Tibet as part of their plan to 'liberate' the whole of Asia. Within one year Tibet would be liberated, within three years Nepal, Sikkim and Bhutan would be liberated, in five years India would be liberated, and thus the East be secured for Communism. He, Pangdatshang, was only a small part in this programme of liberation and if he tried to resist or defy the Communist army he would be swept out of existence.

This was shattering news. The Pangdatshangs had, at the most, expected only the usual odd remnants of the Chinese Army divisions to come this way, as they swept clean for a new administration; and this the tough, fearless Khambas with all the advantages of terrain and altitude could have coped with easily enough in guerrilla warfare for a year or two while the Tibetan Government in Lhasa made up its mind what to do. This news of Asian 'liberation' was overwhelming for it meant that even national resistance would be useless. Tibet alone could not stand against the might of China if that country had decided to throw its five-million-strong army into the conquest of Asia.

The Pangdatshangs were in a quandary. To the west the Tibetan Government was antagonistic and suspicious because of their past history, to the east the Communists demanded collaboration and revolution against their own countrymen. There was no way out. Topgyay was known as the leader of the Khambas, and as such would be held responsible for them. If he ordered them to fight they would fight; if he ordered them to submit they would submit; if he gave no decision at all and the Chinese came in, the Khambas, with their centuries-old racial hatred of the Chinese, would still fight, without the leadership of Topgyay, and the Communists would still hold him responsible for the fighting. It was no use, then, trying to avoid the responsibility of deciding.

We talked far into the night, by the light of the spluttering butter lamps, but the only definite conclusion that Topgyay could come to was that they had at the most six months in which finally to decide. The distances beyond Kangting in West China were vast and the Communists had no idea where the Pangdatshangs were to be found in the mountains. The only post offices were in Litang and Batang and the Communists had no way of knowing how, where or when their ultimatum would be delivered. By the time they consolidated their position in Chengtu and Kangting and then began to turn their attention farther west and make deliberate attempts to find the Pangdatshangs, six months might be expected to pass. In the meantime they would pretend that the letter was never received.

Geoff and I, too, faced a crisis. It was no longer any use thinking that this would only be a small-scale battle in which God would overrule by helping the Khambas defeat the Chinese and so allow us to remain and spread the gospel of Jesus Christ through the influence of friendly, helpful Topgyay. China was set on the conquest of Kham, of Tibet, of Asia. Even if their present time schedule of five years to liberate Asia was arrogant and presumptuous, it was still only a question of time and not of intent. Lenin had stated the course that international Communism must take to reach its goal: 'The road to Paris lies through Peking and Calcutta.' China must be expecting—and would get—help from Russia, for the Chinese economy, after the National Government fiasco, was in ruins and would be even in normal circumstances for years to come, yet here she was anticipating further advances westwards. Confucianism, Buddhism, Mohammedanism, and an empty Christianity, had been swept away before this new dynamic religion of 'dimatism', dialectical materialism. What was there left in Asia to stop it? For that matter, what was there left anywhere in the world to stop it? The western nations had nothing more to offer than they had already provided in their occupation of the East—the same complacency with hypocrisy and exploitation, the same empty platitudes, the same denominational hierarchies, the same vitiated gospel. The only difference was that in the West the people had enough food and better living conditions to keep them from thinking too deeply about other things. The same well-fed, well-clothed people who could afford to attend the theatre to satisfy other appetites than that of food, and applaud the performance of a Hamlet they had heard declaiming:

> *What is a man,*
> *If his chief good and market of his time*
> *Be but to sleep and feed? a beast, no more.*
> *Sure he that made us with such large discourse,*
> *Looking before and after, gave us not*
> *That capability and god-like reason*
> *To rust in us unus'd. Now, whether it be*
> *Bestial oblivion, or some craven scruple*

The Ultimatum

Of thinking too precisely on th' event,—
A thought which, quarter'd, hath but one part wisdom
And ever three parts coward,—I do not know
Why yet I live to say, 'This thing's to do';
Sith I have cause, and will and strength and means
To do't.

—these same people were those who would leave the theatre, go to a restaurant, ease the physical demands of the body where they could and go to sleep. Life for them was a vessel to be drained and not a cup to be filled. There was no vision, no meaning or objective for them in life, and where there was no vision the people perished.

All over the world the standards of nations were rapidly deteriorating, the law of the jungle was being introduced and practised because of the thoughtlessly accepted belief that that was man's original habitat anyway. The sense of creature responsibility to a Creator had gone and men and nations now lived by the law of the Curse of Creation, the survival of the fittest. Even Britain, who at one time had established a reputation for integrity which made it possible to cash an English cheque in almost any great city of the world, and which found expression in some foreign languages, such as the '*mot anglais*' of the French, denoting a promise that would not in any circumstances be broken— even Britain had deteriorated to the point where one social survey could record that an average of one citizen in every eighty-three committed an indictable offence.

And China had just been laid naked to the world in one of the greatest exposures of national corruption in history. Confucianism with its misplaced loyalties to rulers and ancestors and fathers lent itself to the exploiting tendencies of the few, and emperors and governments and landlords had ruthlessly used their power for selfish interests, and imposed on the people a doctrine that fatalistically perpetuated the oppression. The art and culture of the few, displayed so proudly to the world, was produced from the suffering and blood of the millions over the centuries. A person's life became the cheapest thing in China—a paradox of Confucianism in which the individual ranked so high. The leaders of Christianity were little better, making formal association with any denomination sufficient ground for bearing the Name of Christ; and so could make no positive contribution to the life of the people. Wasn't Chiang Kai Shek a Christian? and look at his government and the state of the country under him, as the people, too weary to be cynical, pointed out.

Could, then, any true Christian wish again upon this land the powers that waged continual civil war between its war-lords, that squeezed a land dry of its wealth, that kept 80 per cent of its population living on a mere handful of rice a day? With a war against the Japanese and a civil war against the Communists just ending was it the place of the compassionate Christian to ask for further defiance from a people who could write:

From break of day,
Till sunset glow,
I toil.
I dig my well
I plough my field
And earn my food
And drink.
What care I
Who rules the land
If I
Am left in Peace?

What should a true Christian do when an unbiased reporter could write of Communist China: 'I could feel the new joy of the peasant in the little bit of land he possessed, his intense pride, and his faith in the Communist Party which had made this change possible. He now walked with his back unbent and his eyes sparkled as he looked straight at you. His wife and daughter too shared in the glory. They were no longer shut up in the home cowering to hide their bodies from the lustful eye of the village lord. There was no incense-burning in the temples before the

inscrutable Buddha attended by saffron-robed priests. New China
had emerged and new men are in charge of her destiny.' Was the
possession of a few acres of land the be-all and end-all of existence
for the people of China? Was sufficient food, a roof over the head,
and an inside water-closet for everyone, the true end of man's
destiny? Most important of all, was man to be the final arbiter as
to how that condition was to be brought about, or God? For
God, too, wished every man to have sufficient food, sufficient
shelter and decent sanitary conditions, but the rules laid down by
Him for obtaining these things were diametrically opposed to the
means proposed by man—particularly Marx-man. The doctrine
of the one necessitated the elimination of the other.

Then there was the prophetic place of Communism in Biblical
eschatology. Was Communism the co-ordinating factor that
would bind Russ and Gomer, interpreted to mean Russia and
Germany, together with others into a confederacy that would
conform to the 'king of the north' spoken of in the Bible as one
of the protagonists of the 'end days' at Armageddon? If this was
so in the purposes of God—and other events seemed to uphold
the theory, such as the return of Israel to their land, the atomic
bomb which gave credence to the possibility of the world being
'dissolved in fervent heat'—then obviously it was futile to look
for any help from God to oppose the Communists. For if that
theory were true He would continue to use them as a scourge on
a disobedient world until their course towards Armageddon was
complete, and only then destroy them according to His word.
The duty of the Christian in such an event would be to flee before
the Communists and pray for divine deliverance as he waited for
the end.

Only one factor stood in the scales against this accumulating
and bewildering weight of political, social and scriptural data, and
yet that one factor outweighed them all. God had sent Geoff and
me to Central Asia to fulfil His purpose for us there and He had
not withdrawn that divine commission. For years now we had
moved forward on this principle of obedience to God in every
detail, allowing Him to direct our steps, and we could not allow

the discretionary 'commonsense' of other missionaries or Christian teachers, the avoidance of imprisonment, the change of governments, the fall of nations, or the theories of men, to direct our steps now in the most important issue of all. God must speak. Until then we must remain in the place to which He had brought us. 'Be thou there until I bring thee word,' was still His command.

And He had. We had prayed as never before, for the foundation of our faith was in the balance, and out of the darkness He spoke to me in the vision.

'I have brought you to this place as I promised but this is not the end of my promise, there are still greater things ahead. I told you that I would send you to Tibet, and other countries of Asia, to communicate to those who have never heard the knowledge you have learned of me, and that no one would be able to stop you from accomplishing my purpose for you as long as you obeyed my voice. I have brought you to Tibet but this is only a very small part of the work I have yet for you to do. Not only Kham or Tibet or Central Asia but the whole world must know that I am still the God of Abraham and of Moses, of David and Elijah, the God and Father of the Lord Jesus Christ. What you have done so far is nothing to what I have yet for you to do. The way in which I have led you has brought you into possession of unique knowledge. You are the only person with the knowledge of Chinese Communist plans to take over Tibet and the other countries of Asia. No one else knows, no one even suspects that China is making for India. Therefore you will go to India and take the knowledge you have gained to the authorities there and I will use you to stop the Communist advance, to frustrate the Communist plans for taking over Asia, for I have sent you there and no man or nation can withstand me. I only require that you should be obedient to my every word. There is no living without dying; there is no dying without living.'

No further revelation was given as I argued throughout the night. The words remained emblazoned on my memory as the command of God, and that was all. I was against participating in politics, had always been since I first started to think things out for myself. Modern politics were not based on principle, but expediency. The modern politician was merely a mouthpiece of his party, and if he had any personal integrity it had to be subordinate to his personal ambition to allow him to continue in office. The structure of government and the existence of party politics demanded it. That was why politics had become 'dirty' and unfit for the Christian. An individual could be held responsible to conform to given standards and principles by those who put him in office, but a 'party' or a 'state' was an abstraction that could not be held responsible for any of its actions, for it admitted no principles but those which governed its continued existence as such. The individual had to agree to one or the other party's policies before putting himself up for election; if he did not agree with the policies afterwards the party would see to it that he ceased to have their approval and support, and his days were numbered.

And all parties sought power. How they got it did not greatly concern them. They all acted on Mao Tse Tung's cynical dictum even if they did not confess it so openly: 'Learn from the masses and then teach them.' Democracy—'the form of government in which the supreme power is vested in the people collectively and is administered by them or by officers appointed by them'—was the inevitable corollary of the glorification of the human being. Communism, or the doctrine of dialectical materialism, was simply a courageous recognition of the implications of such a belief. Christian Democracy was a pardox in terms; the true Christian set Christ as Lord over every part of his life and acknowledged no other authority as greater, not even the 'rule of the people' who still said by lip and life: 'We will not have this man to reign over us.' Christian Autocracy was the only acceptable form of government for the Christian and this would not be set up until Christ Himself returned and ruled the people 'with a rod of iron'. Polybius's cyclic law of the government of states, that it passes from monarchy through aristocracy and democracy to monarchy again, was a law long before Polybius thought about it or taught it. Daniel had left it on record as the revelation of God that such was the divine purpose in history when he gave the

interpretation of Nebuchadnezzar's dream of the image as showing monarchic autocracy in the Babylonian rule of Nebuchadnezzar, through the aristocratic rule of the nobles of the Medo-
Persian empire, through the democracy of the Greek and Roman
empires, to the monarchic autocracy of Christ when the 'times of
the nations' had been fulfilled.

When Christ came as king to set up His kingdom in peace and
righteousness and love then the faithful Christian would share in
a government that involved no compromise and admitted no
expediency. Till then His kingdom was not of this world and
therefore His disciples could not fight—either on the battlefields
for the ambitions of governments, or at the polls for the ambitions of parties. The duty of the Christian was to recognize and
obey whatever party was in power where the dictates of that
party were in accord with his conscience and did not conflict
with his greater loyalty to God; where there was conflict on this
issue the command was sharp and clear—'obey God rather than
man'. An individual going into politics in the first place at the
command of God, of course, would naturally be in a different
category from one going into politics as a career or 'to do good',
for then he with God would be sufficient to overthrow the policies of expediency, introduce moral values, and then lay the foundation for the 'righteousness' of a nation which was exalted in the
sight of God. That would only be party politics if a group of such
individuals took a stand on the 'platform' of the principles laid
down in the Word of God, acknowledging their allegiance to
them and their responsibility to abide by them. They would then
not just give God *a* place in their speeches but *the* place in their
everyday lives. Until such a man or such a party came along it
was the duty of the Christian to remain law-abiding, pay the
taxes asked of him, and love his neighbour as himself—to 'render
unto Caesar the things that are Caesar's, and unto God the things
that are God's'. It was not his responsibility to choose between
the Labour Party offering the poor free medical treatment or the
Conservative Party offering the poor free enterprise; that was to
have confusion of testimony to the glory of God when either of

these parties did anything within their other activities that compromised the Name of Christ. The true Christian had access to God's presence, to the very mind of God, and it was his particular glory that he could share in the counsels of God's Will and work with Him to the fulfilment of His purposes, whether in the control of his family, or in the control of the nation. The powers-that-be are ordained of God; it was dishonouring to God when those that used His Name, and consequently admitted the possibilities of knowing God's mind and Will, were divided amongst Conservatives and Liberals, Communists and Labour, each exerting his puny strength to put his own particular group into office as the powers-that-be. For that reason I had never voted for any party. The Christian could not touch politics in its present state.

If it was impossible for the Christian to take part in politics it was even more so for the missionary going to a foreign country. His concern was not with the type of government in power in the country to which he was sent by God, nor with the conditions and exploitation of the people, not even with the *souls* of the people. His first and continuing concern was to do the Will of God. The words of his Master must be his words: 'I am come to do Thy Will, O God.' When he spoke it must not be to voice his own opinions. His Master never did—and the servant is not greater than his lord—and He said when on earth: 'I have not spoken from myself, but the Father who sent me has Himself given me commandment what I should say and what I should speak, and I know that His commandment is life eternal. What therefore I speak, as the Father has said unto me, so I speak.' It was not the function of the missionary to preach in every open place and give out booklets in every spare minute, but to be ready to do so if his Lord commanded. It was the same Lord who wept over people, who gave His life for the sins of those people, who said (Moffat's translation): 'Truly, truly, I tell you the Son can do nothing of his own accord, nothing but what he sees the Father doing; for whatever He does the Son also does the same. The Father loves the Son and shows him all that He is doing Himself. . . . I can do nothing of my own accord . . . because my aim

is not my own will but the will of Him who sent me. . . . I accept
no testimony from man . . . but I possess a testimony greater than
that of John (the Baptist) for the deeds which the Father has
granted me to accomplish, the very deeds on which I am engaged,
are my testimony that the Father has sent me. You know me?
You know where I come from? But I have not come on my own
initiative; I am sent, and sent by him who is real.' The disciple
with the words of his Master constantly in his ears was never
allowed to forget that 'as the Father has sent me even so send I
you.'

Sent . . . to do the will of God. I had tried my best to obey over
a stormy pathway in the past, but now what was being asked of
me was too much. To do something which all my thinking life I
had believed to be wrong, which I still believed to be wrong; to
take part in politics. To be pointed at and condemned by those
who were ready to pounce on any opportunity to prove departure
from obedience to Scripture. That was bad enough, but it was a
thousand times worse to be the means perhaps of bringing suspicion on many hundreds of innocent missionaries throughout
the world if it became known ultimately, as it must. Yet the command of God remained inexorable.

There could be no confusion in the mind of God, though, for
God is not the author of confusion but of peace. When my will
was finally broken, and the storm of protest stilled, the voice of
God came once more calmly and reasonably to point out that I
had for some time been aware of, and contending, the inherently
'political' character of the modern professional missionaries with
their government protection, title deeds to houses and lands, and
imposition of western culture and Scriptural interpretation in the
countries in which they worked; so that my argument about participating in politics could only be one of degree. As far as God
was concerned the modern word 'missionary' meant nothing at
all and I could call myself what I liked as long as I remained
obedient to the heavenly vision and divine control. On the other
hand, I seemed to have forgotten that Communism was not politics but a religion. A religion with a hierarchy and doctrine, faith

and vision, dogmas and heresies. A militant belief that tolerated no opposition, sought converts and advocated conquest, and openly proclaimed the annihilation of anything that postulated the thought of God. I, and all other Christians, would have to face this issue some time for there could be no co-existence. Some time, somewhere, Christians would be able to run away from Communism no longer and would have to stand and face the implications of defiance. I was simply being asked to do it now instead of some years later.

The struggle ended in the early hours of the morning but I put off telling Geoff about it, so fantastic did it all seem in the hard grey light of a Tibetan dawn and the drowsy peace of its valleys. The days passed, slipping away quietly while we continued to discuss the future and Geoff continued to make preparations for departure to India for supplies, and still I could not bring myself to tell Geoff of the vision. It required a further prompting from God.

One day Topgyay and Rapga sent for me to have a further talk on the situation and then Topgyay told me what he had been thinking of. The Communists would not come into Tibet for another six months or so and if anything was to be done it would have to be done within that time. It wasn't possible to get word about the Communist plans all the way to Lhasa and back within that time, for it would take more than six months for a suitable party to ride to Lhasa and back; the Tibetan Government would not believe an ordinary message or messenger but would think it was an attempt of the Pangdatshangs to curry favour with the government in Lhasa. Only three people were aware of the Communist plans and those were Topgyay, Rapga and myself. (I had not discussed all the details with Geoff in case some unexpected event should happen which might place us in a questionable position; in which situation only one of us could then be found guilty and the other would be free to carry on, and in this way God's work would not be disastrously affected.) He, Topgyay, was required in Kham to handle affairs and lead the Khambas in any fighting, Rapga could not go for he was suspected by the Tibetan

Government and forbidden to enter India by the Indian Government, so that left only myself. If I went to India over South-East Tibet instead of Geoff there was a possibility of reaching India in two months, if I travelled quickly. That would give me time to contact the authorities in India about the Communist plans, and also to contact the Tibetan Government in Lhasa through some of the Tibetan officials who were usually to be found in Kalimpong, on the Indo-Tibetan border. They could get word up to Lhasa in a few days from there, the Tibetan Government could decide on what action was to be taken, and then if they wanted the Pangdatshangs to fight the Communists they could send word to them by special messenger and it would arrive before the six months were up. In the meantime I could be buying my supplies and making arrangements to send them into Kham, and by returning back again over the route I had taken into India I too could arrive within the six months.

However, he could not ask me to do it; it was far too dangerous. There was no information available about the trail over South-East Tibet to Sadiya, only a rumour that there used to be a way through. I might be killed by bandits, by floods, by avalanches, by cold, by exposure, by starvation. I would have to travel light to travel fast, yet if I travelled too light I might die of starvation if there were no villages at which to find fresh supplies. Also, I might have to send the horses back if at any time the trail got too bad for us to ride further and take to carrying the loads myself with my few men. Even if I got through to India I might never get back again through avalanches, or landslides, or rising rivers. These were only a few of the reasons why he could not ask me to attempt the journey, but he had to point it out as the only possible chance. The alternative was for them to accept the Communists' demand, resigning themselves to the destruction of their religion and customs and nation, and for the two of us to escape before the Communists arrived. He would be sorry to see us go, for although our beliefs in God were different from his, yet they did believe in God, while the Communists coming in neither believed in God nor believed in letting other people believe in Him.

I could no longer avoid telling Geoff of the vision and God's command to me. Geoff listened in silence and amazement and then, even as I had done on the night of the vision, began to argue its impossibility for many reasons. I admitted them all wearily, pointing out that I had fought each one out with God only to be beaten back again on to that command. I did not want to go, the whole idea fairly shrieked of the fantastic; and also, much subtler to combat, it also appealed to me from the human standpoint, with my liking for the audacious and spectacular. The only way in which we could prove whether it was really of God, and not an hallucination, was for Geoff to pray and wait before God for an answer; Geoff was so different in temperament and training, so hesitant and cautious, it could no longer be classed as an hallucination or the reckless idea of an individual, but only as the considered purpose of God. In the meantime, we would refrain from discussing the subject lest Geoff should be influenced in any way by my conversation and convictions.

It was several days later when Geoff came and quietly said that God had revealed to him that it was His Will for me to go ahead. He, too, could not understand why it had to be in this way but neither could he argue with God. He would remain in Bo, studying the language against the day when it would be required to make God known, and doing what medical work he could from what he had picked up over the past few years. If no more was heard from our caravan making for India he would assume that we had perished on the way and that after all we must have misinterpreted the Will of God, and carry on as best he could alone. God would then always have one witness and the work gained so far not be wholly lost. If the Communists came in before anything could be done then he would remain to face whatever the future held with God, if necessary in prison. If we were right, then both of us would one day meet again to preach with greater assurance than ever before the wonderful glory of God.

We prayed together and then opened the Bible at the place we had reached in our readings for that day. It was in the Old Testament, in the second Book of Kings, chapters 18 and 19:

The Ultimatum

'And Rab-shakeh said to the children of Israel, "Say now to Hezekiah, Thus says the great king, the king of Assyria: What confidence is this wherein thou trustest? Thou sayest—but it is a word of the lips—There is counsel and strength for war. Now on whom dost thou rely that thou hast revolted against me? Now behold, thou reliest upon the staff of that broken reed Egypt, on which if a man lean, it goes into his hand and pierces it: so is Pharaoh King of Egypt to all that rely upon him. And if ye say to me, We rely upon Jehovah our God: is it not he whose high places and whose altars Hezekiah has removed, saying to Judah and Jerusalem, Ye shall worship before this altar in Jerusalem. Hear the word of the great king, the King of Assyria! Thus says the King: Let not Hezekiah deceive you; for he will not be able to deliver you out of the king's hand. Neither let Hezekiah make you rely upon Jehovah, saying, Jehovah will certainly deliver us, and this city shall not be given into the hand of the king of Assyria. Hearken not to Hezekiah, for thus says the king of Assyria: Make peace with me, and come out to me; and eat every one of his vine and every one of his fig-tree, and drink every one the waters of his own cistern until I come and take you away to a land like your own land, a land of corn and wine, a land of bread and vineyards, a land of olive trees and honey, that ye may live and not die; and hearken not to Hezekiah when he persuades you saying, Jehovah will deliver us. Have any of the gods of the nations delivered at all his land out of the hand of the king of Assyria? Where are the gods of Hameth and of Arpad? Where are the gods of Sepharvaim, Hena, and Ivvah? and have they delivered Samaria out of my hand? Which are they among all the gods of the countries, who have delivered their country out of my hand, that Jehovah should deliver Jerusalem out of my hand" . . .

'And the servants of King Hezekiah came to Isaiah. And Isaiah said unto them, "This shall ye say to your master: Thus saith Jehovah, Be not afraid of the words that thou hast heard, wherewith the servants of the king of Assyria have blasphemed me. Behold I will put a spirit into him, and he shall hear tidings, and shall return to his own land; and I will make him to fall by the sword in his own land. . . . That which thou hast prayed to me concerning Sennacherib king of Assyria, I have heard. This is the word that Jehovah has spoken against him: . . . Hast thou not heard long ago that I have done it? And that from ancient days I formed it? Now have I brought it to pass, that thou shouldest lay waste fortified cities into ruinous heaps. And their inhabitants were powerless, they were dismayed and put to shame; they were as the growing grass; and as the green herb, as the grass on the house-tops, and grain blighted before it has grown up. But I know thine abode, and thy going out, and thy coming in, and thy raging against me. Because thy raging against me and thine arrogance is come up into mine ears, I will put my ring in thy nose, and my bridle in thy lips, and I will make thee go back by the way by which thou camest. And this shall be the sign unto thee: they shall eat this year such as groweth of itself, and in the second year that which springeth of the same; but in the third year sow ye and reap, and plant vineyards and eat the fruit thereof. And the remnant that is escaped of the house of Judah shall again take root downward, and bear fruit upward. For out of Jerusalem shall go forth a remnant, and out of mount Zion they that escape: the zeal of Jehovah of hosts shall do this." '

We closed our Bibles, but the words hung still in the air. Shift the time and the names and the circumstances across the centuries to the present and the picture remained the same—the boasts of conquests, the defiance of God, the appeal to the people to overthrow their rulers, the deceitful promise of land and Utopia. But would God find a Hezekiah and a remnant in these days who would humble themselves before Him, obey Him implicitly in all that He said, believing that He must triumph for His own great Name's sake?

Telling Geoff that I would have made my final decision by the time I returned, I went outside and up the mountainside to a rocky promontory where there was space and silence in which such a decision could be made. . . .

Chapter Twelve

THE DECISION

I rose to ease the cramp out of my legs and back. Someone once said: 'The value of knowledge is determined by the value of the end it will help us to reach.' In that case it was easily settled after all, not by a laborious process of induction and deduction from an aggregate of circumstances but by the simple words of Solomon the Wise: 'Let us hear the end of the whole matter: Fear God and keep his commandments; for this is the whole of man. For God shall bring every work into judgement, with every secret thing, whether it be good or whether it be evil.'

The sun was warm. The air was keen and clear with a light, intoxicating quality. The giant mountain peaks were high and distant; but not too high and not too distant. It was good to be alive in such a world.

Well, I thought, I had better get back to Geoff and begin my preparations for leaving.